TAVERN

ON THE

GREEN

COOKBOOK

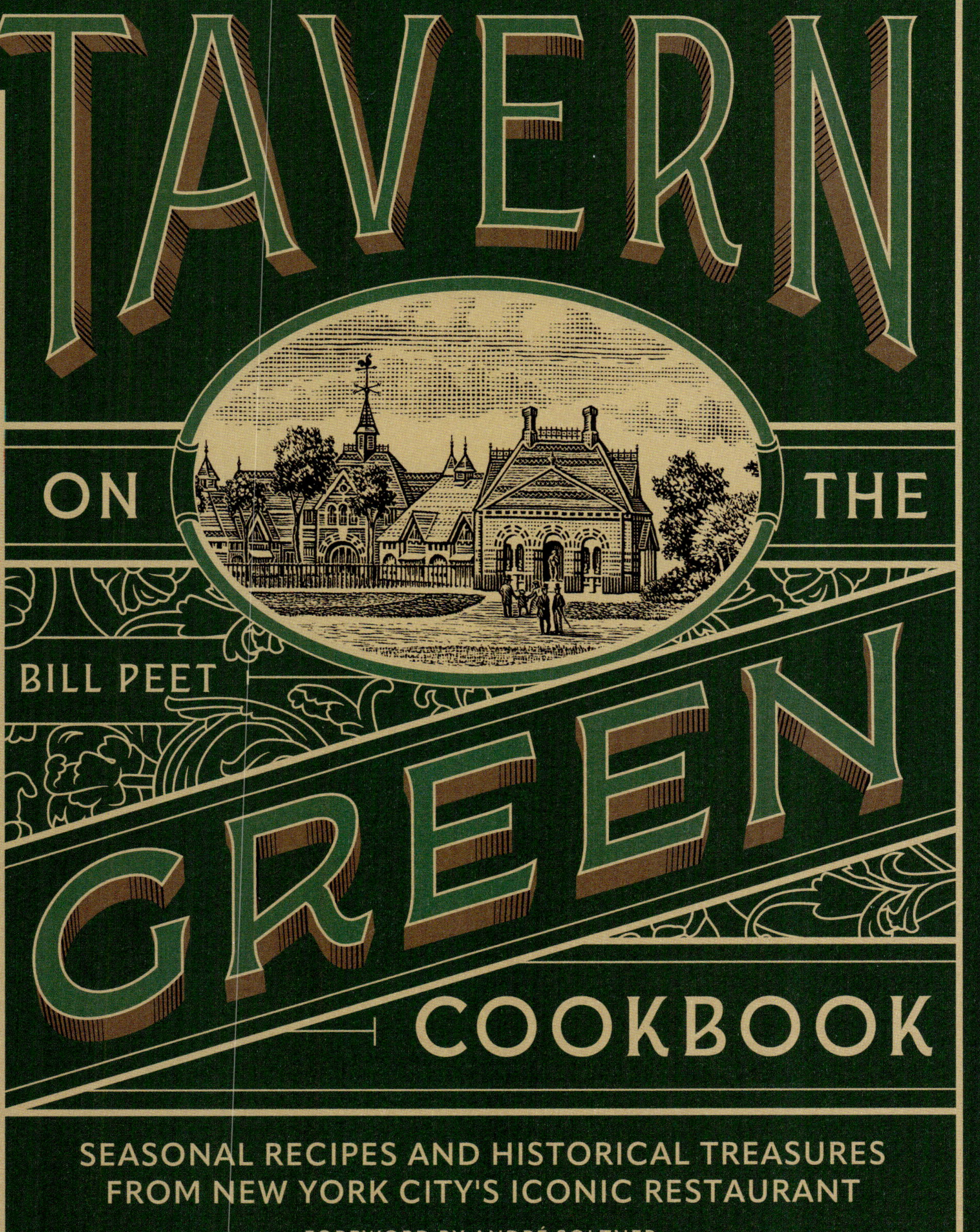

TAVERN
ON
THE
GREEN
COOKBOOK
BILL PEET
SEASONAL RECIPES AND HISTORICAL TREASURES
FROM NEW YORK CITY'S ICONIC RESTAURANT
FOREWORD BY ANDRÉ SOLTNER
Globe Pequot

Globe
Pequot

An imprint of The Globe Pequot Publishing Group, Inc.
64 South Main Street
Essex, CT 06426
www.globepequot.com

British Library Cataloguing in Publication Information available

Library of Congress Cataloging-in-Publication Data
Names: Peet, Bill (Writer on cooking) author | Llewellyn, Deborah
  Whitlaw photographer | Soltner, André, 1932–2025 writer of foreword
Title: Tavern on the Green cookbook : seasonal recipes and historical
  treasures from New York City's iconic restaurant / by Bill Peet;
  photography by Deborah Llewellyn ; foreword by André Soltner.
Description: Essex, Connecticut : Globe Pequot, [2026] | Includes index. |
  Summary: "This cookbook is designed for both the home cook and the
  accomplished chef and will replicate the dining experience at New York's
  famous Tavern on the Green. With clear instructions and beautiful
  photographs, fans can re-create delicious meals at home, as well as read
  historical snapshots about the restaurant's nearly 100-year history"—
  Provided by publisher.
Identifiers: LCCN 2025022185 (print) | LCCN 2025022186 (ebook) | ISBN
  9781493091249 hardcover | ISBN 9781493091256 epub
Subjects: LCSH: Tavern on the Green (New York, N.Y.) | Seasonal cooking |
  LCGFT: Cookbooks
Classification: LCC TX714 .P441538 2026 (print) | LCC TX714 (ebook) | DDC
  641.5/7209747—dc23/eng/20250702
LC record available at https://lccn.loc.gov/2025022185
LC ebook record available at https://lccn.loc.gov/2025022186

To my wife, Anna Maria,
you are both my greatest champion and
my toughest critic.
I love you.

CONTENTS

FOREWORD

I am happy to see Bill Peet finally put his savoir faire in a book. Over a long career, Billy has become an expert in fine cooking as well as in organization of big events. It all started many years ago . . .

Billy came to me as a young cook in 1980, sent from a friend at another French restaurant, Maurice Bertrand at Clos Normand on 52nd Street. In those days, you put the word out that you were looking for a cook, and the cooks who showed up came with good references.

We met one afternoon when Billy came to Lutèce after lunch service for an interview. Maurice had told me that Billy was a hard worker and very enthusiastic, that he came early every day to see and learn as much as he could. Maurice had seen something in this young cook and was willing to pass him on to a restaurant with more opportunities.

We sat and talked for about an hour. There was something about him. He was very curious and asked a lot of questions. I hired him on the spot and told him to start the next Monday. Billy told me he would have to talk with his current boss about starting. I agreed. He did not know that I had already spoken to Maurice about his starting date.

Billy was only the second American cook to work at Lutèce in the almost twenty years we had been open. We had a staff that had been there many years, with very little turnover. So a job at Lutèce came around only once in a while. We had many young cooks coming in to ask about working there, but there were just no openings, so I often reached out to other chef friends to try to place them.

Billy was a graduate of the Culinary Institute of America (CIA), a renowned culinary school with talented chefs and instructors. I was friendly with many of the chefs and executives at the school. It is a very close-knit industry. The American cooks were hungry to work in better restaurants, and quite a few of my colleagues had many in their kitchens. We would eventually hire more Americans. We also started to bring in extern students from the CIA, with the requirement that they had to stay a minimum of one year.

Billy started on the cold line as a garde-manger, working salads and desserts; he was also responsible for about eighty to ninety hot soufflés each night. Most soufflés were ordered after dinner at the last moment, so it was very busy. He got a real education just by working each service.

Over the years, Billy worked most of the stations before becoming a sous chef, responsible for the production of the food that would be served in the restaurant. He also took care of all the desserts and pastries.

Billy was part of the Lutèce family for fifteen years, from 1980 to 1995, the busiest time in Lutèce's history. We closed only on Sundays and for vacation, the entire month of August each year. As busy as we were, Billy was able to balance his work and family life. His wife, Anna, and their boys, Will and Tim, visited often.

Since Billy left Lutèce in 1995, either I would call him or he would call me each week and just catch up. We never went more than a couple of weeks without speaking. I loved to hear all the stories about the restaurants he was working at— wonderful stories. Now I am always impressed with the quality of food he makes for the many diners at Tavern on the Green. Billy is really the perfect chef for Tavern; there are not that many who could handle it. I consider him one of my adopted sons, both in the culinary world and in my affections.

His enormous savoir faire in fine cuisine and his great organizational skills make him a unique chef. The next generation of chefs will learn a lot from "Billy's" book.

Thank you, Bill.

André Soltner
Former Chef Proprietor, Lutèce
Meilleur Ouvrier de France

INTRODUCTION

The reservations list—now at an all-time high—at New York City's restored and flourishing Tavern on the Green is not restricted to celebrities. New Yorkers and gleeful out-of-towners with an appetite for memorable experiences all delight in the landmark space and elegant American menu—with a robust cocktail and wine list, of course.

This book is a celebration of the iconic restaurant throughout the year, from the first cold days of January, when Split Pea and Country Ham Soup and Dark Beer Braised Short Ribs are a must-have, through sultry summers in Manhattan's Central Park, which demand Yellowfin Tuna Burgers and Oreo Ice Cream Sandwiches. It winds into November, one of the biggest months at the Tavern, where the whole city—if not the country—gathers just outside to celebrate the New York City Marathon and the annual Macy's Thanksgiving Day Parade. And then, of course, there's Christmas, when the restaurant is adorned with thousands of twinkling lights and an enormous gingerbread house beckons diners in and the kitchen turns out holiday dishes like Coconut Lobster Bisque, Honey Roasted Christmas Duck, and Eggnog Crème Brûlée.

If only this could be re-created it at home, you say? It can.

This cookbook is designed for both the home cook and the accomplished chef and replicates the Tavern dining experience, sharing the delicious recipes prepared with the flair of a French-trained chef: Bill Peet, a distinguished protégé of French culinary superstar André Soltner. His view of hospitality was shaped during his fifteen-year association with Soltner, the Alsatian chef who turned New York City's Lutèce (which was open from 1961 until 2004) into a four-star sensation.

Despite his formidable pedigree, Chef Peet knows how to make dishes that satisfy people from all walks of life. His revolving menu is seasonal, approachable, playful, and simply delicious. It's a daily effort that keeps diners coming back for more.

We are delighted to share our restaurant with you.

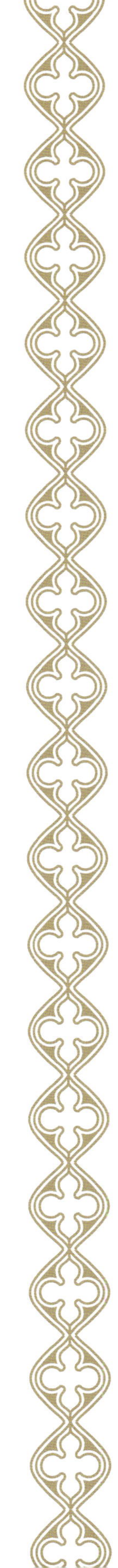

HISTORY

Tavern on the Green was originally designed in 1880 by Calvert Vaux, who worked alongside Frederick Law Olmsted to design Central Park. The building once housed two hundred Southdown sheep that grazed in Sheep Meadow, a large expanse of grass just across the park's West Drive from the Tavern building. In 1934, legendary power broker Robert Moses renovated Central Park and elevated its stature by turning the sheep's home into a restaurant.

The Tavern operated for forty years, but it was a lavish $10 million renovation by New York City businessman Warner LeRoy in 1976 that put the former little pub on the global map. LeRoy brought in Tiffany stained glass and Baccarat chandeliers and built the iconic Crystal Room. The showman transformed the Tavern on the Green into one of the highest-grossing restaurants in America. For decades, the Tavern was a hot spot for famous actors, musicians, and public figures who came in to dine, drink, and celebrate in one of country's most over-the-top restaurants.

In 2009, after three decades, the Tavern closed its doors. This development was due to several factors, including the US financial crisis at the time. The family of the late Warner LeRoy was forced to close and auction all furnishings after the city parks department refused to reissue an operating license.

David Salama was quite sure Tavern on the Green could not be restored after he visited the site that same year at the behest of his partner, Jim Caiola. "Jim had this crazy idea that one day he'd own this place," said Salama.

This was a dream of Caiola's born in the 1980s, when Caiola studied under the famed Lee Strasberg. During one rehearsal, he had a thrilling moment: The Maestro, not a man prone to praise fledgling actors, complimented Caiola's work in front of the entire class.

"As a reward I took myself out for lunch to the iconic Tavern on the Green," said Caiola. "As I enjoyed my lunch, I looked around the room and counted at least eleven foreign languages being spoken. The people at the other tables were full of energy, laughing as they toasted, sang, and celebrated both special moments and the simple joy of being alive.

"I had the thought . . . I told myself that if I ever decided to leave acting, I wanted to own this place, the most magical place on earth. And here I am!"

Salama, however, didn't have the same vision, and he was not at all convinced when he set foot into the space. "I looked at it and thought, no way. The woodwork was rotted, the slate roof had to come down, there were cables all over the place," he said. "The original

flooring was destroyed, there were leaks everywhere, odors, the carpet, the décor—everything—was rotting and smelled."

"I told Jim it would be cheaper to blow the place up," Salama said.

But in 2013, Salama and Caiola left behind their small and very successful Philadelphia restaurant, Beau Monde, to take another look at the vacant Tavern on the Green. The Parks Department and Conservancy had restored the building to its original footprint and registered it as historic. With the structure repaired, Salama and Caiola went to work on a very detailed and in-depth proposal to take over the space and make it their own. It took a whole team of architects, landscapers, designers, and financiers to win the bid from the city.

With a seasonal menu reflective of Greater New York, they reopened Tavern on the Green in April 2014.

As you approach the Tavern and come inside,
something happens. Magic happens. To everybody.
People gasp when Tavern on the Green is mentioned.
It's about place, history, and iconic New York City.

-JIM CAIOLA

THE TAVERN TIMELINE

1870: Tavern on the Green begins life as a Gothic Revival sheepfold housing 200 Southdown sheep.

1934: The sheepfold becomes a restaurant as part of a Robert Moses renovation of Central Park. The sheep are banished to Brooklyn's Prospect Park.

1940s–1950s: The dance floor is enlarged and a large outdoor patio is added; in addition, the Elm Tree Room is built.

1976: The Tavern is lavishly reincarnated by Warner LeRoy, who adds the Crystal Room. Celebrities dine amid brass, Tiffany stained glass, and Baccarat chandeliers.

2014: Tavern on the Green returns to its inviting, tavern-inspired roots. Local and artisanal food become the forefront of the experience. Live sheep are still unwelcome.

There were restrictions, however, and to some degree they were imposed so that the Salama/ Caiola tenure did not replicate LeRoy's flamboyance and disregard for city building codes.

New codes prevented Salama and Caiola from building any additions to the property, for example. They were not permitted to play loud music after 10:00 p.m. or to host overly large parties. They also lost the use of the parking lot. Yes, Tavern on the Green had a parking lot for many years, which was a big benefit. It lured diners from New Jersey, Connecticut, and New York who could drive into the city knowing that parking would be provided in front of the restaurant. But that also created headaches. A large tent was often erected in the lot for private parties and holiday bashes, and the loud music and chaos disturbed neighbors.

Regardless of the restrictive contract, Salama found freedom in discipline. The renovation of the Tavern drew from history, and the goal was to make the space feel like it had always been there. He describes his renovation as "Victorian Gothic on a budget." It's not fuzzy. The design doesn't include pillows or table lamps or things that are too precious. A specific plastering technique called scagliola was used to create special features of the restaurant, like the fireplace and entrance tables. *Verre églomisé* (a centuries-old French technique) was used to make gilded mirrors with leaves and birds highlighting Central Park. Parquet floors, polished daily, create a whimsical sheen brightened by abundant natural light in a room that looks out on the park. The only element retained from the past? The ceiling beams.

"I've had this experience before," Salama said. "You have a vision, you build, and then it takes on a life of its own."

With a new contract in hand and a refreshing design complete, the Salama/Caiola team still had another challenge: They needed a chef who could create delicious food while also mastering the fiscal demands of maintaining quality while keeping costs down.

Several chefs tried but did not make their mark. Finally, Bill Peet was recommended. He came, he conquered budget overages, and, most important, he stayed.

In keeping with Chef Peet's view of running a classic French kitchen and maintaining the Tavern's traditional, flexible, and extraordinary menu, these cookbook recipes reflect his modern view of elegant food, including all the Tavern specials that lure diners back.

HOLLYWOOD DINES AT TAVERN ON THE GREEN

Reinforcing its iconic status and cinematic style, Tavern on the Green has been prominently featured or mentioned in numerous films over the years, and many famous people have come in to dine.

An Unmarried Woman (1978)

It's My Turn (1980)

Arthur (1981)

Only When I Laugh (1981)

Ghostbusters (1984)

Heartburn (1986)

Wall Street (1987)

Arthur 2 (1988)

Beaches (1988)

New York Stories: Oedipus Wrecks (1989)

Crimes and Misdemeanors (1989)

Stella (1990)

Whispers in the Dark (1992)

The Night We Never Met (1993)

The Out-of-Towners (1999)

It Had to Be You (2000)

Hall of Mirrors (2001)

Made (2001)

Alfie (2004)

New York, I Love You (2008)

Mr. Popper's Penguins (2011)

CHEF PEET'S EQUIPMENT LIST

These are some of the tools I use in the kitchen. They help me and will definitely help you too.

IMMERSION BLENDER

An immersion blender (or stick blender) is a game changer when it comes to making soups. Its size makes it easy to purée soup directly in the pot rather than blending it in batches, as you would with a full-size blender. It is also very easy to clean and always at the ready.

SILICONE BAKING SHEETS

Silicone baking sheets are another game changer! During the early part of my career, I baked a lot, and I always used parchment paper. Sometimes these sheets would have to be greased, which always made a mess. When I tried to use less grease, the parchment paper would stick and I had to peel off each sliver that remained. Then came silicone sheets (introduced by Silpat), and it instantly became easier. These oven-proof sheets can be used thousands of times and are quickly cleaned and easily stored until next time.

CHINOIS

A chinois is a cone-shaped strainer with very fine mesh, 8 to 10 inches in diameter, used for straining liquids and soft foods.

CONICAL TEA STRAINER

This tool is similar to a chinois but smaller, about 3 inches in diameter—great for quickly straining a sauce before serving.

DOUBLE MESH STRAINER

A stainless-steel double mesh strainer has an attached support loop that allows for resting over a bowl or pot with ease and provides additional grip if necessary. Many sizes are available; I like a 10-inch diameter. This tool is good for quickly sifting dry ingredients, straining pasta and vegetables, or pushing a thick purée through.

MANDOLINE

Chefs in almost every restaurant use mandoline slicers to cut thin and very even slices of fruits and vegetables. There is no better tool for quickly slicing or cutting a julienne of fruit and vegetables. Mandoline slicers are essential for creating uniform and precise cuts, but they can also be dangerous. The blade is sharp and can easily slice a fingertip. When using one, it's important to use the guard that is included with it—and to focus and take your time.

I like two different types of mandoline: a large, heavy French model (Bron) that is a workhorse for French fries, shredded root vegetables, thick slices of potato for gratin potatoes, and so on, and a more compact and lighter plastic Japanese model (Benriner) that is great for thinly slicing and shredding smaller vegetables. Purchase one of these, and you will see a difference in the finished plates.

MICROPLANE GRATER

The design of the microplane grater came from woodworkers who just needed to take a little off very quickly. This is a zester and a grater in one, and its length allows you to get whatever cooking task you need done quickly. There are many options for microplane graters with varying hole sizes that produce large gratings down to the smallest gratings. These are useful for zesting citrus peels, nutmeg, hard cheeses, coconut—almost anything you can think of. Watch your knuckles!

INSTANT-READ THERMOMETER

Every cook needs an instant-read thermometer in the kitchen, even though some people will dig it out only once or twice a year to make a turkey. It is great for any kind of roast meat, as well as for deep frying, poaching, grilling, and baking—having an instant-read thermometer will help you avoid over- and undercooking.

GRAM/OUNCE SCALE

A kitchen scale is a necessary piece of culinary equipment. Volume measures, like cups and tablespoons, are notoriously imprecise, but the best kitchen scales allow you to be exact about the amount of any ingredient, which means more consistent results. Using a kitchen scale also cuts down on cleanup: Rather than using many cups and spoons, you can measure ingredients in a single bowl or container. I always used spoons and cups until I started working at Lutèce, where we had a little balance beam gram scale. It is definitely more precise, and eventually I revised many of my recipes to be just in grams.

KITCHEN SPOONS: SLOTTED, PERFORATED, AND SOLID

Always use the spoon meant for the job! Perforated and slotted serving spoons have different holes/slots. Perforated spoons have small holes to drain excess juice, syrup, or water, and they are also handy to pick up smaller pieces of food like peas, chopped onion, or minced garlic that you want to keep in the dish. Slotted spoons have large slots to drain thicker liquids (like sauces) and bigger foods. When I was a young cook, we all had our own spoons in our kit. I was always on the lookout for more spoons; flea markets and antique shops are great places to find them.

FOOD PROCESSOR

Food processors come in all different sizes and strengths, and they are common to most households. I like a basic Cuisinart with interchangeable blades and plates. They're great for chopping, but not for super-smooth purées, which requires a tapered blender that pulls ingredients down toward the blade.

BLENDER/VITAMIX

A food blender is primarily used for creating smooth liquids like smoothies and purées by blending ingredients together. A blender is best for liquids. Vitamix blenders are powerful enough to pulverize a full container of ingredients, and you can add ingredients through the lid opening while the machine is running. The Vitamix also has variable speeds. Professional kitchens use these tools quite a bit, but they are very expensive. A regular bar blender can be the right fit for an average kitchen.

STANDING MIXER

If you cook and bake a lot, a standing mixer is indispensable in the kitchen. The difference in the finished product using a standing mixer versus beating ingredients by hand is like night and day, and the range of attachments available is staggering—including a pasta rolling and cutting attachment, juicer, meat grinder, and many others. It is a good investment; the KitchenAid mixer I bought in 1981 still runs great.

KNIVES: 4- TO 6-INCH PARING KNIFE, 8- TO 10-INCH CHEF KNIFE, SERRATED KNIFE

Knives are the kitchen workhorses. You absolutely need a good serrated knife when cutting bread, which will dull a regular knife very quickly. The size of the chef knife is a personal preference; I like a 10-inch knife. The serrated knife should be 10 inches or longer. And remember, when you cut, it should be like cutting with a saw, with long draws.

RUBBER SPATULAS: LARGE AND SMALL

Spatulas are very useful for everything in the kitchen. You want to get everything out of the containers, leaving nothing behind. They're also very handy for folding ingredients into each other. You should get heat-resistant rubber spatulas; otherwise, they will melt over time—which is not a great ingredient.

PEPPERMILLS WITH BLACK AND WHITE PEPPER

I like fresh ground pepper, and I have peppermills for both white and black pepper. The brand that I use is Peugeot; I find the grind and feel of the peppermill ideal. My primary peppermill is at least fifty years old, given to me by Chef André Soltner—and it was his before that. I use it almost every day.

PASTRY BRUSHES

There is no substitute for a pastry brush when you need to apply a light layer of glaze or egg wash. Buy an assortment: 1 inch, 2 inch, and a larger 4 inch. The bristles come in different materials, including nylon and silicone; I prefer boar's hair.

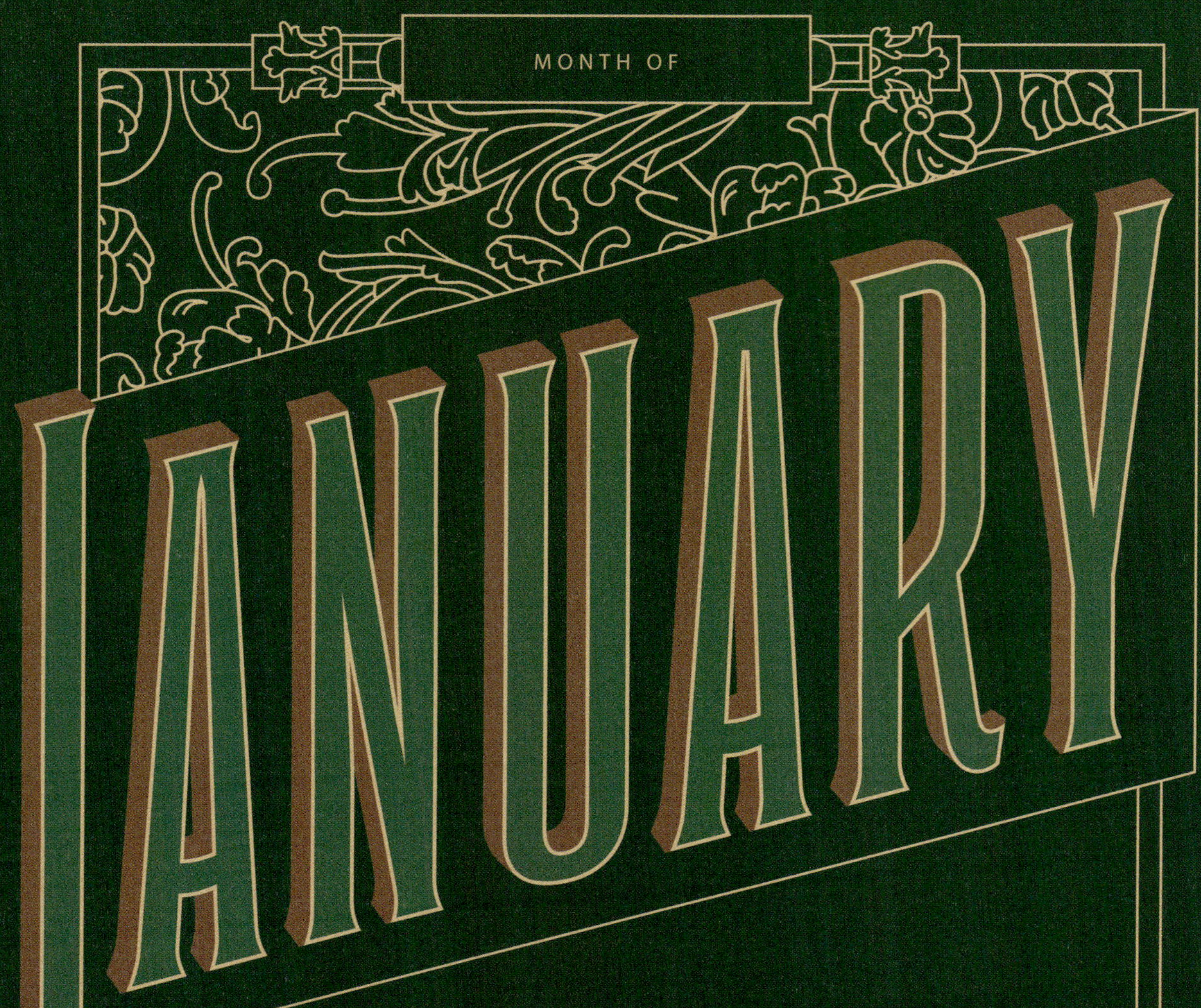

The New Year begins by taking a breather from the previous month's holiday indulgences.

Despite the sprawl of winter, Tavern diners will enjoy the views of the park from the Central Park Room. Winter is magical, with an extra layer of twinkle to everything. It is a wondrous time to be reminded how delicious and satisfying simple fare can be. The park is quiet this time of year, but there is a gentle hum indoors as forks clink on plates and diners converse over the hearty, warming dishes of winter.

The first day of the year is a busy one, and the Tavern team drags themselves in after the big night. It's one of the few holidays that Chef Peet takes off, but the kitchen team is prepared to churn out all sorts of dishes, many of which check off that perfect "day-after-drunk-food" requirement. Coffee is brewed, Bloody Marys are served, and diners dig into specials like prime rib hash, egg sandwiches with maple bacon, and Disco fries topped with cheese and gravy.

A Tavern favorite that customers have come to expect on the menu at this time of year is the Roasted Fig Salad. The combination of sweet honey-roasted figs with meaty bresaola and tangy goat cheese wakes up the palate with a brilliant balance of texture and flavor. Others might begin the new year transition with Split Pea and Country Ham Soup, which is redolent with smoky ham and topped with crisp, buttery croutons.

Appetizers include French Country Flatbread, a close cousin to Alsatian tarte flambée: a very thin, crisp dough topped with fromage blanc, bacon, and onions. The alluring aroma of the tarte fills the dining room and entices diners to order it. The other delicious-smelling appetizer wafting through the dining room? Roasted Garlic Shrimp, which comes served in bowls alongside toasty baguette slices for dipping into the smoky, garlicky butter.

When it comes time for main courses, Beer-Battered Fish and Chips are a source of pride for Chef Peet, who spent fifteen years perfecting the batter so that the fried fish comes out of the fryer irresistibly crispy. Beer is also a key component in Dark Beer Braised Short Ribs with Aligot Mashed Potatoes.

Despite many New Year's resolutions to the contrary, January does not demand that you skip dessert. Since January is prime citrus season, a perfect choice is Grapefruit Gratin with Sabayon Sauce, a bright, tangy dessert with a warming jolt of Grand Marnier in the sabayon. And for chocolate lovers, nothing compares to a hot Chocolate Peanut Butter Lava Cake, its molten core oozing salty peanut butter.

ROASTED FIG SALAD

This dish is a fantastic balance of textures and flavors, with sweet caramelized figs, tangy and rich goat cheese crème, meaty bresaola, and peppery arugula dressed with a lemony dressing. At one point, Chef Peet took the salad off the Tavern menu, but after many diners complained, it was brought back. It's now a signature dish for the restaurant.

SERVES 4

8 fresh figs, split

⅓ cup wildflower honey

6 ounces soft fresh goat cheese, preferably from Laura Chenel (see note)

¼ cup heavy cream

2 tablespoons white balsamic vinegar

Fresh ground black pepper

3 cups baby arugula

1 tablespoon lemon juice

1 teaspoon extra virgin olive oil

Kosher salt

4 thin slices of bresaola (air-cured beef)

Light the broiler. Lay the figs cut side up on an aluminum foil–lined baking sheet. Drizzle half of the honey over the figs and broil for 1 to 2 minutes, watching carefully, until they soften and start to brown and caramelize. Let cool.

Meanwhile, in a small bowl, stir the goat cheese with the cream until smooth. In another bowl, combine the remaining honey with the white balsamic vinegar and season with pepper. In a medium bowl, combine the baby arugula with the lemon juice and olive oil, and season with salt and pepper.

Spoon the goat cheese mixture onto 4 plates and top each with 1 slice of bresaola, pressing down to flatten it. Place 4 fig halves around the goat cheese on each plate. Arrange the arugula on top of the bresaola. Drizzle the honey mixture around the perimeter of the plate and over the salad and serve.

NOTE

Chef Peet's favorite goat cheese to use in this salad is from Laura Chenel, who started making her outstanding farmstead goat cheese in California's Sonoma County in 1979. She is credited with launching goat cheese onto the American food scene, popularizing it throughout the United States.

SPLIT PEA AND COUNTRY HAM SOUP

This dish is a staple of Chef Peet's—so much so that he occasionally finds that one of his family or friends has mailed him a ham bone with a message to make the soup! He says using a ham bone is optional, but it adds an extra layer of flavor. This is one of those soups that improves the longer it sits, as it absorbs more and more of the rich country ham goodness over time.

SERVES 4 TO 6

2 tablespoons unsalted butter

1 small yellow onion, cut into small dice

1 celery stalk, cut into small dice

1 small carrot, cut into small dice

Kosher salt and fresh ground black pepper

6 cups Vegetable Stock (page 341) or store-bought broth

1 ham bone or ham hock (optional)

2 cups green split peas, rinsed

1 bay leaf

7 ounces country ham, cut into small dice (1½ cups)

Croutons, for serving (see note)

In a heavy-bottomed saucepot or a Dutch oven, melt the butter over medium heat. Add the onion, celery, and carrot; season with salt and pepper; and cook until starting to soften but not brown (about 5 minutes). Add the vegetable stock and ham bone (if using), and bring to a boil. Add the split peas and bay leaf, cover, and simmer over low heat until the peas fall apart (about an hour).

Remove the ham bone and bay leaf. Blend the soup using an immersion blender or a standard blender. (You may also pass it through a food mill.) Add the diced ham and any meat that can be pulled off the ham bone.

Bring the soup back to a simmer. If it is too thick, add a little more stock or water. Season with salt and pepper. Serve hot with croutons.

The soup can be refrigerated for 4 days.

NOTE

To make your own croutons, cut a baguette into ½-inch pieces. Melt butter in a large skillet and toast the croutons until golden brown.

FRENCH COUNTRY FLATBREADS

Tarte flambée, also known as flammekueche, is an Alsatian specialty composed of a very thin, crisp dough covered with fromage blanc, bacon, and onions. Chef Peet learned to make it at NYC's Lutèce, where it was quite beloved. As simple as it is, it's packed with flavor and is delightful alongside a glass of Alsatian Riesling. This is Chef Peet's take on the classic tart.

MAKES FOUR 9-INCH FLATBREADS

FOR THE DOUGH:

2½ cups/354g all-purpose flour, plus more for dusting

2 teaspoons active dry yeast

⅛ teaspoon kosher salt

¾ cup lukewarm water (additional water if needed)

FOR THE TOPPINGS:

1 cup full-fat cottage cheese, drained

1 tablespoon all-purpose flour

1 teaspoon extra virgin olive oil

Pinch cayenne pepper

Kosher salt

12 ounces smoked bacon, cut into ½-inch pieces

2 tablespoons water

1 large yellow onion, thinly sliced

1 sprig fresh thyme

Fresh ground black pepper

¼ cup cornmeal, for dusting

2 teaspoons finely cut flat-leaf parsley (see notes)

Make the dough. In the bowl of a stand mixer fitted with the dough hook (see notes), combine the flour, yeast, and salt. Mix on low to combine; then, with the machine still on low speed, slowly add the lukewarm water until the dough is smooth and pulls away from the side of the bowl, scraping down the bowl occasionally—about 6 minutes. (You may need to add an additional tablespoon of water.) Transfer the dough to a lightly oiled bowl, cover with plastic wrap, and let rise at room temperature until doubled in size—about an hour. (See notes.)

Uncover the dough, punch it down, and then cover again and let rise for 1 more hour.

Meanwhile, prepare the toppings. In the bowl of a food processor, pulse the cottage cheese with the flour, olive oil, cayenne, and a pinch of salt until combined. Set aside.

In a large skillet, cook the bacon with 2 tablespoons of water over medium-high heat, stirring often, until the bacon is softened and the fat is rendered (6 to 8 minutes). Add the onion and thyme, season with salt and pepper, and cook until the onion is transparent (about 5 minutes). Discard the thyme sprig, and let the bacon mixture cool to room temperature.

FRENCH COUNTRY FLATBREADS

continued...

Preheat the oven to 450°F. Dust two large baking sheets with the cornmeal. Turn the dough out onto a lightly floured work surface. Divide the dough into four even pieces and roll each into a ball; then roll each ball into a round, about ⅛ inch thick and roughly 9 inches in diameter. Transfer two rounds each to the prepared baking sheets.

Spread each round thinly with the cheese mixture, leaving a ¼-inch rim around the edges. Scatter the bacon mixture over the top. Bake for 9 to 11 minutes (or until the dough is baked and golden and the tops start to brown and bubble). Sprinkle with parsley and serve hot.

The flatbreads can be reheated on a baking sheet in a 375°F oven for 5 minutes.

NOTES

- If you prefer, you can make the dough by hand. In a large bowl, whisk the flour, yeast, and salt and stir in the water with a wooden spoon until most of the flour is absorbed. Transfer the dough to a lightly floured work surface and knead for 7 minutes, until a smooth ball forms. Proceed with the recipe as written.
- We cut the parsley in a specific way at Tavern; it will be the same for most of the flat-leaf parsley in recipes. We cut a fine chiffonade, which is a French knife technique for cutting leafy greens and herbs into long, thin strips that resemble ribbons—but this is cut finer.

ROASTED GARLIC SHRIMP

Made with salted butter, fresh garlic, and smoky spices, these shrimp are full of flavor. They are easy enough for a weeknight dinner but special enough for a weekend dinner party. Don't skimp on the toasted baguette slices, which are excellent for mopping up the buttery sauce.

SERVES 4

1 stick salted butter, at room temperature

3 garlic cloves, finely chopped

1 tablespoon sherry vinegar

1 teaspoon fresh lemon juice

⅛ teaspoon smoked paprika

⅛ teaspoon Espelette pepper

Small pinch cayenne pepper (or to taste)

2 pounds jumbo shrimp (32 shrimp), peeled and deveined, tails left on

Kosher salt

1 teaspoon finely cut flat-leaf parsley

1 large baguette, sliced and toasted

In the bowl of a food processor, pulse the butter, garlic, vinegar, lemon juice, paprika, Espelette, and cayenne until blended and smooth, scraping down the blade and sides of the bowl as needed to fully incorporate. (The garlic butter can be prepared a few hours ahead and kept at room temperature.)

In a large skillet, lay half the shrimp in a single layer, season with salt, and cook over medium heat until the shrimp start to lightly brown (about 2 minutes). Add half the garlic butter and swirl the pan. Increase the heat to medium-high, turn the shrimp over, and continue to cook, swirling the pan a bit, until the butter browns and foams and the shrimp are cooked through (about 2 to 3 minutes longer). Transfer to a plate, cover loosely with foil and keep warm. Repeat with the remaining shrimp and butter.

Divide the shrimp into bowls and top with the parsley. Serve with toasted baguette slices.

BEER-BATTERED FISH AND CHIPS

Chef Peet experimented with his batter recipe for fifteen years before he was satisfied. The challenge was to develop a batter that was crispy and not mushy. For flavor, he adds nonalcoholic beer so that children can also enjoy this dish, though a lager or light beer can be used as well.

SERVES 4

FOR THE BEER BATTER:

1¾ cups all-purpose flour

½ cup potato starch

1¼ cups light beer, lager, or nonalcoholic beer

1 cup whole milk

2 tablespoons canola oil

1 large egg yolk

FOR THE FISH:

1 cup all-purpose flour

½ teaspoon kosher salt

¼ teaspoon smoked paprika

¼ teaspoon fresh ground black pepper

4 cups canola oil, for frying

2 pounds cod fillet, cut into eight 4-ounce pieces

1 bunch watercress, cleaned and dried

Malt Vinaigrette, for serving (recipe follows)

Kosher salt

Potato "Chips" (recipe follows; see note)

Make the beer batter. In a large bowl, mix all the ingredients well. Strain into another bowl and let rest for an hour.

Make the fish. In a shallow bowl, mix the flour with the salt, paprika, and pepper. In a heavy pot or electric deep fryer, heat the canola oil to 360°F over medium heat. Working in 2 or 3 batches (depending on the size of your fryer), dip the cod fillets in the seasoned flour and then immediately in the batter. Deep fry, turning a couple of times with a slotted spoon, until golden brown and cooked through (5 to 7 minutes). Remove from the pot with a slotted spoon and drain on a paper-towel-lined plate. Season with salt and pepper. Repeat with the remaining cod, maintaining the oil temperature at 360°F.

Toss the watercress with some of the Malt Vinaigrette and season lightly with salt and pepper. Divide the fish, chips, and salad onto four plates and serve right away.

NOTE

To make the fish and chips together, start by making the chips. After they're fried and drained, transfer them to a wire rack set over a baking sheet and keep warm in a 250°F oven. Proceed with the fish in the same pot, adding a little more oil to maintain 4 cups/1 quart.

MALT VINAIGRETTE

MAKES ABOUT 1 CUP

3 tablespoons malt vinegar

2 tablespoons Dijon mustard

3 tablespoons water

¾ cup extra virgin olive oil

Kosher salt and fresh ground
black pepper

In a small bowl or in a jar, whisk (or cover and shake the jar) to combine the vinegar, mustard, water, and oil. Season with salt and pepper.

The vinaigrette can be refrigerated for 3 months.

TIP Whenever Chef Peet is almost done with a jar of Dijon mustard, he adds a bit of vinegar (whatever he is feeling like using in the moment), olive oil, and salt and pepper. He closes the jar, shakes it, and has a nice bit of vinaigrette to use . . . no wasting any mustard!

POTATO "CHIPS"

4 large Idaho potatoes, peeled
Canola oil, for frying
(about 4 cups)

Kosher salt

Cut the potatoes lengthwise into ½-inch strips and wash in cold water until rid of all starch; drain. Transfer to a clean kitchen towel and lay in a single layer to dry; you may have to pat dry further ahead of frying.

In a heavy pot or electric deep fryer, heat the canola oil to 300°F over medium heat. Fry the potatoes for 6 to 7 minutes, until soft. Remove with a slotted spoon and drain on a paper-towel-lined plate; cool slightly.

Bring the oil up to 360°F. When the oil is hot, add the chips; fry for 5 to 6 minutes, until golden and crisp. Remove from the pot with a slotted spoon and drain again on a fresh paper-towel-lined plate. Season with salt and serve.

NOTE

For the ultimate crispy chips, the potatoes must be fried twice. First, they are blanched at a low temperature to cook through, and then they're fried a second time at a higher heat so they get extra crispy.

"

DARK BEER BRAISED SHORT RIBS WITH ALIGOT MASHED POTATOES

Of all the many different meats that are braised at Tavern on the Green, Chef Peet's favorite is this one. It's even on the menu in the hottest part of summer! Depending on the season, he uses a variety of different types of alcohol for braising, from dark beer (stout) to white wine, red wine, and even champagne.

SERVES 4

¼ cup canola oil

4 pounds boneless beef short ribs, trimmed of fat

Kosher salt and fresh ground black pepper

1 large white onion, thinly sliced

4 garlic cloves, smashed

¼ cup tomato paste

½ cup all-purpose flour

Two 12-ounce bottles dark beer, such as stout

2 celery stalks, trimmed of leaves, washed, and halved

2 fresh thyme sprigs

1 bay leaf

4 cups beef broth

16 baby carrots, peeled (about 1 pound) (see note)

Aligot Mashed Potatoes (recipe follows)

Preheat the oven to 350°F. In a large Dutch oven, heat the oil over medium-high heat until shimmering. Season the short ribs with salt and pepper, and sear until browned on all four sides (about 2 minutes per side). Transfer to a plate and set aside. (Depending on the size of your Dutch oven, you may have to brown the ribs in batches for the best sear; you will not need to add more oil between batches.)

Add the onion and garlic to the pot and cook, stirring constantly, until the onion starts to brown (4 to 5 minutes). Stir in the tomato paste and then the flour, cooking until slightly browned (about 2 minutes). Add the beer and cook, scraping up the browned bits from the bottom of the pot, until the beer is reduced by half (about 4 minutes).

Tie the celery, thyme, and bay leaf into a bundle in a piece of cheesecloth. Add to the pot with the beef broth and bring to a boil. Return the beef to the pot. Cover the pot and place in the oven for an hour. Add the carrots, cover, and continue to braise in the oven for about 1 hour and 45 minutes (or until the meat is fork tender).

DARK BEER BRAISED SHORT RIBS WITH ALIGOT MASHED POTATOES *continued...*

Transfer the beef and carrots to a plate and cover with aluminum foil to keep warm. Discard the celery bundle.

Skim off any fat on the surface of the braising liquid. Simmer the liquid for 15 minutes over medium-high heat to thicken it slightly. Season with salt and pepper.

Place the beef on a platter with the carrots, ladle the sauce on top, and serve hot with the mashed potatoes on the side.

The short ribs can be refrigerated for 3 days.

NOTE

Baby carrots are those that have been harvested while still quite small; they're typically 4 to 5 inches in length. They're not to be confused with baby-cut carrots sold in bags, which are made by cutting down larger carrots into little nubs.

MASHED POTATOES/ALIGOT MASHED POTATOES

Aligot Potatoes (known as pommes Aligot in central France, where the dish originates) is akin to a cheesy potato fondue. When the cheese is added, the texture becomes stretchy, silky, and so smooth. If you prefer basic mashed potatoes, you can omit the cheese and extra cream altogether. Both versions of the potatoes are divine with the rich short ribs.

SERVES 4

FOR THE MASHED POTATOES:

2½ pounds Idaho potatoes, peeled and cut into 2-inch chunks

Kosher salt

1 stick unsalted butter, at room temperature

1½ cups heavy cream, heated

Fresh ground white pepper

FOR THE ALIGOT MASHED POTATOES:

½ cup/2 ounces grated Comté cheese

½ cup/2 ounces grated Gruyère cheese

½ cup heavy cream, heated

Make the mashed potatoes. In a medium pot, add the potatoes and enough water to cover by 2 inches. Add 1 tablespoon salt. Bring to a boil, and then briskly simmer over medium heat until the potatoes are tender when pierced with a knife (15 to 20 minutes).

Drain the potatoes and return to the pot. Using a wire whisk or potato masher, break up the potatoes, leaving no big pieces. Gradually add the butter and heated heavy cream, stirring with the whisk until smooth. Season with salt and white pepper.

If you are making Aligot potatoes, stir both cheeses into the hot potatoes along with the cream and check for seasoning before serving. Serve right away.

GRAPEFRUIT GRATIN WITH SABAYON SAUCE

When developing the sabayon for these tangy grapefruit gratins, Chef Peet was inspired by glaçage (a savory whipped egg and cream mixture used to glaze oysters Rockefeller). In addition to glazing citrus, he says that very ripe fruit, such as peaches and strawberries, will work in this dessert.

SERVES 4

3 large grapefruits

2 tablespoons granulated sugar

1 teaspoon Grenadine

Sabayon Sauce, for serving (recipe follows)

1 tablespoon finely sliced mint leaves

Cut off the top and bottom of each grapefruit. Standing the grapefruit upright on a cutting board, cut along the sides of each grapefruit to remove the peel and pith. Holding one grapefruit over a bowl, cut between the membranes to separate and release the segments, letting the juices drip into the bowl; squeeze any extra juice from the grapefruit into the bowl. Strain the juice into a measuring cup.

In a small saucepan, simmer the sugar and 1 tablespoon of water over medium heat for about 5 minutes, until thickened and lightly browned. Add the grapefruit juice and Grenadine and bring back to a boil over medium-high heat. Pour over the grapefruit in the bowl. Cool, and then refrigerate for an hour.

Preheat the broiler and arrange the rack about 4 inches from the heat source. Using a slotted spoon, transfer the grapefruit segments to four shallow bowls. Arrange the segments in each bowl all in the same direction, like a spiral; don't overlap the segments, and leave a small space in between each. Spoon about ½ cup of sabayon in the center of each bowl.

Place the bowls on a rimmed baking sheet and broil, watching carefully, until the sabayon is golden brown (1 to 1½ minutes). Let rest for 1 minute, and then sprinkle with mint and serve, noting that the bowls will be hot to the touch.

SABAYON SAUCE

MAKES 2 CUPS

⅔ cup granulated sugar

1 teaspoon light corn syrup

1 large egg

2 large egg yolks

¼ cup/2 ounces Grand Marnier

1 teaspoon pure vanilla extract

1¼ cups/10 ounces heavy cream, lightly whipped

In a small saucepan fitted with a candy thermometer, combine the sugar and corn syrup with ¼ cup water. Bring to a boil over medium-high heat, and then lower the heat slightly and cook until the temperature reaches 280°F (about 8 minutes).

Meanwhile, in the bowl of a stand mixer fitted with the whisk attachment, whip the egg and yolks at high speed until they are pale and fluffy (3 to 5 minutes). With the machine on, carefully drizzle the hot sugar mixture down the side of the bowl, being careful not to pour the sugar syrup directly onto the eggs. Continue to whip for 5 to 7 minutes, until the mixture is very pale and thick. Whip in the Grand Marnier and vanilla. When cool, fold in the whipped cream and refrigerate for 3 hours (or until ready to use).

CHOCOLATE PEANUT BUTTER LAVA CAKES

Chef Jean-Georges Vongerichten is credited with creating the chocolate lava cake (aka molten chocolate cake), with its warm, oozy chocolate center, in 1987. It was an instant hit that is now ubiquitous on menus all over the country. Chef Peet wanted to make his own version, doing something a little different, so he created a version using peanut butter. He says the dessert gives Funny Bones vibes more than Reese's Cups. He especially likes to serve peanut brittle on the side for a double dose of peanutty goodness.

SERVES 4

2 tablespoons/24g granulated sugar

6 ounces/170g high-quality semisweet chocolate (66%), chopped

1 stick/114g unsalted butter

⅓ cup/45g confectioners' sugar

2 tablespoons/16g all-purpose flour

¼ teaspoon kosher salt

2 large eggs

2 large egg yolks

4 tablespoons/64g smooth peanut butter

Chocolate Sauce (recipe follows)

Peanut Brittle, for serving (page 289)

Lightly sweetened whipped cream, for serving

Preheat the oven to 425°F. Liberally spray four 6-ounce ramekins with baking spray and dust with the granulated sugar: Add the sugar to one ramekin and rotate the ramekin to cover the

CHOCOLATE PEANUT BUTTER LAVA CAKES *continued...*

inside all over with the sugar. Pour the excess sugar into another ramekin and repeat the process for all the ramekins.

In a medium heatproof bowl, combine the chocolate and butter. Set the bowl over a pan of simmering water (make sure the bowl doesn't touch the water) and melt the chocolate and butter, stirring now and then.

In a small bowl, whisk the confectioners' sugar, flour, and salt. Add to the bowl with the chocolate, and then slowly whisk in the eggs and egg yolks until incorporated; do not overmix. The batter will be a little thick.

Spoon the batter evenly into the ramekins. Put 1 tablespoon of peanut butter on top of each filled ramekin; push the peanut butter down slightly but not all the way under.

Set the ramekins on a rimmed baking sheet and bake for 12 to 14 minutes (see note), until the sides of the cakes look firm (the tops may look soft). Let cool for 3 to 4 minutes, and then carefully invert each cake onto a plate. Serve right away with Chocolate Sauce, Peanut Brittle, and a dollop of whipped cream.

NOTE

The cakes will continue to set as they cool. If you like a gooey, molten texture, aim to bake the cakes for around 12 minutes. For a more brownie-like texture, bake for closer to 14 minutes.

CHOCOLATE SAUCE

This is a quick and tasty homemade chocolate sauce, and, as with a lot of three-ingredient recipes, the better quality your cocoa powder is, the better your chocolate sauce will taste.

MAKES 1 CUP

¾ cup granulated sugar

⅔ cup Dutch-processed cocoa powder

2 tablespoons unsalted butter

In a small saucepan, whisk 1 cup of water with the sugar and cocoa over medium-high heat. Bring to a boil, stirring now and then. Reduce the heat slightly and let simmer for 1 minute. Whisk in the butter and bring back just to a boil. Pass the sauce through a fine-mesh sieve and refrigerate for at least 3 hours, until cooled and thickened slightly.

The sauce can be refrigerated for 3 months.

NOTE

If your cocoa powder has lumps, whisk the cocoa powder and sugar together in the saucepan before adding the water.

FEBRUARY

While a quiet hush falls over Central Park in winter, there is always something happening in the Tavern.

As diners approach the restaurant, warm lights glow from within, and once they've escaped the cold, the fireplace roars by the bar as glasses clink and conversation hums.

Cold midwinter brightens in anticipation of romance with Valentine's Day, when the Tavern dims the lights and provides a romantically curated menu of sumptuous soups, appetizers, and mains, all coupled with sparkling wines. A chilly February dinner might start with Black Bean Soup with Bacon or Steak Tartare that gets piled onto crisp garlic toast. For vegetarians, Wild Mushroom Toasts are not to be missed. Chef Peet's trick is making them with Boursin, the soft and creamy cheese spread flavored with garlic and herbs. It adds that same something special that sherry would, but the cheese helps hold the creamy sauce together (and it's more kid friendly). He serves the mushrooms in brioche boxes, like a little gift at the table.

The menu continues with seasonal salads such as Roasted Beet and Burrata, as well as Winter Frisée and Crispy Poached Egg, studded with crisp and chewy bacon lardons. As the meal shifts into the main course, options include hearty Tavern Turkey Chili (a favorite dish among the staff) or Duroc Pork Chop Milanese. Chef gets the best rack of pork, marbled with fat for the ultimate flavor and texture. He pounds each chop thinly, leaving the bone in, so when the chop is pan-fried, it stays juicy and moist. The chops are finished with a tangy, fresh mixture of arugula, red onions, tomatoes, and apples dressed in an alluring reduction of apple juice with balsamic vinegar.

The evening meal is complete with Tahitian Vanilla Crème Brûlée—a longtime favorite of Chef Peet's—or Chocolate Challah Bread Pudding with Peanut Butter Sauce, which is simultaneously deeply chocolatey and light as a feather.

The Tavern has a long history of promoting special events throughout the year. Events in February might include an Oscar party, where sightings of Broadway performers and Hollywood celebrities are the norm, which harkens back to the Warner LeRoy era. Starting in 1976, LeRoy's vision for the Tavern evolved from his love of Hollywood and celebrity. He put the former sheep barn on the map and attracted Manhattan socialites and stars throughout his twenty-five-year tenure. That aura of celebrity still pervades the Tavern, and even in deep winter, the Tavern hosts galas and parties, welcoming partygoers into its festive arms.

BLACK BEAN SOUP WITH BACON

This is a two-part recipe. It starts with cooking the dried beans, which are then added to the vegetables in the second part of the recipe. This is how the team cooks the soup in the restaurant, ensuring that everything is cooked correctly. You can also use the method that follows for cooking black beans to eat on their own or to use in other recipes.

SERVES 8 TO 10

FOR THE BEANS:

2 cups dried black beans, picked over and rinsed

1½ quarts water

One 6-ounce slab smoked bacon (see note)

1 large bay leaf

2 teaspoons kosher salt

FOR THE SOUP:

½ stick unsalted butter

3 celery stalks, finely chopped

1 large onion, finely chopped

1 large carrot, finely chopped

Kosher salt

3 garlic cloves, minced

1½ tablespoons ground cumin

2 quarts Vegetable Stock (page 341) or low-sodium broth

3 tablespoons cornstarch mixed with ¼ cup water to dissolve and form a slurry

Juice of 1 lime

FOR THE GARNISH:

½ cup sour cream

Juice of ½ lime

¼ teaspoon hot sauce, preferably Tabasco (use more for a spicier kick)

Make the beans. Place the beans and water in a pot. Add the bacon and bay leaf. Bring to a boil over medium-high heat, and then reduce the heat to medium, add the salt, and simmer for about 1½ hours, stirring occasionally, until the beans are tender; add more water as needed. Skim any scum from the surface.

Remove the beans from the heat and discard the bay leaf. Cut the bacon into small pieces (if there is any skin on, discard it) and set aside.

Make the soup. In a heavy-bottomed Dutch oven, melt the butter over medium heat. Add the celery, onion, and carrot, seasoning with salt. Cook, stirring occasionally, until the vegetables are softened and start to brown slightly (8 to 10 minutes). Add the garlic and cumin, and cook for 2 minutes. Stir in the beans and their cooking liquid, along with the stock and reserved bacon. Bring to a boil, and then simmer for about 30 minutes, until the flavors are blended.

BLACK BEAN SOUP WITH BACON

continued...

Remove the pot from the heat. Ladle 3 cups of beans and liquid into a food processor and purée; return this mixture to the pot. (You can also use an immersion blender to purée some of the beans right in the pot.) Stir the cornstarch slurry into the soup and bring back to a simmer to thicken the broth. Season the soup with salt and add the lime juice.

Make the garnish. In a small bowl, combine the sour cream with the lime juice and Tabasco. Spoon the soup into bowls and dollop with the sour cream mixture to serve.

The soup can be refrigerated for 3 to 4 days.

NOTE

If your slab bacon comes with the skin still on, it's fine to leave it as is.

WILD MUSHROOM TOASTS

Chef Peet turns to Boursin cheese to amp up flavor in a variety of dishes, like these super savory wild mushroom toasts. If you get this at the Tavern, it's typically served in brioche that has been cut into boxes, but at home a simple slab of toast is just as good.

SERVES 4 TO 6

1 tablespoon canola oil

2 cups cremini mushrooms, cleaned and sliced

2 cups oyster mushrooms, trimmed, cleaned, and sliced

2 cups shiitake mushrooms, trimmed, cleaned, and sliced

1½ cups heavy cream

2 tablespoons Boursin cheese

Kosher salt and fresh ground black pepper

4 to 6 thick slices brioche, trimmed of crusts and toasted

1 teaspoon snipped chives

In a large skillet, heat the oil over medium heat. Add all the mushrooms and cook, stirring occasionally, until softened and the juices have been released (about 10 minutes); do not brown the mushrooms.

Add the heavy cream and bring to a boil; then lower the heat and simmer for 3 minutes. Turn off the heat and stir in the cheese. Season with salt and pepper.

Put the toasts on plates and spoon the mushrooms over. Garnish with chives and serve.

STEAK TARTARE

Many recipes for steak tartare use filet mignon, but Chef Peet finds it too mushy. He prefers using top round of beef, which has a better chew and more flavor.

SERVES 4

1 garlic clove, halved

8 baguette slices, cut on a bias

12 ounces ground top round of beef

2 large egg yolks (see note)

2 oil-packed anchovies, drained and chopped to a paste

2 cornichons, finely chopped

2 teaspoons minced shallot

2 teaspoons finely cut flat-leaf parsley

1 teaspoon Dijon mustard

1 teaspoon finely chopped drained capers

½ teaspoon Worcestershire sauce

Kosher salt and fresh ground black pepper

Rub the garlic clove over the baguette slices and toast until lightly browned.

In a bowl, combine the beef with the egg yolks, anchovies, cornichons, shallots, parsley, mustard, capers, and Worcestershire. Using a fork, gently mix; you don't want to overmix the tartare. Taste and season with salt and pepper. Add a little cold water to lighten the tartare; it shouldn't be pasty. Taste again and check for seasoning. Spoon into ramekins or small bowls and serve with the garlic-rubbed baguette toast.

NOTE
Because the eggs in this recipe will be consumed raw, you can use pasteurized eggs to reduce the risk of foodborne illness.

Courtesy of Andrew Federico

WINTER FRISÉE AND CRISPY POACHED EGG SALAD

There are many salads with poached eggs out there, but Chef Peet thought it would be fun to mix this one up by making a version of a Scotch egg, which is a hard-boiled egg that's wrapped in sausage meat, breaded, and deep fried. Here he skips the sausage and breads a poached egg and then delicately fries it until crisp.

SERVES 4

1 pound slab bacon, cut into 1½-inch-by-½-inch strips

5 large eggs

1 tablespoon white vinegar

¼ cup all-purpose flour

Kosher salt and fresh ground black pepper

½ cup panko breadcrumbs

1 cup canola oil

4 cups frisée, trimmed and cleaned

Dijon Vinaigrette (recipe follows)

Put ¼ cup of water in a medium skillet and bring to a boil. Stir in the bacon. Reduce the heat to low and cook, stirring occasionally, until the water evaporates, the bacon browns, and the fat renders (about an hour). Using a slotted spoon, transfer the bacon to a paper-towel-lined plate. Reserve 2 tablespoons of the rendered bacon fat for the Dijon Vinaigrette.

Bring a medium saucepan of water to a low simmer and fill a bowl with ice water. Add the vinegar to the saucepan. Using a slotted spoon, stir the water in a circular motion. One at a time, crack 4 of the eggs into the moving water. Cook gently for 4 minutes, and then transfer the eggs to the ice water. Let cool for 10 minutes before transferring to a paper-towel-lined plate; let dry thoroughly.

Place the flour in a small bowl and season with salt and pepper. Put the remaining egg in another bowl and beat it lightly. Put the panko in a third bowl. Carefully dredge each poached egg in the flour and then in the beaten egg. Finish by coating in the panko breadcrumbs, being sure to coat all over. Transfer the eggs to a plate.

Heat the oil in a small pot over medium-high heat until a few breadcrumbs sprinkled in bubble and brown (about 3 minutes). Gently add one egg into the hot oil and fry about 1 minute; then turn the egg over with the slotted spoon and continue to fry until golden brown (about 1½ to 2 minutes total). Transfer to a paper-towel-lined plate and repeat with the remaining eggs. Keep warm.

In a medium bowl, toss the frisée and bacon with 2 tablespoons of the Dijon Vinaigrette. Season with salt and fresh ground black pepper. Divide the salads on four plates and top with the fried eggs. Drizzle the remaining vinaigrette over the finished salads and around the plates.

DIJON VINAIGRETTE

MAKES ⅓ CUP

1 tablespoon Dijon mustard

2 tablespoons white wine vinegar

¼ cup canola oil

2 tablespoons rendered
bacon fat

Kosher salt and fresh ground
black pepper

In a small bowl or in a jar, whisk (or cover and shake the jar) to combine the mustard, vinegar, oil, and bacon fat. Season with salt and pepper.

The dressing can be refrigerated for 2 weeks.

ROASTED BEET AND BURRATA SALAD

Soft, fresh burrata cheese has received a lot of attention in the past couple of decades as more and more is imported from Italy. It lends itself to so many simple and delicious preparations. The outside of the cheese is a thin shell of mozzarella, while the inside is creamy and rich. Chef Peet combines it with beautifully roasted red beets, velvety carrot purée, and a perfectly tangy vinaigrette for a compelling contrast of colors, flavors, and textures.

SERVES 4

4 medium red beets,
trimmed of greens

1½ cups kosher salt

4 pieces of fresh burrata cheese
(½ pound total)

Carrot Purée (recipe follows)

1 bunch watercress, stemmed
(about 2 packed cups)

1 Belgian endive, split lengthwise
and sliced crosswise ¼-inch thick

Champagne Vinaigrette
(recipe follows)

Kosher salt and fresh ground
black pepper

Preheat the oven to 425°F. Spread the salt on a baking sheet and set the beets on the salt, leaving space between each beet. Roast for about an hour (or until the beets are soft when pierced with a knife). Transfer the beets to a plate to cool.

Peel each beet with a paring knife and then slice ½-inch thick. Keep the beets in four piles.

Place a spoonful of Carrot Purée each onto four separate plates and draw the spoon through the purée. Arrange a beet on each plate, next to or just overlapping the purée. Place 1 burrata next to the beets, and then cut an X in the top of the burrata.

Combine the watercress and endive in a bowl and toss with some of the vinaigrette; season with salt and pepper. Divide the salad among the plates. Drizzle the remaining vinaigrette over the beets and burrata, and serve.

CARROT PURÉE

MAKES ABOUT ⅔ CUP

½ cup half-and-half

1 small Yukon Gold potato,
peeled and cut into ½-inch dice

1 large carrot, peeled and
cut into ½-inch dice

1 garlic clove,
split and germ removed

1 fresh thyme sprig

Kosher salt and fresh ground
white pepper

In a small saucepan, combine all the ingredients except the salt and pepper and bring to a simmer over medium heat. Cover and simmer over medium-low heat until the potato and carrot are softened (about 15 minutes); do not let the half-and-half boil, or it will curdle. Discard the thyme sprig.

Using a slotted spoon, transfer the potato, carrot, and garlic to a mini food processor or a glass measuring cup. Return the half-and-half to the heat and simmer over medium until reduced by half (1 to 2 minutes). Add the liquid to the vegetables and purée; alternately, use an immersion blender to purée. Let cool, and then season with salt and pepper.

The purée can be refrigerated for up to 2 days.

CHAMPAGNE VINAIGRETTE

MAKES A SCANT ½ CUP

2 tablespoons champagne
vinegar

1 teaspoon Dijon mustard

⅓ cup extra virgin olive oil

Kosher salt and fresh ground
black pepper

In a small bowl or in a jar, whisk (or cover and shake the jar) to combine the vinegar, mustard, and oil. Season with salt and pepper.

The vinaigrette can be refrigerated for 3 months.

TAVERN TURKEY CHILI

Chef Peet switched from beef to turkey chili several years ago when the staff requested it, since so many of them liked having it during their work hours but didn't want to be eating so much beef. Since then, it has become a staple for staff and customers alike. It's a perfect dish to make ahead, as the flavors only get better after a day or two.

SERVES 6

2 tablespoons canola oil

2 pounds ground white meat turkey (93% lean)

Kosher salt and fresh ground black pepper

1 large onion, chopped

6 celery stalks, chopped

2 red bell peppers, seeded and chopped

2 garlic cloves, chopped

½ jalapeno, seeded and finely chopped

1 tablespoon chopped fresh oregano

1 tablespoon chili powder

1½ teaspoons ground cumin

1 bay leaf

Three 14½-ounce cans chopped tomatoes with their juices

2 tablespoons tomato paste

One 28-ounce can red kidney beans, drained and liquid reserved

Shredded cheddar cheese and chopped red onion, for serving (optional)

In a large heavy pot or Dutch oven, heat the oil over medium-high heat. Add the turkey and season with salt and pepper. Cook, stirring occasionally, until lightly browned and the meat is broken up (5 to 7 minutes). Using a slotted spoon, remove from the pot and transfer to a bowl; leave any fat behind in the pot.

Reduce the heat to medium. Add the onion, season with salt and pepper and cook, stirring often, until softened and lightly browned (about 5 minutes). Add the celery, red peppers, garlic, jalapeno, oregano, chili powder, cumin, and bay leaf. Cook, stirring occasionally, until the celery and peppers are softened (12 to 15 minutes).

Stir in the tomatoes and their juices along with the tomato paste and 1 cup of the bean liquid from the can (if you don't have 1 full cup, you can add water). Add the turkey back to the pot. Bring up to a boil, and then cover partially and simmer over medium-low heat for 15 minutes, stirring occasionally. Add 2 cups of the drained beans (reserve the remainder for another use) and simmer for 15 minutes longer, stirring occasionally, until heated through. Check for seasoning and serve with shredded cheddar and chopped red onion, if desired.

DUROC PORK CHOP MILANESE

Chef Peet sources the best pigs he can for the Tavern because he knows that quality pork means the best flavor. The two kinds he uses most often are Duroc and Berkshire. Once Chef breaks down the rack of pork, he pounds the chops thinly and leaves the bone in for frying, which helps keep the meat moist and tender during cooking. He tops the crispy breaded chops with a refreshing salad of arugula, onions, tomatoes, and fresh apples that have been dressed in a tangy vinaigrette made with reduced apple juice.

SERVES 4

Four 10-ounce bone-on pork chops, preferably Duroc

Kosher salt and fresh ground black pepper

1 cup all-purpose flour

3 cups panko breadcrumbs

3 large eggs, beaten

⅔ cup canola oil

3 cups arugula, stemmed and washed

2 ripe plum tomatoes, split lengthwise, seeded, and cut in ½-inch slices

1 small red onion, thinly shaved into rings

1 small ripe Golden Delicious apple, seeded and cut into ¼-inch wedges

½ cup Apple Balsamic Vinaigrette (recipe follows)

Preheat the oven to 400°F. With a meat tenderizer or a rolling pin, lightly pound each pork chop between 2 sheets of plastic wrap until the meat is ½-inch thick. Be careful not to put any holes in the meat. (This process takes a bit of patience, but keep pounding, being sure to get up against the bone for an even thickness.)

Separately place the flour, breadcrumbs, and beaten eggs in three small cookie sheets or wide, shallow bowls. Lightly season each chop with salt and pepper. Working with one chop at a time, dredge in the flour, being sure to coat well and shake off any excess. Next, dip the chop in the egg, coating it all over and letting any excess drip back into the bowl. Finish by coating in the breadcrumbs, patting to help the crumbs adhere. Repeat with the remaining chops.

In a large skillet, heat the oil over medium-high heat until it starts to shimmer and smoke (3 to 4 minutes). Add one pork chop at a time to the hot oil, cooking until browned (about 1½ minutes per side). Transfer to a baking sheet and fry the remaining chops. Season with salt and pepper. Transfer the chops to the oven and bake for 10 minutes.

Meanwhile, in a bowl, toss the arugula with the tomatoes, onion, and apple and season lightly with salt and pepper. Toss with some of the vinaigrette.

Place the chops on four warmed plates and top with the salad. Drizzle the remaining vinaigrette over each plate and serve.

APPLE BALSAMIC VINAIGRETTE

MAKES ¾ CUP

1 cup apple juice (not cider)

2 tablespoons balsamic vinegar

1 teaspoon Dijon mustard

½ cup extra virgin olive oil

Kosher salt and fresh ground black pepper

In a small saucepan, simmer the apple juice over medium heat until reduced to ¼ cup (about 15 minutes). Pour the apple reduction into a bowl with the balsamic vinegar and mustard and let cool. Whisk in the olive oil in a steady stream until incorporated. Season with salt and pepper.

The vinaigrette can be refrigerated for 2 weeks.

CHOCOLATE CHALLAH BREAD PUDDING WITH PEANUT BUTTER SAUCE

The key here is using challah, a type of bread that is simultaneously tender and hearty and holds up perfectly to the custard.

SERVES 4

Unsalted butter, softened

2 packed cups (5 ounces/141g) challah bread, cut into 1-inch cubes

3½ ounces/100g bittersweet chocolate (64%), roughly chopped

Scant ¼ cup/15g unsweetened Dutch-processed cocoa powder

2 cups/454ml heavy cream

3 tablespoons plus 1 teaspoon/40g granulated sugar

4 large egg yolks

½ teaspoon pure vanilla extract

Peanut Butter Sauce, for serving (recipe follows)

Preheat the oven to 325°F. Lightly butter four 8-ounce ramekins and set aside. Spread the bread on a baking sheet and toast for 10 to 12 minutes, stirring once, until lightly toasted; cool, and then transfer to a large bowl. Increase the oven temperature to 350°F.

In a double boiler, melt the chocolate and cocoa powder. (You can also melt this mixture in a microwave-safe bowl in the microwave, stopping to stir every 20–30 seconds until melted.) In a small saucepan, combine the heavy cream and sugar and bring just to a boil over medium heat to dissolve the sugar (about 3 minutes). Pour over the melted chocolate and stir until smooth and combined.

In a medium bowl, whisk the egg yolks and vanilla. Slowly whisk in the melted chocolate mixture, whisking constantly. Pour over the toasted challah and fold gently with a rubber spatula. Let stand for 20 minutes.

Spoon the bread pudding into the prepared ramekins and set the ramekins in a casserole or roasting pan. Add enough boiling water to come halfway up the sides of the ramekins. Carefully slide the pan into the preheated oven and bake until set and just cooked through (35 to 45 minutes). Serve right away with the Peanut Butter Sauce drizzled on top.

PEANUT BUTTER SAUCE

1½ cups whole milk

6 tablespoons granulated sugar

5 large egg yolks

2 tablespoons smooth
peanut butter

½ teaspoon pure vanilla extract

In a small saucepan over medium heat, bring the milk and 3 tablespoons of the sugar to a simmer for 2 minutes to dissolve the sugar; do not let it boil. Meanwhile, in a medium bowl, whisk the egg yolks with the remaining 3 tablespoons of sugar. Slowly whisk the hot milk into the yolk mixture until fully incorporated. Pour this mixture back into the pot and cook over medium heat, stirring occasionally, until the sauce starts to thicken and coats the back of a spoon (about 5 minutes).

Strain the sauce into a medium bowl through a fine-mesh strainer. Whisk in the peanut butter and vanilla extract, and continue to whisk until completely incorporated and smooth.

The sauce can be refrigerated for 5 days.

TAHITIAN VANILLA CRÈME BRÛLÉE

They make a variety of different flavors of crème brûlée at the Tavern, changing the dish with the seasons. Tahitian vanilla is the first crème brûlée Chef Peet learned to make, and it has always been special for him because, although it is simple, it packs so much flavor. Start with this recipe and experiment by adding other ingredients to customize to your tastes.

SERVES 6

2 cups heavy cream

1 Tahitian vanilla bean, split, seeds scraped

½ cup/100g granulated sugar

6 large egg yolks

¼ cup plus 2 tablespoons/ 75g turbinado sugar (Sugar in the Raw)

Preheat the oven to 300°F. Set six 6-ounce crème brûlée dishes in a lipped sheet pan or roasting pan and place a kettle of water on to boil.

In a small saucepan, simmer the heavy cream and vanilla bean over medium heat for 10 minutes; do not let it boil.

Meanwhile, in a medium bowl, mix the white sugar and vanilla bean seeds, rubbing the seeds into the sugar with your fingertips. Whisk in the egg yolks until the eggs are pale. Remove the cream from the heat, and remove and reserve the vanilla bean (see note). While whisking constantly, slowly add the hot cream into the egg mixture and continue whisking until completely combined. Strain through a fine-mesh strainer into a clean bowl or large heatproof measuring cup.

Carefully pour the custard into the brûlée dishes, being sure to scrape out any vanilla seeds that may have settled on the bottom of the bowl. Pour the boiling water into the pan, halfway up the side of the dishes. Carefully slide the pan into the oven and bake for 35 to 40 minutes, until firm.

Remove the custards from the water and set on a rack to cool for an hour; then refrigerate until completely chilled.

To serve, sprinkle about 1 tablespoon of turbinado sugar over the surface of each custard in a thin layer. Using a torch, heat until the sugar melts and browns evenly. You can also broil the custards as close to the heat source as possible to brown and melt the sugar. Serve immediately.

The custards can be covered and refrigerated for 2 days. Brown the sugar just before serving.

NOTE

Rinse and dry out the used vanilla bean. Place in a jar with sugar (approximately 1 cup sugar to 1 used vanilla bean) to infuse the vanilla flavor into the sugar. Use a jar with a lid.

MONTH OF
MARCH
If ever there were a time for Irish Soda
Bread, it arrives in March . . .

St. Patrick's Day is a big holiday at Tavern on the Green, and not just for the delicious food. New York City hosts an annual parade that includes a long list of local bagpipe and drum bands. The musicians dress in plaid kilts and other traditional garb. They begin late in the morning at East 44th Street in Manhattan and proceed north on Fifth Avenue to East 79th Street. But the festivities don't end there.

Every year, David Salama invites the St. Patrick's Day parade marching band into the Tavern with their brass and bagpipes blaring. Newcomers are delighted when the regiment of pipe and drum musicians suddenly comes marching into the Central Park Room: No one knows when they will show up. The marching band has

Courtesy of Bill Peet

upward of seventy people, many of whom are local carpenters who helped rebuild the restaurant. They come into the Tavern, play three songs in each room, and then sit down to eat.

If the St. Patrick's Day Parade anchors the month, a multitude of quieter daily events dot the calendar. Early each morning, Chef Peet delights in handwriting the menu of that day's specials. Monday and Tuesday mornings are fun because he knows there will be that Maple and Brown Sugar Smoked Bacon left over from Sunday brunch. (There is always excess bacon because the restaurant chefs dare not run out of it due to its popularity.) Tavern diners love it, and some people even say it's life changing. There is little wonder why. The half-inch-cut smoked bacon is marinated and baked until it comes out like candy. The bacon is served with a small green salad dressed with a sharp vinaigrette and a drizzle of maple syrup. The sweetness of the bacon and tanginess of the vinaigrette emerge as an extravagance for all seasons. Yet each bite is thick with Chef's kitchen management philosophy: Waste not. Make something special with what you have.

Before writing the menu, Chef Peet does an inventory of what sold the previous night and what remains. Since he knows what to expect on Monday, he will use the bacon to create a flatbread for lunch.

Whatever is plentiful will inspire one of that day's specials. During Lent, a flatbread recipe may include roasted mushrooms or cream spinach with cheddar cheese. On another day, specials may feature Grilled Rainbow Trout, Blistered Green Beans, and Garlic Fingerling Potatoes with a Toasted Walnut and Arugula Pesto, or perhaps slow-roasted Shaved Prime Rib Steak Sandwich with Caramelized Onions and Provolone and Horseradish. Leftovers? Never!

APPETIZERS

Soup Du Jour 15

Jumbo Lump Crab Cake
Remoulade Sauce 28

Tavern Country Salad (GF)
Baby Oakleaf Greens, Roasted Kabocha Squash,
Maple Bacon Lardons, Crispy Poached Egg,
Whole Grain Mustard Vinaigrette 21

Honey Roasted Figs (GF)
Laura Chenel Goat Cheese,
Honey-White Balsamic Dressing,
Air Cured Beef, Baby Arugula 24

Chopped Vegetable Salad (VG, GF)
Haricots Verts, Radish, Jicama, Asparagus,
Butternut Squash

DINNER MENU

MAIN COURSES

Seared Diver Sea Scallops (GF)
Roasted Pumpkin & Sage Paella Rice, Arugula Pesto

Organic Scottish
French Lentils with

Bar Menu

Caramelized French Onion Soup
Gruyère & Parmesan Cheese
19

French Country Flatbread
Smoked Bacon, Onions, Farmers Cheese
20

Giant Soft Pretzel
Warm Cheese Sauce, Mustard
15

Chilled Jumbo Shrimp Cocktail
Cocktail Sauce, Lemon
29

Crabmeat Cocktail
Lemon Truffle Vinaigrette, Avocado, Chives
32

Tavern Burger
American Cheese, Dill Pickle, Salt & Vinegar Chips
32

Braised Beef Short Rib Sandwich
Pickled Red Onions, Horseradish Sauce
28

Cheese & Charcuterie Plate
House Mustard, Cornichons, Toasted Bread
31

Meatball Sliders
Parmesan, Marinara Dipping Sauce
16

Pork Confit & Broccoli Rabe Sandwich
Ciabatta Roll, Provolone
29

BILL PEET, EXECUTIVE CHEF
Consuming raw or undercooked meats,
shellfish or eggs may increase your risk...
Our fish dishes may contain small bones.

APPETIZERS

Kids Menu

Tavern Beef Sliders
Two Mini Burgers, American Cheese, Dill Pickle, Chips 17
Bow Tie Pasta
Tomato & Basil Sauce or Butter & Parmesan 14
Grilled Cheese Sandwich
American Cheese Brioche 14
Kid's Macaroni & Cheese
White Cheddar & Fontina 14
Crispy Chicken Fingers
Tomato Sauce 16

Warm Chocolate Brownie
Vanilla Bean Ice Cream

DELUXE
TIC-TAC

LUNCH MENU

Chopped Vegetable Salad (VG, GF)
Jicama, Asparagus, ... Tomato, Corn,
Avocado, Carrot, ... Paper Dressing 24

Apple Bacon
... Black Rice
... Vinaigrette 19

Mushroom Toast
Creamy Garlic

RAW BAR SELECTIONS

10oz

Curried Crab

Shredded Duck

Lemon
Italian Farro Pilaf

Shrimp Cocktail (GF)
Avocado, Chives 32

APPETIZERS

... Basket (V)
Butter & Preserves

Honey

Dessert Menu

Blueberry Crumble Tart (V)
Crème Anglaise, Vanilla Ice Cream 16
Caramelized Apple Tart (V)
Cardamom Sauce, Cinnamon Ice Cream 16
Lemon Crème Brûlée (V)
Blackberry Shortbread Cookie 16
Molten Peanut Butter Chocolate Lava Cake (V)
Peanut Butter Custard Sauce, Vanilla Ice Cream, Peanut Brittle 16
New York Style Cheesecake (V, GF)
Meringue Kisses, Raspberry Coulis 16
Sticky Toffee Pudding (V)
Sundried Date Compote, Salted Caramel Ice Cream 16
A Slice Of Birthday Cake (V)
Confetti Layer Cake, Ice Cream 16
Artisanal Cheese Plate (V)
Chef's Selection of 3 Cheeses, Fresh Honeycomb, Toasted Baguette 23

Dessert Wines

Sauternes
Petit Guiraud-Bordeaux, France 2016 17
Tokaji
Royal Tokaji Aszú 5 Puttonyos-Tokaj, Hungary 2013 18
Zinfandel
... Cellars, Late Harvest-Sonoma, California 2016 14
Port
... Tawny Port, Portugal NV. 14

Brunch Menu

COCKTAILS

Beau Monde Bloody Mary 19

Cranberry Clementine Spritz 22

BILL PEET, EXECUTIVE CHEF
Consuming raw or undercooked meats...
increase your risk of foodborne illness...
may contain small bones.

Taverngreen.com · Taven on the Green

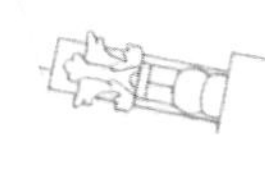

Smoked Brisket
Shredded

Tavern
Strawberries, Caramel

Classic
Canadian Bacon, Hollandaise

Add:
Substitute For: Maine

Grilled Organic
Baby Red Mustard

Baked Vegetable
Parmesan Cheese,
Roasted Tomato
22

Steak & Eggs
Sliced Sirloin, Breakfast
37

Organic Scottish Salmon
Black Beluga Lentils with Roasted Mini
Chive Beurre Blanc
38

Grilled Chicken Salad
Deviled Eggs, Baby Oakleaf Lettuce
Sun-dried Dates, Toasted Almonds
Red Wine Vinaigrette
33

Tavern Burger
10 oz Burger, American Cheese, Dill
Salt & Vinegar Chips
32

IRISH SODA BREAD WITH RAISINS

Traditional Irish soda bread is a brown bread made with just whole wheat flour, baking soda, buttermilk, and salt. This version is far lighter in color and a little sweet. Chef Peet prepares it in a cast-iron skillet, which gives it a great crust. He got this recipe from his childhood friend Freddy Monaghan, who used to make it every year for the local church. If you're not a fan of raisins, Chef says it's fine to skip them.

MAKES ONE LOAF

2 cups/284g raisins

4 cups/520g sifted all-purpose flour, plus more for greasing and dusting

3 teaspoons caraway seeds

1 teaspoon baking powder

1 teaspoon kosher salt

1 stick/112g unsalted butter, cut into cubes and chilled, plus more for greasing

½ cup/100g sugar

1⅓ cups/314ml buttermilk

3 large eggs

1 teaspoon baking soda

Preheat the oven to 325°F. Lightly butter and flour a medium cast-iron skillet. In a large bowl, toss the raisins with 1 cup of the flour to separate them. Add the remaining 3 cups of flour along with the caraway seeds, baking powder, and salt.

In a medium bowl, using your hand, blend the butter with the sugar until a coarse mixture forms. Add to the flour and raisins.

In another bowl, combine the buttermilk with 2 eggs and the baking soda.

Form a well in the center of the flour mixture. Pour in the wet mixture in three increments, stirring with a wooden spoon, until a rough, sticky dough forms. Flour a work surface and scrape the dough onto it. With well-floured hands (the dough will be sticky), knead the dough for about 1 minute, forming a rough mound. Turn the dough seam side down and flatten so it's about 1½ inches high.

Transfer the dough to the prepared cast-iron skillet. In a small bowl, mix the remaining egg with 1 tablespoon of water and brush it all over the top of the dough. Using a sharp knife, cut a deep X into the top of the dough.

Bake for an hour. Increase the oven temperature to 375°F and continue to bake for another 5 to 10 minutes (or until the top is golden brown). You can check whether it's finished by inserting a thermometer in the center; it should be around 200°F. Let the bread cool in the skillet before serving.

CHICKEN VEGETABLE SOUP

Chef Peet grew up with chicken vegetable soup, so this recipe is near and dear to his heart. What makes it really stand out is adding a squeeze of fresh lemon juice at the end, which brightens up the soup.

SERVES 4 TO 6

2 tablespoons unsalted butter

1 cup diced onions

½ cup diced carrots

½ cup diced celery

¼ cup diced white turnips

1½ quarts Chicken Stock
(page 342)

One 6-ounce boneless,
skinless chicken breast

¼ cup drained canned tomatoes,
coarsely chopped

¼ cup frozen peas

1 teaspoon fresh lemon juice

Kosher salt and fresh
ground black pepper

2 teaspoons finely cut
flat-leaf parsley

In a heavy saucepan, melt the butter over medium heat. Add the onions, carrots, celery, and turnips and cook, stirring occasionally, until softened but still a bit crunchy (10 to 15 minutes). Add the stock and bring to a boil; skim off the scum that rises to the surface.

Add the chicken breast to the pot and simmer for 10 minutes. Remove the chicken and let cool; then dice the meat. Simmer the vegetables until just cooked. Add the tomatoes, peas, and chicken, and bring up to a simmer. Add the lemon juice and season with salt and pepper. Add the parsley just before serving.

The soup can be refrigerated for 4 days.

MAPLE AND BROWN SUGAR SMOKED BACON WITH WATERCRESS SALAD

This dish is so popular that it can't be removed from the Tavern brunch menu. It's served at both brunch and lunch, but the difference is that at lunch it's grilled, giving it a barbecue-like flavor. At brunch, the marinated bacon is baked, making it taste more like candy.

SERVES 4

½ cup pure maple syrup

¼ cup light brown sugar

⅛ teaspoon cayenne pepper

12 slices (1½ pounds)
thick-cut smoked bacon

3 packed cups (about 4 ounces)
watercress, cleaned and dried

1 cup frisée, trimmed and cleaned

¼ cup Sherry Vinaigrette (recipe
follows)

Kosher salt and fresh
ground black pepper

Preheat the oven to 350°F. In a small pot, simmer the maple syrup, brown sugar, and cayenne over low heat, stirring until the sugar dissolves (2 to 3 minutes). Transfer to a dish large enough to hold the bacon in a single layer (a little overlap is okay) and let cool for 15 minutes. Add the bacon, being sure to coat each slice well. Marinate for an hour.

On a foil- or parchment-paper-lined baking sheet, lay the bacon strips in a single layer, leaving any excess marinade in the dish. Bake the bacon for 30 to 40 minutes; turn and brush with the leftover marinade every 10 minutes. The finished bacon will be caramelized and nicely browned.

In a medium bowl, toss the watercress and frisée with the vinaigrette and season lightly with salt and pepper. Divide the bacon and greens onto four plates and serve.

SHERRY VINAIGRETTE

This is a great base recipe for a variety of vinaigrettes. Feel free to change the type of vinegar you use, or consider adding chopped capers, olives, different ground peppers, or even sriracha.

MAKES A SCANT 1 CUP

3 tablespoons sherry vinegar

2 tablespoons Dijon mustard

⅔ cup extra virgin olive oil

Kosher salt and fresh ground black pepper

In a small bowl or in a jar, whisk (or cover and shake the jar) to combine the vinegar, mustard, and oil. If the vinaigrette seems too thick, thin it with a little cool water. Season with salt and pepper.

The vinaigrette can be refrigerated for 2 months.

CHARRED OCTOPUS AND CHORIZO SALAD

This is a very popular lunch dish at the Tavern. It's made with cured chorizo, a smoky Spanish-style seasoned sausage. It's not to be confused with fresh chorizo, which needs to be fully cooked before eating.

SERVES 4

2 frozen cooked octopus legs (about 4 ounces each)

1 large or 2 small cooked (cured) chorizo links, cut into 1-inch pieces (about ⅔ cup)

1 tablespoon extra virgin olive oil

¼ teaspoon smoked paprika

1 pinch cayenne pepper

Kosher salt

2 tablespoons Sherry Vinaigrette (page 70)

1 teaspoon sriracha hot sauce

1 shallot, thinly sliced into rings

1 tender inner celery stalk, thinly sliced on a bias

¼ cup flat-leaf parsley leaves

2 small ruby grapefruits, peeled and segmented (1½ cups) (see notes)

In a medium bowl, combine the octopus and chorizo with the olive oil, paprika, and cayenne and refrigerate for at least an hour and up to overnight.

Preheat the broiler. Season the octopus and chorizo with salt, and arrange on a baking sheet. Broil 4 to 5 inches from the heat source until the octopus and chorizo start to char (3 to 4 minutes). Turn the octopus and chorizo over and char on the other side. Remove from the heat and allow to cool slightly. Slice the legs on a 2-inch-long bias about ½ inch thick. Transfer to a bowl with the chorizo and keep warm.

In a small bowl, combine the vinaigrette with the sriracha.

In another bowl, toss the shallot, celery, and parsley leaves with half of the sriracha vinaigrette and a pinch of salt. Gently mix in the warm octopus and chorizo. Divide between four plates and arrange the grapefruit segments on each plate. Drizzle the remaining sriracha dressing around each plate and serve.

NOTES

- To segment a grapefruit, trim the bottom and top, and then peel and trim away all the bitter white pith. Cut between the segments, following the curve of the fruit and releasing the segments into a bowl to catch the fruit.
- 1 tablespoon of Pickled Wild Ramps (recipe in the "Pantry" section) can be cut up and added to the salad for a nice flavor pop.

PAN-ROASTED BABY BLACK SEA BASS

Chef Peet fell in love with this fish as a young cook because the taste was so clean. Black bass has very white flesh and black skin, and while this recipe calls for baby, larger black bass are easier to get. If you are unable to source baby black bass, look for another round fish, such as striped bass, red snapper, or grouper.

SERVES 4

Kosher salt

1 pound small fingerling potatoes

½ cup extra virgin olive oil

Sea salt and fresh ground black pepper

Four 8-ounce baby black sea bass fillets, with skin

6 ounces fresh baby sweet pea shoots, with tendrils (about 6 cups)

Fresh lemon juice, for seasoning

Preheat the oven to 400°F. In a medium pot of salted water, bring the potatoes up to a boil, and then simmer until the potatoes are tender (10 to 12 minutes). Drain the potatoes, transfer to a bowl, and crush with the back of a fork. Add ¼ cup of the olive oil and season with salt and pepper. Cover and keep warm.

In a large oven-safe skillet, heat 2 tablespoons of the oil over medium heat until it just starts to shimmer and smoke. Season the fish with salt and pepper. Place two of the fillets in the hot pan, skin side down, and let cook for 1 minute. Transfer the pan to the oven and cook for another 5 minutes (or until opaque and cooked through). Using a large spatula, flip the fillets and cook in the pan (not in the oven) for 1 minute longer. Transfer to a warm platter, tent with foil, and keep warm while you cook the remaining fillets. (You do not need to add more oil to the pan.) Transfer the fillets to the platter and keep warm.

Place the potatoes on plates and set the fillets on top. Toss the pea shoots in the warm pan and cook just until wilted; season with lemon juice, salt, and pepper. Add to the plates. Drizzle the remaining 2 tablespoons of olive oil (see note) over each dish and serve immediately.

NOTE

An alternative to just extra virgin olive oil at the end is a drizzle of Balsamic Vinaigrette (recipe in the "Pantry" section).

NEW YORK–STYLE CHEESECAKE WITH RASPBERRY COULIS

Chef Peet refers to this delicious cheesecake as "plain." That's not a criticism but an invitation. Try the recipe as is, and then get creative. For example, before baking, Chef sometimes adds chocolate sauce to the mixture and swirls it to create a marbled texture. The "get creative" challenge comes with one caveat: Slicing the soft cheesecake could be problematic if you use a hard ingredient, such as nuts.

MAKES ONE 9-INCH ROUND CHEESECAKE

FOR THE CRUST:

1½ sticks plus 1 tablespoon unsalted butter, melted

1 sleeve/126g graham crackers, finely crushed (scant 1¼ cups crumbs)

FOR THE FILLING:

1 pound/453g cream cheese, at room temperature

3 large eggs at room temperature, lightly beaten

1 cup/200g sugar

1 tablespoon pure vanilla extract

3 cups/680g sour cream, at room temperature

½ cup/118ml heavy cream, at room temperature

Raspberry Coulis, for serving (recipe follows)

Make the crust. Brush the inside of a 9-inch springform pan with 1 tablespoon of the melted butter. Wrap the bottom of the pan with a single sheet of heavy-duty aluminum foil, and then tie a piece of kitchen string around the pan to secure it (you may also use a large rubber band).

Put the graham cracker crumbs in a medium bowl and stir in the 1½ sticks of melted butter until it looks like wet sand. Add the cracker mixture to the prepared pan and, using the flat bottom of a glass or measuring cup, gently press to create a uniform thickness. Refrigerate the crust for an hour.

Preheat the oven to 300°F. Fill a roasting pan with water to come 1½ inches up the side. Carefully set the pan in the oven on the middle rack.

Make the filling. In the bowl of a food processor or in the bowl of a stand mixer (or in a medium bowl using a handheld mixer), blend the cream cheese, eggs, sugar, and vanilla until smooth, stopping once to scrape down the sides of the bowl.

NEW YORK–STYLE CHEESECAKE WITH RASPBERRY COULIS *continued...*

In a large bowl, whisk the sour cream with the heavy cream until combined. Add the cream cheese mixture, and whisk until fully incorporated.

Scrape the cheesecake mixture into the chilled crust and smooth the top. Transfer the pan to the hot water bath in the oven and bake for 1 hour and 45 minutes to 2 hours (or until the cake is set but still slightly jiggly in the center and a toothpick inserted in the middle of the cake comes out clean).

Carefully take the entire pan of water out of the oven. Let the cheesecake cool to room temperature in the pan (about 3 hours).

Remove the pan from the water bath, and then refrigerate the cheesecake for at least 4 hours (preferably overnight). Serve chilled with the Raspberry Coulis.

The cheesecake can be wrapped in plastic and refrigerated for 3 days.

NOTE

If the cheesecake begins to brown too much during baking, reduce the oven temperature to 275°F. If the cheesecake begins to puff toward the end of baking, open the oven door to let out some heat and lower the temperature to 275°F to finish baking.

RASPBERRY COULIS

This versatile coulis can be served with cheesecake, angel food cake, sponge cake, chocolate cake—any cake you like, really. It's also superb over ice cream.

MAKES 1½ CUPS

½ cup granulated sugar

½ cup water

2 cups raspberries, picked through and any softer ones kept together

1 teaspoon fresh lemon juice

1 teaspoon pure vanilla extract

In a small saucepan, simmer the sugar and water over medium heat until the liquid begins to thicken and form large bubbles, browning slightly at the edges. Reduce heat to low, add 1 cup of the raspberries (include the softer ones), cover, and cook for 10 minutes.

Give the mixture a good stir, and then pass it through a fine-mesh strainer into a small bowl, pushing on the solids with a rubber spatula. Discard the seeds. Stir in the lemon juice and vanilla, and mix the remaining raspberries into the sauce. Let cool before serving.

The coulis can be refrigerated for 1 week.

TRIPLE CHOCOLATE CHIP COOKIES

The good news is that these monster-sized cookies can be underbaked for a softer final product (ideal for lovers of cookie dough) or baked a bit longer for a firmer and crunchier cookie. They make the ultimate coffee or tea dunkers.

MAKES 8 TO 9 COOKIES

3 cups/425g all-purpose flour

⅛ teaspoon baking soda

¾ teaspoon kosher salt

1¾ sticks/198g unsalted butter, at room temperature

⅔ cup/141g granulated sugar

1 cup/198g light brown sugar

2 large eggs

½ teaspoon pure vanilla extract

5 ounces/142g semisweet chocolate (64%) pistoles or bar, roughly chopped into ¼-inch pieces

5 ounces/142g milk chocolate (38%) pistoles or bar, roughly chopped into ¼-inch pieces

5 ounces/142g white chocolate (29%) pistoles or bar, roughly chopped into ¼-inch pieces

Preheat the oven to 350°F. In a medium bowl, combine the flour, baking soda, and salt. In a large bowl or in the bowl of a stand mixer, cream the butter and both sugars together until fluffy and combined, stopping to scrape down the side of the bowl with a rubber spatula once or twice (2 to 3 minutes). Beat in the eggs and vanilla. Mix in the dry ingredients until combined, and then mix in the chocolate until just incorporated into the dough.

Line a baking sheet with a silicone liner or parchment paper. Scoop the dough into ¾ cup (170g each) balls. Working in batches, arrange the balls on the sheet and press down to flatten to a rough ½ inch thickness; there should be 3 to 4 inches between each cookie. Bake for 8 to 10 minutes (or until the cookies have spread a bit and start to turn golden brown around the edges). Allow to cool on the baking sheet for 7 minutes, and then, with a wide spatula, carefully transfer the cookies to a wire cooling rack to finishing cooling.

The cookies can be kept in an airtight container for 5 days.

CHEF PEET'S IRISH CREAM

This Irish cream is more potent than Bailey's and is as good enjoyed as an after-dinner shot as in a cup of coffee. Chef makes it at home during the holidays to gift to friends. He puts it in clean repurposed bottles from the restaurant, but you can easily keep the drink in jars.

MAKES ABOUT 1 QUART

One 14-ounce can sweetened condensed milk

1½ cups heavy cream

¾ cup Jameson Irish Whiskey

1½ tablespoons chocolate syrup, preferably Fox's U-Bet brand

⅛ teaspoon coconut extract

In a blender, combine all the ingredients, using a rubber spatula to get all the condensed milk out of the can. Blend completely, and then allow to sit for 5 minutes. Scoop off and discard the foam from the surface.

Slowly pour the drink into a clean quart bottle (or jars), just up to the base of the neck. Seal the bottle and refrigerate until chilled.

The Irish cream can be refrigerated for 2 months.

Spring has sprung and al fresco dining in the courtyard opens as Central Park blooms with daffodils and tulips.

The Chopped Vegetable Salad is very popular. The generous assortment of veggies—including fingerling potatoes, baby asparagus, and chopped tomato—is prepared in a manner Chef Peet says keeps the quality and satisfaction high. However, the veggies are not merely chopped and then tossed onto a plate. Some vegetables are raw while others are cooked, whether blanched, grilled, or roasted. Each item brings a different texture, flavor, and dimension to the dish.

Some diners may choose to savor a Pork Confit and Broccoli Rabe Sandwich or partake in the Tavern Cobb Salad, an ideal lunch or dinner; deviled eggs are a highlight of the salad that make it a real hit among diners. Guests who celebrate Passover (or Pesach) can feast on White Wine Braised Beef Brisket, which is cooked until it's fall-apart tender. To finish, sweets include Rhubarb and Strawberry Tarts and Carrot Layer Cake, which is lightly spiced with cinnamon and nutmeg and topped with an irresistible cream cheese frosting.

To celebrate Easter, David Salama builds a corral and brings in sheep from a local farmer, who drives them to Manhattan in a little pickup truck. The annual event harkens back to the origins of the area, when the Tavern was a sheepfold housing the sheep that grazed in nearby Sheep Meadow. Salama considers it a tribute to the animals who were evicted in 1934, when Robert Moses converted the building into a restaurant. To make the holiday feel especially festive, the sheep are dressed up with garlands and flowers and set up in their corral in front of the glass in the main dining room, where everyone can see them.

Those who have been to the Tavern at this time of year know that there is no shortage of flowers. Salama plants between three and five thousand tulip bulbs that come into full bloom in April, in every color imaginable. The park, which has been relatively quiet through the winter, starts to come alive again with runners, bikers, and dog walkers, along with tourists who meander along its winding paths. Spring is definitely in the air.

CREAM OF ASPARAGUS SOUP WITH **BLACK TRUFFLE OIL**

A good asparagus soup is so satisfying, but there are simple ways to turn it into something truly great. Chef Peet tops the creamy soup with asparagus tips in black truffle oil, which accentuates the rich earthy flavor of the soup and adds a very appealing crunchy finish to the dish.

SERVES 4 TO 6

2 tablespoons unsalted butter

16 jumbo asparagus spears (about 1 pound)—peeled, woody stems trimmed and discarded, tips cut into 2-inch pieces, stalks cut into 1-inch pieces

1 small white onion, sliced

1 garlic clove, smashed

2 small Yukon Gold potatoes, peeled and diced

5 cups Vegetable Stock (page 341)

½ cup crème fraîche

Kosher salt and fresh ground black pepper

1 teaspoon black truffle oil

In a heavy-bottomed stockpot, melt the butter over medium-high heat. Add the asparagus stalks, onion, and garlic and cook, stirring often, until the onions are transparent (about 5 minutes). Add the potatoes and stock and bring to a boil. Reduce heat to medium and simmer until the vegetables are completely soft and tender (25 to 30 minutes).

Meanwhile, in a steamer set in a saucepan of boiling water, steam the asparagus tips until crisp-tender (2 to 3 minutes). Fill a small bowl with ice water and transfer the cooked asparagus to the bowl to stop them from cooking further. Once cool, drain and dry the tips and slice them in half lengthwise.

Using an immersion blender, purée the soup (you may also use a blender or food processor and purée the soup in batches). Add the crème fraîche and blend to combine. Season with salt and pepper. When ready to serve, toss the asparagus tips with the black truffle oil. Top each bowl with a few of the tips and serve.

The soup can be refrigerated overnight.

GRILLED ASPARAGUS VINAIGRETTE

The chopped hard-boiled eggs mixed into this vinaigrette are called a "Mimosa" garnish, a classic garnish resembling the yellow flowers of the Mimosa tree. Jumbo spring asparagus is both tender and toothsome. Peeling the stalks is necessary to eliminate the tough, woody exterior, but it takes just a couple of minutes and is well worth it.

SERVES 4

¼ cup white wine vinegar

2 tablespoons sherry wine vinegar

2 teaspoons Dijon mustard

¾ cup canola oil

Kosher salt and fresh ground black pepper

20 spears jumbo asparagus, woody ends trimmed and stalks peeled

2 large hard-boiled eggs, chopped

1 teaspoon finely cut flat-leaf parsley

Using a handheld mixer or a wire whisk, blend both vinegars with the mustard. Whisk in the oil slowly, until emulsified; add 2 teaspoons of water to thin the vinaigrette. Season with salt and pepper.

Meanwhile, bring a wide saucepan of water to a boil. Place the asparagus in a steamer basket, cover, and steam until the asparagus is tender but still firm (6 to 8 minutes, depending on how thick the spears are). Lightly grill the asparagus for around 1 minute to change the flavor.

Transfer the spears to four plates. Add the chopped eggs and parsley to the vinaigrette and spoon across the spears, just following the tips. Serve at once.

CHOPPED VEGETABLE SALAD

This compound salad uses a variety of vegetables, both raw and cooked. Because the vegetables are all chopped, it's easy to eat and very pretty on the plate. When you take a bite, the combination of textures and flavors is enormously appealing. Chef Peet created it for a very practical reason: Many of the salads served at lunch were being sent back to the kitchen by customers requesting their salad be chopped up. The simple solution was to give them this! The salad is admittedly a bit time consuming to prepare, but, unlike many salads, it can be prepared ahead of time.

SERVES 4

1 small butternut squash, peeled and cut into small dice (about 2 cups)

2 teaspoons olive oil

4 ounces haricots verts

10 ounces fingerling potatoes

8 ounces thin asparagus spears

1 medium sweet onion, preferably Bermuda, sliced into rings

1 ear of corn, shucked

3 tablespoons vegetable oil

1 tablespoon drained capers

4 ounces breakfast radishes, trimmed and thinly sliced

1 medium avocado, pitted, peeled, and diced

1 small jicama, peeled and diced

1 medium tomato, diced

2 carrots, peeled and shredded (preferably on a box grater)

Grated zest of 1 lemon

Kosher salt and fresh ground black pepper

Finely cut flat-leaf parsley

Tangy Caper Dressing (recipe follows)

Preheat the oven to 425°F. Arrange the squash on a baking sheet and toss with the olive oil. Roast the squash until tender, tossing once (about 30 minutes). Set aside.

Meanwhile, bring a medium pot of water to a boil and add the haricots verts. Simmer until bright green (about 1 minute). Fill a small bowl with ice water, and, using a slotted spoon, transfer the haricots verts to the bowl to stop them from cooking further. Drain and pat dry. Cut into small dice, put into a large bowl, and keep chilled.

Add the potatoes to the boiling water and cook until tender when pierced with a fork (about 20 minutes). Drain. When cool enough to handle, peel and slice the potatoes. Add to the haricots verts.

CHOPPED VEGETABLE SALAD

continued...

Heat a large grill pan. Grill the asparagus, onion rings, and ear of corn (in batches, if necessary) until lightly charred. Dice the onion and asparagus, and add to the bowl with the haricots verts. Cut the corn off the cob and add to the bowl.

Heat the vegetable oil in a small skillet until shimmering. Add the drained capers and fry, stirring a bit, until they start to open and get a bit dark (about 45 seconds). Use a slotted spoon to transfer the capers to a paper-towel-lined plate. They will crisp as they cool.

In the large bowl, combine all the vegetables with the lemon zest and season with salt and pepper. Add some of the vinaigrette and season again to taste. Divide the salad onto plates, top with the parsley and capers, and serve.

The dressed salad can be refrigerated for 4 hours; top with the fried capers and parsley before serving.

TANGY CAPER DRESSING

MAKES 1 CUP

⅓ cup sherry vinegar

2 tablespoons Dijon mustard

⅔ cup extra virgin olive oil

Kosher salt and fresh ground black pepper

2 tablespoons chopped drained capers

In a small bowl, whisk the vinegar and mustard. Slowly whisk in the olive oil until emulsified. Season with salt and pepper and stir in the capers.

The dressing can be refrigerated for one week.

TAVERN COBB SALAD

Chef Peet says that people like the deviled eggs in this hearty salad more than anything, though the salad also includes creamy, pungent Stilton blue cheese instead of just any blue cheese. Chef makes the salad with chicken, but it can also be made with duck confit.

SERVES 4

1 cup cooked chicken breast, cut into ½-inch dice

8 cups romaine lettuce, cleaned and cut into 2-inch pieces

2 ripe plum tomatoes, seeded and cut into ½-inch dice

12 strips crisp-cooked bacon, cut into 1-inch pieces

Kosher salt and fresh ground black pepper

½ cup Cabernet Vinaigrette (recipe follows)

2 ripe avocados, halved, pitted, peeled, and cut like a fan

8 Deviled Egg halves (recipe follows)

⅔ cup crumbled Stilton blue cheese

In a large bowl, combine the chicken, lettuce, tomatoes, and bacon. Season lightly with salt and pepper. Toss with ¼ cup of the vinaigrette. Divide the salad into four large, chilled bowls. Garnish each bowl with 2 deviled egg halves and a fanned half avocado. Sprinkle with the crumbled cheese, and drizzle the remaining dressing over the salads.

CABERNET VINAIGRETTE

MAKES 1 CUP

¼ cup cabernet vinegar
(or another high-quality
red wine vinegar)

½ tablespoon Dijon mustard

¾ cup extra virgin olive oil

Kosher salt and fresh ground
black pepper

In a small bowl or in a jar, whisk (or cover and shake the jar) to combine the vinegar, mustard, and oil. Season with salt and pepper.

The vinaigrette can be refrigerated for 1 month.

DEVILED EGGS

MAKES 8 HALVES

4 large hard-boiled eggs,
peeled and halved lengthwise

1½ tablespoons mayonnaise

½ teaspoon Dijon mustard

¼ teaspoon Worcestershire
sauce

¼ teaspoon hot sauce,
preferably Cholula

¼ teaspoon dry mustard

Kosher salt and fresh
ground white pepper

Paprika or finely cut parsley,
for garnish

Remove the egg yolks from the whites and push through a small fine-mesh strainer into a bowl. Add the mayo, mustard, Worcestershire, hot sauce, and dry mustard, and stir to combine; season with salt and white pepper. Spoon into a pastry bag (or plastic bag with the corner snipped off) fitted with either a star tip or a plain round tip, and fill the egg white halves. Garnish with a sprinkling of paprika or parsley, or leave plain.

The deviled eggs can be refrigerated overnight.

PORK CONFIT AND BROCCOLI RABE SANDWICH

Confit is a process of cooking food (meat, fish, or vegetables) slowly in fat. It's a means of preservation, as the food can typically be stored for a good amount of time. In this case, the pork can be refrigerated for up to a month in the duck fat.

SERVES 4

5 ounces broccoli rabe

1½ pounds pork shoulder, cut into 4 equal pieces

1 tablespoon Confit Spice (recipe follows)

3 cups rendered duck fat (see notes)

4 garlic cloves, peeled and smashed

2 fresh thyme sprigs

Kosher salt and fresh ground black pepper

4 ounces provolone cheese, shredded

4 ciabatta hoagie rolls, split horizontally (but not all the way through)

In a pot of boiling salted water, blanch the broccoli rabe until just crisp-tender and bright green. Transfer to a bowl of ice water to cool. Drain and cut into 2-inch pieces and refrigerate for later.

Season the pork shoulder pieces all over with all the confit spice. Transfer to a baking sheet lined with plastic wrap, and cover the pork with another sheet of plastic wrap. Top with another baking sheet and put a 2–3-pound weight on top (see notes). Refrigerate overnight.

Preheat the oven to 300°F. Wipe any moisture off the pork. In a large Dutch oven or heavy-bottomed ovenproof pot, heat the duck fat over low heat. Add the pork, thyme, and garlic (they should be submerged in the fat) and cook until the fat reaches a temperature of 125°F or until you start to see a few little bubbles in the oil (about 15 minutes). Transfer to the oven and braise until the pork is super tender and falling apart (2½ to 3 hours). Check from time to time to make sure the fat isn't too hot (see notes), or the pork will fry and dry out; if this happens, lower your oven temperature a bit. Remove from the oven and let the pork and garlic cool in the fat.

PORK CONFIT AND BROCCOLI RABE SANDWICH *continued...*

Transfer 1 tablespoon of the fat to a medium skillet with the garlic. Add the broccoli rabe and cook until the garlic is broken up and mixed with the broccoli rabe (about 2 minutes). Season with a little salt and a generous amount of fresh ground black pepper.

To assemble the sandwiches, reheat the pork in the fat. Spread the shredded provolone in the crease of the ciabatta rolls and divide the broccoli rabe between the four sandwiches. Lift the pork out of the fat with a slotted spoon, allowing the meat to drain, and then divide the pork between the four rolls. Push down with a knife to close the roll. Cut in half, serve, and have a great time!

CONFIT SPICE

MAKES ABOUT 1 CUP

¾ cup kosher salt

2 tablespoons granulated sugar

2 tablespoons ground
white pepper

1 tablespoon ground nutmeg

1 tablespoon ground bay leaves

Mix everything together and store in an airtight container.

The spice mix can be stored at room temperature for 2 years.

NOTES
- Duck fat is available at gourmet markets and online.
- If you need ideas for weights, consider using a few bottles of wine or oil or some heavy cans.
- You can tell the fat is too hot if it starts to bubble; if that occurs, add more cold fat to bring the temperature down and lower the oven to 275°F.

ROASTED LEG OF SPRING LAMB WITH POTATOES AND MINT PESTO

Why is mint so commonly paired with lamb? Along with radishes and chives, mint is the first aromatic herb to bloom in the garden come spring, and it's a perfect accompaniment to the rich meat. At the Tavern, the lamb is seared in a hot roasting pan to get a good crust and to help seal in the juices. This is a little harder to do at home, so instead the lamb is seared in a very hot oven for 10 minutes. Chef Peet shifts the lamb over the potatoes once or twice to give the potatoes ample time to cook and to give them an extra boost of lamb flavor. To serve, the meat can be sliced right off the leg into large pieces and then more thinly sliced into uniform pieces.

SERVES 6 TO 8

One 5–7-pound bone-in leg of lamb, hip bone removed, leg trimmed of excess fat and tied (see notes)

1 tablespoon canola oil

Kosher salt and fresh ground black pepper

6 medium Idaho potatoes, peeled and sliced ⅛-inch thick

1 medium onion, thinly sliced

1 bunch wild ramps, cleaned and roughly chopped (see notes)

2 thyme sprigs and 2 rosemary sprigs, tied together with twine

4 cups Chicken Stock (page 342) or prepared chicken broth

4 tablespoons unsalted butter, melted

Mint Pesto (recipe follows)

Remove the lamb from the fridge 30 minutes before cooking. Preheat the oven to 450°F.

In a roasting pan, heat the oil over medium-high heat until it shimmers and just begins to smoke. Season the meat all over with salt and pepper, and place in the roasting pan. Transfer to the oven and cook for 5 minutes, and then turn the lamb over and cook for another 5 minutes. Remove from the oven and transfer the lamb to a large plate.

In the roasting pan, combine the potatoes, onion, ramps, and herb bundle and season with salt and pepper. Add the chicken stock, just covering the potatoes. (You may not need all the stock.) Set the lamb on top of the potatoes and pour half of the melted butter over the lamb. Lower the oven temperature to 350°F and place in the oven.

Cook for 30 minutes. Turn the lamb over and move to another position on the potatoes. Pour

ROASTED LEG OF SPRING LAMB WITH POTATOES AND MINT PESTO

continued...

the remaining butter over the lamb and continue to cook until a thermometer inserted in the thickest part of the lamb reaches 130–135°F, about 45 minutes longer. (This takes about 15 minutes per pound.) The internal temperature will continue to rise another 10 degrees as it rests.

Transfer the meat to a platter and remove the twine. Let the meat rest loosely covered with aluminum foil for 10 minutes, and finish cooking the potatoes in the oven during this time.

Season the potatoes with salt and pepper and discard the herb bundle. Slice the lamb and serve with the potatoes and a drizzle of the pesto.

NOTES
- Have your butcher trim and tie the lamb for you.
- Ramps are a type of wild spring onion sometimes called wild leeks. They're in season only for a short time, so if you can't find them, scallions or baby leeks can be substituted.

MINT PESTO

MAKES 1 CUP

1 cup packed mint leaves, stems off

1 cup packed spinach, stems off

1 tablespoon freshly grated Parmesan cheese

½ garlic clove, finely chopped

¾ cup extra virgin olive oil

Pinch cayenne pepper

Kosher salt and fresh ground black pepper

Bring a medium pot of boiling water to a boil and blanch the mint and spinach for 20 seconds; then drain and immediately plunge the leaves into a bowl of ice water. (This method will help preserve the color.) After a minute or two, remove the mint and spinach and squeeze dry.

Add the mint, spinach, Parmesan, garlic, and olive oil to a blender or food processor and purée until blended. Season with salt and pepper to taste. If the sauce is too thick, add a little hot water until you have the right consistency. Serve at room temperature with the lamb.

The pesto can be refrigerated for 3 days. Serve at room temperature.

WHITE WINE BRAISED BEEF BRISKET

While red wine seems to be the wine of choice when it comes to cooking beef, Chef Peet is a big believer in white wine. This is because the bulk of his professional training was spent in the kitchens of Alsatian chef André Soltner, and white wine—especially Riesling—is a staple of Alsatian cuisine. Their Rieslings are not too sweet and have great acidity, making a great accent to a rich beef dish like brisket. Chef Peet also likes using vegetable stock for a cleaner flavor in the dish.

SERVES 6

¼ cup canola oil

One 4-pound beef brisket, trimmed of fat

Kosher salt and fresh ground black pepper

1 large onion, cut into small dice (2 cups)

1 large carrot, cut into small dice (1 cup)

1 celery stalk, cut into small dice (⅔ cup)

4 garlic cloves, smashed

¼ cup tomato paste

¼ cup all-purpose flour

2 cups dry white wine

8 cups Vegetable Stock (page 341)

2 fresh thyme sprigs

1 bay leaf

Preheat the oven to 350°F. In a roasting pan, heat the oil over medium-high heat until shimmering. Season the brisket all over with salt and pepper and add to the pan. Cook, browning on both sides (about 8 minutes). Transfer the brisket to a plate.

Add the onion, carrot, celery, and garlic to the pan and cook, stirring, until the vegetables start to brown (about 7 minutes). Add the tomato paste and flour and cook for 3 minutes, stirring, until lightly browned. Add the wine and cook, scraping up the browned bits from the bottom of the pan, until the wine is reduced by half (about 10 minutes).

Add the vegetable stock, thyme, and bay leaf and bring to a boil. Add the brisket to the pan fat side up. Cover and roast for 3 to 3½ hours (or until the meat is fork tender).

Gently transfer the brisket to a plate and cover with foil. Meanwhile, strain the sauce through a sieve into a medium saucepan; discard the solids. Bring the sauce to a boil, skimming off any scum that rises to the surface. Season with salt and pepper.

Thinly slice the meat against the grain and serve with the sauce.

The brisket can be left whole and refrigerated in the sauce for 2 days. Slice, reheat in the sauce, and serve hot.

CARROT LAYER CAKE WITH CREAM CHEESE FROSTING

This recipe is a riff on a fantastic carrot cake that Chef Peet's wife, Anna Maria, makes at home. It's lightly spiced and loaded with carrots, resulting in a very moist crumb. The cake is served in rectangles at the Tavern, but the home version is a classic round "naked" cake, meaning the cake is frosted between the layers and on the top, but not around the sides.

MAKES ONE 9-INCH LAYER CAKE

FOR THE CAKE:

2 cups/260g all-purpose flour, plus more for dusting

2 teaspoons cinnamon

¼ teaspoon nutmeg

2 teaspoons baking soda

1 teaspoon kosher salt

½ cup/100g dark brown sugar

½ cup/100g granulated sugar

1 cup/238ml vegetable oil

4 large eggs

½ cup/6 ounces honey

2 teaspoons pure vanilla extract

6 medium carrots, shredded and squeezed dry (4 cups)

FOR THE NUTS AND CREAM CHEESE FROSTING:

1 cup/100g walnuts

2 sticks/226g unsalted butter at room temperature

1 pound/453g cream cheese at room temperature

⅓ cup/85g granulated sugar

1 teaspoon pure vanilla extract

Make the cake. Preheat the oven to 325°F. Line two 9-inch springform pans with parchment paper; grease/butter and flour the paper.

In a medium bowl, whisk together the flour, cinnamon, nutmeg, baking soda, and salt. In a large bowl, using a handheld mixer or in the bowl of a standing mixer fitted with the paddle attachment, combine both sugars. With the mixer on, slowly mix in the vegetable oil, scraping down the side of the bowl once or twice. Mix in the eggs, one at a time, and then mix in the honey and vanilla. Add the dry ingredients and mix just until combined. Fold in the carrots until just incorporated.

Scrape the batter into the prepared pans. Bake in the center of the oven for 35 to 45 minutes, rotating the pans halfway through baking, until a toothpick inserted in the center of each cake comes out clean. Transfer to wire racks to cool for at least 1 hour.

Meanwhile, make the nuts and frosting. Place the walnuts on a small baking sheet and toast at 350°F for about 7 minutes (or until golden and fragrant). Let cool, and then chop.

CARROT LAYER CAKE WITH CREAM CHEESE FROSTING *continued…*

In a medium bowl, using a handheld mixer (or in the bowl of a standing mixer fitted with the whisk), whisk the remaining ingredients until fluffy (about 3 minutes).

Invert one of cooled cakes onto a plate and spread to the edge with some of the frosting. Top with the other cake and frost the top. Garnish with the toasted walnuts and serve.

The cake can be stored in an airtight container at room temperature for 3 days.

RHUBARB AND STRAWBERRY TARTS

Rhubarb is in season only a short time and captures the essence of spring and Easter. Chef Peet makes it into this versatile compote, which can be served over ice cream, angel food cake, or pound cake. It's also great over your morning yogurt. Since the recipe calls for making a few cups of it, the compote is perfect to freeze and have later in the year when you have a hankering for rhubarb.

SERVES 4

FOR THE TART SHELLS:

1 cup plus 3 tablespoons/163g Wondra flour, chilled, plus more for rolling

1 stick/114g unsalted butter, cubed and frozen

5 teaspoons/20g granulated sugar

⅛ teaspoon kosher salt

¼ cup ice water

⅛ teaspoon pure vanilla extract

FOR THE COMPOTE FILLING:

½ cup sugar

½ cup water

1 pound rhubarb stalks (4 medium), sliced ½-inch thick (4 cups)

10 ounces strawberries, cleaned and sliced ½-inch thick (2 cups)

1 teaspoon pure vanilla extract

1 teaspoon fresh lemon juice

Whipped cream, for serving

Make the tart shells. In the bowl of a food processor, pulse the flour, butter, sugar, and salt until the mixture resembles small crumbs. In a small bowl or measuring cup, mix the ice water and vanilla. With the processor running, add the water in a steady stream until just incorporated. The mixture will look dry but should hold together when pinched. Transfer the dough to a work surface and pat into a thick square. Wrap in plastic and refrigerate for an hour.

Meanwhile, make the compote filling. In a medium saucepot, cook the sugar and water over medium heat until the mixture thickens and large bubbles starts to form (8 to 10 minutes). Add the rhubarb and strawberries, and bring to a simmer. Cover and simmer over low heat, stirring occasionally, until slightly thickened but still chunky (10 to 15 minutes). Stir in the vanilla and lemon juice, and transfer to a bowl. Refrigerate.

Spray four jumbo muffin pan slots with cooking spray. On a lightly floured surface, roll out the dough ¼ inch thick. Cut out four 5-inch rounds. Lay each round into a muffin cup and press the dough into the corners. Refrigerate for 20 minutes.

RHUBARB AND STRAWBERRY TARTS

continued . . .

Preheat the oven to 350°F. Roll up four balls of aluminum foil, one to fill each muffin cup. Delicately place each foil ball into the prepared dough cups, being careful not to poke any holes in the dough. Bake for 8 minutes (or until the tart shells are set and start to brown just slightly). Gently lift out the foil balls and bake another for 12 to 15 minutes longer, until the dough is fully baked and golden brown. Let cool on a rack before unmolding.

To serve, add about 2 tablespoons of the compote to each shell and top with whipped cream.

The compote can be refrigerated for 3 days and frozen for 3 months. The tart shells can be stored in an airtight container overnight.

Mother's Day is a very popular holiday to celebrate at the Tavern, with families flocking to the sunny dining room or—weather permitting—the patio.

No matter the month or seasonal influence, every day is a birthday at the Tavern. A large slab of buttermilk Confetti Birthday Cake (with plenty of colorful sprinkles) is always on the menu. The slices are cut from a giant round cake decorated with the name of a significant person who was born that day. Chef Peet chooses who to celebrate from a broad spectrum of luminaries (both famous and infamous)—scientists, artists, politicians, athletes, and actors. If for any reason he forgets to name names, the staff is quick to remind him: "Hey, Chef, whose birthday do we use today?" This playfulness helps the staff interact with their customers.

If it's your birthday at the Tavern, they will send you a free slice of this colorful cake along with a sparkling candle. It's no surprise that many people take advantage of this perk as yet another reason to celebrate at the restaurant.

The takeout window, located in the rear of the restaurant and facing the park drive, is open year-round, but May starts its busy season. Now it's not just locals walking their dogs who pop by for hot coffee on cold winter mornings but also tourists, kids, runners, bikers, and anyone who happens to be in the vicinity. They come by for breakfast treats like homemade muffins and pastries, banana bread, and egg sandwiches. At lunch, they pick up hot sliders, crispy chicken sandwiches, or salads.

Not even the pets are left out: The kitchen makes oatmeal-based Scooby snacks for dogs. Some people pop by with the pooches just for that!

CHILLED SWEET PEA SOUP

This pretty spring-green soup has a light, fresh taste and is far more elegant than the sum of its humble parts. Since it's prepared ahead of time and chilled, it's ideal to make for a late spring or summer dinner party.

SERVES 4 TO 6

1 tablespoon canola oil

1 small onion, sliced

1 garlic clove, smashed

Kosher salt and fresh ground black pepper

10 fresh mint leaves

½ cup dry white wine

2½ cups Vegetable Stock (page 341) or low-sodium broth

4 cups frozen peas

Sweet pea shoots, for garnish

In a large saucepan, heat the oil over medium heat. Add the onion and garlic, season with salt, and cook until the onion is softened (about 3 minutes). Stir in half the mint to infuse the mint scent (about 1 minute). Add the wine, and then add the stock and bring up to a boil. Add the peas, bring back to a boil, and simmer until the peas are cooked (3 to 5 minutes). Remove the soup from the heat.

Using an immersion blender (or working in batches in a blender), purée the soup with the remaining mint leaves until smooth. Strain the soup through a fine strainer into a medium bowl set over a larger bowl of ice water. Chill the soup in the ice bath for about 2 hours, stirring occasionally, and then refrigerate to chill completely (about 6 hours).

When the soup is cold, season with salt and pepper. Serve in chilled bowls, garnished with sweet pea shoots.

The soup can be refrigerated for 4 days.

AVOCADO TOASTS WITH FRESH HERB SALAD

These crowd-pleasing avocado toasts get a tiny bit of heat from hot sauce and a punch of tangy sweetness from the vinaigrette.

SERVES 4

2 ripe avocados, pitted, peeled, and crushed with a fork

1 tablespoon extra virgin olive oil

½ teaspoon hot sauce, preferably Tabasco

Kosher salt and fresh ground white pepper

4 slices whole grain toast

2 cups Herb Salad Mix (recipe follows)

2 tablespoons Sherry Vinaigrette (page 70)

In a small bowl, mix the crushed avocado, oil, and hot sauce and season lightly with salt and white pepper. Divide the avocado mash between the slices of toast, smoothing it out with the back of a fork.

In a medium bowl, toss the herb mix with the vinaigrette and season with salt and pepper. Divide the salad over the toasts, fluffing it up when arranging it. Serve immediately.

HERB SALAD MIX

With the variety of herbs and greens here, each bite of this mixture is like a little surprise. Don't hesitate to swap in different things if you prefer or if you can't find an ingredient. Mint and dill are both lovely, and other neutral greens can stand in for the frisée, arugula, and celery if need be.

MAKES 2 CUPS

¾ cup curly frisée, torn small

¾ cup baby arugula

2 tablespoons yellow celery leaves (from the center of the stalks)

1 tablespoon chervil leaves

1 tablespoon tarragon leaves

1 tablespoon flat-leaf parsley leaves

Combine all the ingredients for the salad mix.

THE TAVERN BURGER

Chef Peet came up with this winning burger recipe through much trial and error and is not afraid to share that he and his team gladly ate all the losing burger recipes in the process. Why is it so good? There are a few secrets: Use a special, juicy blend of beef; use a very hot grill to seal in the juices; don't press on the burgers while grilling (so you don't squeeze out the fatty juices); and butter the finished burgers before letting them rest, treating them like you would a steak.

SERVES 4

4 ripe plum tomatoes, sliced lengthwise and seeds squeezed out (see notes)

¼ cup extra virgin olive oil, plus more for brushing

1 fresh thyme sprig, leaves stripped

1 garlic clove, smashed and finely chopped

Kosher salt and fresh ground black pepper

1 large red onion, cut into 4 thick slices

2½ pounds ground beef mix (see notes)

2 tablespoons unsalted butter, at room temperature

Pinch sea salt

4 hamburger rolls/buns of your choice

Preheat the oven to 250°F. In a small bowl, toss the tomatoes with 2 tablespoons of the olive oil, the thyme, and the garlic; season with salt and pepper. Arrange the tomatoes cut side up in a shallow casserole dish and drizzle any remaining oil from the bowl over them. Bake for about 2½ hours, until the tomatoes have softened and a collapsed a good bit. Let cool.

Light a grill. Rub the onion slices with the remaining 2 tablespoons of olive oil and season with salt and pepper. Cover and grill over low heat, turning once (about 15 minutes per side), until the onions are cooked through and nicely browned.

Meanwhile, divide the meat evenly into 4 patties, each about 1 inch thick. When the onions are finished, get your grill very hot. Brush the outside of the burgers with oil and season liberally with salt and pepper. Grill for 5 minutes, and then flip and grill for 6 to 7 minutes longer for medium-rare (or longer if you like your burgers more well done).

Transfer the burgers to a plate and brush with some of the butter; sprinkle with sea salt and let rest for 5 minutes.

THE TAVERN BURGER *continued...*

Meanwhile, brush the buns with the remaining butter and grill cut side down until toasted (about 2 minutes). Set the burgers on the toasted buns and top with the onion and tomato; serve hot.

The tomatoes can be refrigerated for a week; bring to room temperature before serving.

NOTES

- The meat is an equal ratio of ground chuck, ground brisket, and ground short rib. The mixture is about 25% fat, making it very juicy. You can ask your butcher to provide this mix, or just use ground chuck, which is typically 80% lean meat and 20% fat.
- An alternative to the roasted plum whole tomatoes is Slow Roasted Tomato Jam (recipe in the "Pantry" section).
- If you want to add cheese, just put it on the cooked patties after they've rested and return the patties to the grill. Close the grill for 1 minute (or until the cheese is melted).

PAN-ROASTED SOFT-SHELL CRABS

Soft-shell crabs have a very short season—typically April through October, depending on where you live. As soon as they're available and diners know they're being served, the Tavern sells out of them at every meal. Even though Chef Peet tends to over-order them from his supplier, they still sell out. The beauty of soft-shell crabs (as opposed to hard shells) is that once they're cleaned, you can eat the entire crab, shell and all.

SERVES 4

1 cup buttermilk

1 cup Wondra flour

¼ teaspoon kosher salt, plus more for seasoning

⅛ teaspoon fresh ground black pepper, plus more for seasoning

⅛ teaspoon smoked paprika

⅛ teaspoon cayenne pepper

Eight 4–4½-inch (hotel-size) soft-shell crabs, cleaned (see notes)

½ cup canola oil

3 tablespoons unsalted butter

¼ cup fresh lemon juice

1 tablespoon capers

½ tablespoon finely chopped flat-leaf parsley

Preheat the oven to 400°F. Place the buttermilk in a wide, shallow bowl. In another wide, shallow bowl, mix the Wondra with the salt, pepper, paprika, and cayenne. Working with one crab at a time, dip the crab in the buttermilk, letting any excess drip back into the bowl, and then dredge both sides in the seasoned flour. Transfer to a baking sheet while you dredge all the crabs.

In two large nonstick oven-safe skillets, heat the oil over medium heat. (The crabs need to fit into the skillets in a single layer.) Gently add the crabs shell side down to the oil and cook undisturbed until light golden (2 to 3 minutes); be careful, as the crabs may pop in the skillet. Turn the crabs over and transfer the skillets to the oven. Cook for 3 minutes longer.

Using a slotted spoon or perforated spatula, transfer the crabs to a serving platter, shingling them. Season lightly with salt and pepper.

Pour off the oil from one of the skillets. Add the butter and cook over medium heat until the butter starts to foam and brown. Add the lemon juice to stop the butter from burning, and then swirl the pan to combine. Let the mixture to reduce a bit, and then add the capers. Spoon the sauce over the crabs. Garnish with parsley and serve immediately.

NOTES

- You can buy precleaned soft-shell crabs from most fish markets, but if you opt to clean your own, use a pair of kitchen shears to cut off the crab's face (behind the eyes). Lift the pointed edges of the shell to remove the gills and cut off the breast plate on the underside. Rinse thoroughly and drain before proceeding to batter and fry.
- Pickled Wild Ramps (recipe in the "Pantry" section) would pair very nicely with the crabs.

SMOKED SALMON TARTINES

These simple open-faced sandwiches get an extra boost of flavor from a spread of garlicky Boursin cheese mixed with punchy horseradish.

SERVES 4

¼ cup Boursin cheese

1 tablespoon prepared horseradish

2 cups Herb Salad Mix (page 115)

2 tablespoons Sherry Vinaigrette (page 70)

Kosher salt and fresh ground black pepper

4 slices toasted whole wheat bread, crusts removed

4 slices thin slices smoked salmon

1 tablespoon Pickled Red Onions (page 208)

In a small bowl, mix the Boursin and horseradish. In another bowl, toss the greens with the sherry vinaigrette and season with salt and pepper.

Spread the cheese mixture onto the toast and top with the smoked salmon. Lightly pile the salad over the salmon, and arrange the pickled onions on top. Serve immediately.

YELLOWFIN TUNA NIÇOISE SALAD

The tuna in this recipe is seared rare, which makes it very easy to cook and serve in the restaurant, but Chef Peet says it can also be cooked all the way through in an olive oil bath, like cooking a confit.

SERVES 4

1 cup haricots verts

8 ounces fingerling potatoes (about 1 cup)

Four 8-ounce yellowfin tuna steaks, cut into 2-by-4-inch rectangles

Kosher salt and fresh ground black pepper

1 tablespoons canola oil

2 cups baby arugula

1 cup frisée, trimmed, cleaned, and cut into 2-inch pieces

16 grape tomatoes, sliced lengthwise

16 pitted Kalamata olives, sliced lengthwise

½ cup Red Wine and Caper Vinaigrette (recipe follows)

4 hard-boiled eggs, peeled and quartered lengthwise

2 ripe avocados, peeled and cubed

1 teaspoon finely cut flat-leaf parsley

Bring a medium pot of water to a boil. Add the haricots verts and simmer just until bright green (about 1 minute). Using a slotted spoon, transfer the beans to a colander to drain and cool.

Add the fingerling potatoes to the water and simmer until tender (about 25 minutes). Drain and cool, and then peel and cut the potatoes into ½-inch coins.

Season the tuna with salt and pepper. In a large skillet, heat the canola oil over medium-high heat. Add the tuna and cook, turning until all 4 sides are seared (no more than 2 minutes total); the tuna should be extra rare.

In a large bowl, mix the arugula, frisée, tomatoes, and olives with the haricots verts and potatoes. Toss with half of the vinaigrette and season with salt and pepper. Divide the salad into four large chilled bowls. Add the eggs and avocado to each bowl, and sprinkle with a little salt.

Slice the tuna crosswise into ½-inch-thick slices and shingle them on top of each bowl. Drizzle the remaining vinaigrette over the tuna, eggs, and avocado. Garnish with parsley and serve.

RED WINE AND CAPER VINAIGRETTE

½ tablespoon Dijon mustard

¼ cup red wine vinegar

¾ cup extra virgin olive oil

1 tablespoon finely chopped capers

Kosher salt and fresh ground black pepper

In a small bowl or in a jar, whisk (or cover and shake the jar) to combine the vinegar, mustard, and oil. Stir in the capers and season with salt and pepper.

The vinaigrette can be refrigerated for 3 weeks.

LEMON CURD MERINGUE TARTS

The best thing about a recipe like this one—other than how good it tastes—is that it can be made in increments. The tart shells can be baked a couple of days ahead and stored in an airtight container, while the curd can be refrigerated for a few days. You can even make the whole tarts a couple of days in advance, and they will still be as silky and lemony as the day they were made.

MAKES 4 TARTS

FOR THE TART SHELLS:

1 cup plus 3 tablespoons/163g Wondra flour, chilled, plus more for rolling

1 stick/114g unsalted butter, cubed and frozen

5 teaspoons/20g granulated sugar

⅛ teaspoon kosher salt

¼ cup ice water

⅛ teaspoon pure vanilla extract

FOR THE LEMON CURD:

6 large egg yolks

⅔ cup granulated sugar

⅔ cup fresh lemon juice, plus finely grated zest of 1 lemon

6 tablespoons unsalted butter, cut into ½-inch pieces

FOR THE ITALIAN MERINGUE:

¾ cup/150g granulated sugar

½ cup/120g egg whites (about 4 large egg whites)

Pinch cream of tartar

Make the tart shells. In the bowl of a food processor, pulse the flour, butter, sugar, and salt until the mixture resembles small crumbs. In a small bowl or measuring cup, mix the ice water and vanilla. With the processor running, add the water in a steady stream until just incorporated. The mixture will look dry but should hold together when pinched. Transfer the dough to a work surface and pat into a thick square. Wrap in plastic and refrigerate for an hour.

Meanwhile, make the curd. In a small heavy-bottomed saucepan, whisk the yolks and sugar until smooth and pale in color (about 2 minutes). Whisk in the lemon juice and zest.

Over medium heat, cook the mixture, whisking constantly and making sure to get into all areas of the pot, until the mixture thickens and starts to bubble just slightly (about 7 minutes). Take the saucepan off the heat right away if it looks like it may boil.

Off the heat, whisk in the butter until melted. Pour the curd into a bowl and cover with plastic wrap, pressing down against the surface so a skin does not form. Let cool for an hour, and then refrigerate until ready to use.

LEMON CURD MERINGUE TARTS

continued . . .

Remove the tart dough from the refrigerator. Spray four jumbo muffin pan slots with cooking spray. On a lightly floured surface, roll out the dough ¼ inch thick. Cut out four 5-inch rounds. Lay each round into a muffin cup and press the dough into the corners. Refrigerate for 20 minutes.

Preheat the oven to 350°F. Roll up four balls of aluminum foil, one to fill each muffin cup. Delicately place each foil ball into the prepared dough cups, being careful not to poke any holes in the dough. Bake for 8 minutes (or until the tart shells are set and start to brown just slightly). Gently lift out the foil balls and bake 12 to 15 minutes longer, until the dough is fully baked and golden brown. Let cool on a rack before unmolding.

Make the meringue. In a small saucepan fitted with a candy thermometer, combine the sugar with 2 tablespoons of water and simmer over medium heat until a syrup forms and the temperature reaches 240°F (about 7 minutes).

Meanwhile, in a stand mixer fitted with the whisk attachment or in a medium bowl using an electric mixer, beat the egg whites and cream of tartar at medium-low speed until the whites start to turn opaque and become frothy. When the sugar has reached 240°F, while whipping at high speed, slowly drizzle the hot syrup into the egg whites between the side of the bowl and the beaters; avoid hitting the beaters. Continue whipping for about 5 minutes, until the meringue is stiff, silky, and glossy. Transfer the meringue to a pastry bag fitted with a star tip.

Fill the tart shells with the lemon curd filling. Pipe the meringue in a circular motion over each tart, covering the entire tart. Use a torch to brown the meringue, or quickly broil until nicely browned. The tarts can be prepared ahead and refrigerated until ready to serve.

The tarts shells can stored in an airtight container for 2 days. The curd can be refrigerated for 4 days. The finished tarts can be refrigerated for 2 days.

NOTE

For an extra boost of lemony flavor in this silky curd, rub the lemon zest directly into the sugar to release the oils and infuse the sugar.

CONFETTI BIRTHDAY CAKE

This confetti cake will please everyone looking for a fun all-occasion celebratory cake, especially those nostalgic for their childhood "sprinkles" birthday cake. It has a nice fluffy crumb with a hint of vanilla, as well as a silky buttercream frosting. Each day at the Tavern, Chef Peet looks up famous birthdays and writes a happy birthday to that person on the cake. It gives the waitstaff something to connect with at their table if someone is celebrating a birthday!

FOR THE CAKE:

2½ cups/295g cake flour

¼ cup/30g cornstarch

2 teaspoons/10g baking powder

1 teaspoon/6g kosher salt

2 sticks/224g unsalted butter, at room temperature

1½ cups/300g granulated sugar

4 large egg whites

¼ cup canola oil

1 tablespoon pure vanilla extract

¾ cup whole milk

½ cup/100g rainbow sprinkles

FOR FROSTING AND FINISHING:

3½ sticks/392g unsalted butter, at room temperature

3½ cups/420g confectioners' sugar

2 tablespoons whole milk

1½ teaspoons pure vanilla extract

⅛ teaspoon salt

½ cup/100g rainbow sprinkles

Make the cake layers. Preheat the oven to 325°F. Grease three 8-inch round cake pans, and then line with parchment paper and grease the paper.

In a medium bowl, whisk the cake flour, cornstarch, baking powder, and salt. In a standing mixer fitted with the paddle, beat the butter and sugar until light and fluffy (about 5 minutes). Add the egg whites one at a time, beating well between each addition. Beat in the oil and vanilla until combined. Working in three batches, alternately beat in the dry ingredients and milk; mix to just barely combine.

Gently fold in the rainbow sprinkles, making sure they are evenly distributed. Divide the batter between the three prepared pans. Bake for about 25 minutes, rotating the pans halfway through baking, until a toothpick inserted in the centers comes out clean and the cakes begin turn golden.

Let the cakes cool in the pans for 20 minutes, and then turn them out and invert (so they are right side up) onto a cooling rack to cool completely.

CONFETTI BIRTHDAY CAKE

continued . . .

Make the frosting. In a standing mixer fitted with the paddle, beat the butter until smooth, scraping down the side of the bowl once or twice (2 to 3 minutes). Add the sugar and beat, scraping down the bowl a couple of times, until combined (2 minutes). Add the milk, vanilla, and salt and beat until thoroughly combined.

Using a serrated knife, trim the domed top of two layers so they are flat. Transfer one cake layer to a plate and frost the top in an even layer. Top with another cake and frost it evenly. Cover with the third layer, rounded side up. Frost the top and all around the sides. Add the sprinkles to the top and sides, and serve.

The cake can be refrigerated for 4 days.

MONTH OF
JUNE
Summer shines with weddings,
graduation celebrations,
and Father's Day.

The warmth of the season makes chilled Yukon Gold Potato Leek Soup, with its cool and creamy texture, an easy pick from the menu—it's also a perfect vegetarian dish. Diners can savor an appetizer of Jumbo Lump Crabmeat Cocktail (a favorite Tavern special), made with tender morsels of fresh crab and dressed in a fragrant lemon truffle vinaigrette. Not to be forgotten is the Grilled Baby Octopus Salad served on an irresistible orzo salad that includes chopped olives, sun-dried tomatoes, feta cheese, and a puckery Roasted Lemon Vinaigrette.

June brings main courses such as Grilled Lamb Meatball Sliders with Tzatziki. The lamb meatballs are flattened like a "smash burger," very juicy and paired perfectly with the cucumber and yogurt sauce. Asparagus Risotto, topped with a baked Parmesan Crisp, or cracker, is another seasonal favorite. The crisp may seem fancy, but those at home will see that it can be made in just 15 minutes with only one ingredient: Parmesan cheese!

For those looking for a healthy option, the Tavern offers a Veggie Burger that's a savory and moist combination of white beans, quinoa, mushrooms, oats, and fresh herbs. Chef Peet slathers the fluffy buns with a sweet-spicy mayo sauce to complement the savory burger.

Sweets also brighten the festivities. Blueberry Lemon Crumble is a crowd-pleaser that screams summer, while on cooler evenings Sun-Dried Apricot Bread Pudding made with sweet Turkish apricots and hints of Earl Grey tea is a perfect way to finish an early summer meal.

New York City has many colleges and universities that graduate in late May and early June, bringing students in gowns of many colors to the Tavern to celebrate their accomplishments along with their families. The menu offers so many options that there is something for everyone. Once they've eaten and toasted, families gather in nearby Sheep Meadow to take photos with the beautiful green Central Park backdrop and the New York City skyline lurking just beyond.

YUKON GOLD POTATO LEEK SOUP

This take on a classic French vichyssoise (a cold potato leek soup) can be served hot as well. Just note that if you opt to serve it hot, it should be tasted and seasoned with salt and pepper while it's hot; once it's cold, it will need more salt and pepper. (It might come as a surprise, but if you heat up a well-seasoned cold soup, it's going to taste too salty.)

SERVES 6

4 tablespoons unsalted butter

4 large leeks, sliced and cleaned (about 4 cups)

Kosher salt and fresh ground black pepper

1½ quarts Vegetable Stock (page 341) or low-sodium broth

2 large Yukon Gold potatoes, peeled and cut into 1-inch chunks

1 bay leaf

1 fresh thyme sprig

½ cup heavy cream

2 teaspoons finely cut flat-leaf parsley

In a heavy-bottomed Dutch oven or cast-iron pot, melt the butter over medium heat. Add the leeks and season with salt and pepper. Cook, stirring now and then, until softened but not browned. Add the stock, potatoes, bay leaf, and thyme spring and bring to a boil over medium-high heat.

Cover the pot slightly, lower the heat to medium, and simmer until the potatoes and leeks are softened (25 to 30 minutes). Remove from the heat and discard the bay leaf and thyme spring.

Using an immersion blender or in batches in a standard blender, purée the soup until smooth. Strain the soup through a medium-mesh strainer into a medium bowl. Refrigerate until well chilled.

Before serving, stir in the heavy cream. Season with salt and pepper. Serve the chilled soup in chilled bowls, garnished with a bit of parsley.

The soup can be refrigerated for 3 days.

JUMBO LUMP CRABMEAT COCKTAIL

This is a dish that Chef Peet has served at many restaurants, but he wanted to change it up at the Tavern and was looking for something to tweak the flavor. After trying citrus and a variety of vinegars, he stumbled on white truffle paste. He doesn't typically push truffle flavoring, but it paired perfectly with the crab, avocado, and white balsamic, and a new dish was born!

SERVES 4

1 pound jumbo lump crabmeat

⅓ cup Lemon Truffle Vinaigrette (recipe follows)

1 ripe avocado, peeled, pitted, and cubed

½ teaspoon snipped chives

Kosher salt and fresh ground white pepper

4 lemon wedges, for serving

Gently mix the crabmeat with the vinaigrette, avocado, and chives; be careful not to break up the jumbo lumps of crab. Season with salt and pepper. Divide the mixture into four small bowls, garnish with a lemon wedge, and serve.

LEMON TRUFFLE VINAIGRETTE

MAKES 1¼ CUPS

¼ cup white balsamic vinegar

2 tablespoons Dijon mustard

1 tablespoon white truffle paste

1 tablespoon fresh lemon juice

¾ cup canola oil

¼ cup extra virgin olive oil

Kosher salt and fresh ground white pepper

In a medium bowl or a tall container, whisk (or cover and shake the container) to combine the vinegar, mustard, truffle paste, and lemon juice. Slowly whisk in the two oils in a steady stream until emulsified. Season with salt and pepper.

The vinaigrette can be refrigerated for 2 weeks.

GRILLED BABY OCTOPUS SALAD

Octopus isn't the easiest thing to cook. There are all sorts of tricks, like freezing and then beating the meat to tenderize it or cooking it with a cork. The good news? This recipe calls for precooked octopus, so no corks necessary.

SERVES 4

FOR THE OCTOPUS:

4 frozen cooked small octopus legs (4 ounces each)

¼ cup extra virgin olive oil

1 teaspoon fresh lemon juice

1 garlic clove, finely chopped

½ teaspoon chopped fresh thyme

Kosher salt and fresh ground black pepper

FOR THE ORZO SALAD:

1½ cups orzo, cooked and cooled slightly

¼ cup sun-dried tomatoes, thinly sliced

1 tablespoon finely chopped flat-leaf parsley

2 teaspoons thinly sliced Kalamata olives

½ teaspoon finely grated lemon zest

3 tablespoons Roasted Lemon Vinaigrette (recipe follows)

Salt and fresh ground black pepper

¼ cup diced feta cheese, cut in small dice

1 cup fresh pea sprouts with tendrils

Marinate the octopus. In a medium bowl, combine the octopus with the olive oil, lemon juice, garlic, and thyme. Refrigerate for at least 2 hours.

Preheat the broiler. Remove the octopus from the marinade, season with salt and pepper, and arrange on a baking sheet. Broil 4 to 5 inches from the heat source until the octopus starts to char (3 to 4 minutes). Turn the octopus over and char on the other side. Remove from the heat and allow to cool slightly. Slice the legs on a 2-inch-long bias about ½ inch thick. Transfer to a bowl and keep warm.

Make the orzo salad. In a medium bowl, combine the orzo with the sun-dried tomatoes, parsley, olives, lemon zest, and 1 tablespoon of the vinaigrette. Season with salt and pepper.

Mound the orzo into the center of four plates. Lay the octopus over and around the orzo. Arrange the feta cheese around the perimeter of the plate. Top the plates with the fresh pea sprouts and season with a little salt and pepper. Drizzle the remaining 2 tablespoons of vinaigrette over the salad and around the plate, and then serve.

ROASTED LEMON VINAIGRETTE

7 lemons, halved

1 teaspoon lemon oil

1 teaspoon white wine vinegar

½ cup extra virgin olive oil

Kosher salt and fresh
ground black pepper

Preheat the oven to 425°F. Arrange the lemon halves cut side up on a baking sheet. Roast until the skins start to brown (12 to 15 minutes). Let the lemons cool slightly, and then juice each half through a fine strainer into a bowl, pushing the pulp through with a ladle or rubber spatula.

Add the lemon oil and white vinegar to the juice. Using an immersion blender or a whisk, drizzle the olive oil into the juice in a steady stream until emulsified. Season with salt and pepper.

The vinaigrette can be refrigerated for 3 weeks.

LAMB MEATBALL SLIDERS WITH TZATZIKI

Lunch at the Tavern is very busy, with a lot of regular customers. As such, Chef Peet likes to change up the specials pretty frequently. Every time these lamb meatball sliders cycle onto the menu, they sell out. We start with meatballs, but they are flattened out to keep the sliders juicy. Diners love the alluring combination of warm, savory lamb with the cooling yogurt and cucumber.

SERVES 4

1½ pounds ground lamb

1 small yellow onion, finely chopped

¼ cup crumbled feta cheese

1 tablespoon finely chopped oregano

1 garlic clove, minced

1 teaspoon kosher salt

Fresh ground black pepper

2 tablespoons canola oil

12 mini burger buns/rolls, split

¼ cup Tzatziki (recipe follows)

Fresh baby spinach leaves (optional)

In a medium bowl, gently mix the ground lamb with the onion, feta, oregano, and garlic; add the salt and a few grindings of fresh pepper. Without overmixing, loosely form 12 balls.

Heat the canola oil in a large skillet over medium-high heat. When it starts to shimmer and smoke, add half of the meatballs, pressing down to flatten them slightly (or else they would roll off the bun). Cook over medium heat until browned (about 2 minutes). Flip and cook for another 1 to 2 minutes, or until browned and medium-rare (or cooked to your liking). Transfer the finished patties to a plate and repeat with the remaining patties.

Place 3 bottom burger buns on each plate. Top with the sliders and Tzatziki (you can also garnish with the spinach leaves, if using), close, and serve.

TZATZIKI

1 cup (8 ounces) full-fat Greek yogurt

½ cup finely grated cucumber, squeezed dry (from one-fourth of an unpeeled English cucumber)

1 tablespoon fresh lemon juice

2 teaspoons extra virgin olive oil

1 teaspoon chopped fresh dill

1 teaspoon chopped fresh mint

1 garlic clove, grated

Sea salt

In a medium bowl, mix all the ingredients and season with salt. Keep refrigerated until ready to use.

The Tzatziki can be refrigerated for 4 days; stir well before using.

NOTES

- Any leftover Tzatziki is excellent served as a dip for crudites.
- If the Tzatziki isn't your favorite, you can add a little Slow Roasted Tomato Jam (recipe in the "Pantry" section) to each slider.

ASPARAGUS RISOTTO

Parmesan Crisps are easy to make and add a special twist to this creamy spring risotto, replacing the more standard garnish of grated Parmesan. They do need to be prepared before the risotto, so as soon as the risotto is cooked it can be served hot and fresh. Asparagus is a great choice here, but sautéed mushrooms and roasted red or golden beets would be equally delicious. You can also add arugula or fresh spinach at the end to wilt in the risotto for an extra pop of green color and flavor.

SERVES 4

3½ cups Vegetable Stock (page 341) or low-sodium broth

10 jumbo asparagus spears (about ½ pound), peeled, top halves sliced on a bias into 1-inch pieces, bottom halves finely chopped

3 tablespoons unsalted butter

1 tablespoon canola oil

1 small onion, finely chopped

1 cup arborio rice

½ cup dry white wine

¼ cup freshly grated Parmesan

Kosher salt and fresh ground black pepper

Parmesan Crisps (recipe follows)

In a medium saucepan, bring the stock to a simmer. Add the asparagus tips and cook until they just begin to soften (1 to 2 minutes). Remove with a slotted spoon and set aside. Keep the stock at a low simmer.

Meanwhile, in a medium heavy-bottomed pot or Dutch oven, heat 1 tablespoon of the butter with the oil over medium heat. Add the onion and finely chopped asparagus and cook until softened (about 5 minutes). Add the rice and stir to coat. Add the wine and cook, stirring constantly, until evaporated (about 2 minutes). Add 1 cup of the hot stock and cook, stirring, until the stock is absorbed (4 to 5 minutes). Continue adding ½ cup of stock at a time and cook, stirring continuously, until the stock is absorbed before adding more (about 20 minutes total). The rice should be cooked through, but if not, add a bit of boiling water and continue to cook until it is done.

Remove the pan from the heat and add the Parmesan and the remaining 2 tablespoons of butter. Season with salt and pepper and stir in the reserved asparagus tips. Divide between 4 warm bowls. Garnish with a Parmesan Crisp and serve right away.

PARMESAN CRISPS

4 tablespoons freshly grated Parmesan

Preheat the oven to 350°F. On a silicone- or parchment-paper-lined baking sheet, spoon 1 tablespoon of the cheese into each corner of the baking sheet (you need room for the cheese to spread). Use your fingers to spread the cheese thinly and evenly into rounds. Bake until the cheese melts and turns golden brown (8 to 9 minutes). Let the crisps cool on the baking sheet for about 5 minutes (they crisp as they cool), and then use a thin spatula to transfer the crisps to a plate until ready to serve the risotto.

The crisps are best eaten within hours of making but can be held and recrisped in a warm oven if needed.

VEGGIE BURGERS

When they first opened, the Tavern had a lot of requests for vegetarian dishes, especially a burger. Chef Peet put this dish together with bits and pieces from the refrigerator, and it was an instant hit. In keeping with the Tavern's commitment to minimizing waste, the resulting burger was a great way to use up extra product.

MAKES 4 BURGERS

6 ounces white mushrooms, diced

One 15-ounce can white beans, drained and mashed (1¼ cups)

1 cup rolled oats

1 cup cooked quinoa

1 large egg, beaten

2 teaspoons finely grated lemon zest

1 teaspoon chopped flat-leaf parsley

1 teaspoon chopped chives

1 teaspoon chopped cilantro

¾ tsp kosher salt

Fresh ground black pepper

1 tablespoon canola oil

¼ cup mayonnaise

¼ cup ketchup

1½ teaspoon hot sauce, preferably Cholula

4 burger buns

1 cup alfalfa sprouts

Heat a large skillet and add the mushrooms. Cook over medium heat, stirring occasionally, until the mushrooms are cooked through and softened.

In a medium bowl, mix the mushrooms with the beans, oats, cooked quinoa, egg, lemon zest, and herbs; add the salt and a few grinds of pepper. Form into four 4-inch patties. Refrigerate for an hour.

When you're ready to make the burgers, let the patties sit at room temperature for 15 minutes. In a large skillet over medium-high heat, heat the canola oil until it starts to shimmer and smoke slightly. Reduce the heat to medium and cook the burgers until browned (about 5 minutes). Flip each patty and cook until browned on the bottom (another 5 to 7 minutes).

Meanwhile, in a small bowl, combine the mayonnaise, ketchup, and hot sauce. Spread the mayo mixture on both sides of the buns. Top with the patties and alfalfa sprouts, close the buns, and serve immediately.

NOTE

A few whole Pickled Wild Ramps (recipe in the "Pantry" section) on the burger will "ramp" up the flavor if desired.

SUN-DRIED APRICOT BREAD PUDDING

These are delicious little bread puddings, made more special by the generous individual servings and a distinct mix of citrus and vanilla. Do take note that the puddings need to be refrigerated overnight before baking.

SERVES 4

1 Earl Grey tea bag

¼ cup sun-dried apricots, cut into small pieces

1 tablespoon unsalted butter, softened, for buttering the baking dish

2 large eggs

1 large egg yolk

1 cup whole milk

1½ cups heavy cream

¾ cup/150g granulated sugar

½ teaspoon finely grated orange zest

½ teaspoon finely grated lemon zest

½ teaspoon pure vanilla extract

8 ounces brioche, crusts removed, bread cut into 1-inch cubes (3 cups)

In a small bowl, combine 1 cup boiling water with the tea bag and add the apricots. Let stand for 10 minutes, and then strain well; discard the liquid and tea bag.

Lightly butter four 8-ounce soufflé cups or ramekins and divide the strained apricots into them. In a medium bowl, whisk the eggs and yolk with ¼ cup of the milk.

In a medium saucepan, combine the heavy cream, sugar, zests, and vanilla with the remaining ¾ cup of milk; bring just to a boil. Whisking constantly, very slowly add the cream mixture to the eggs until fully combined. Using a fine-mesh strainer, strain the mixture back into the saucepan. Add the brioche cubes. Allow to soak a few minutes undisturbed.

Spoon the brioche mixture into the soufflé cups; the cups will be full. Cover each soufflé cup and refrigerate overnight.

Preheat the oven to 350°F. Let the puddings stand for 30 minutes at room temperature before baking. Arrange the soufflé cups in a shallow casserole or roasting pan and add enough boiling water to come halfway up the side of the soufflé cups. Carefully slide the pan into the oven and bake for 40 to 50 minutes, until firm on top and cooked through. Serve hot.

BLUEBERRY LEMON CRUMBLE

This crumble is super easy to make and perfect when you want to serve a hot, fresh, right-out-of-the-oven dessert to your guests. The crumble topping and the filling can be prepared several hours in advance and refrigerated separately. Just put the crumble over the filling and pop into the oven about an hour before you want to serve it.

SERVES 6

FOR THE TOPPING:

1 cup/100g rolled oats

½ cup/65g all-purpose flour

½ cup/100g packed light brown sugar

1 teaspoon finely grated lemon zest

½ tsp ground cinnamon

⅛ teaspoon kosher salt

1 stick/114g unsalted butter, melted

FOR THE FILLING:

1 tablespoon unsalted butter, softened, for buttering the baking dish

5 cups/750g blueberries

½ cup/100g granulated sugar

2 tablespoons cornstarch

1 tablespoon fresh lemon juice

½ teaspoon pure vanilla extract

Confectioners' sugar, for serving

Lightly sweetened whipped cream or vanilla ice cream, for serving

Make the topping. Preheat the oven to 375°F. In a large bowl, combine the dry ingredients and stir in the butter. Using your hands, mix the topping into hazelnut-sized clumps.

Make the filling. Butter a 2-quart baking dish. In a large bowl, toss the blueberries with the granulated sugar, cornstarch, lemon juice, and vanilla. Pour the mixture into the baking dish. Crumble the topping over the filling.

Bake until the filling is bubbling at the edges and the topping is golden brown (about 45 minutes). Let rest for 20 minutes, and then dust with confectioners' sugar and serve with whipped cream or ice cream.

The crumble is best eaten the day it's made, but it can be refrigerated for 2 days and reheated gently at 300°F for 30 minutes.

MONTH OF
JULY
Firecrackers and hot dogs are not the only signs of summer excitement and fun.

A bounty of fresh produce inspires all kinds of seasonal dishes, while the warm weather makes way for chilled soups like Chilled Garden Gazpacho, a summertime staple. The soup is prepared with three colors and types of peppers—red, yellow, and green poblano—as well as tomatoes and cucumbers. These ingredients are chopped and then marinated with extra virgin olive oil, salt, pepper, and a bit of vinegar, which brings out the most flavor. The concoction is poured into a meat grinder so that all the vegetables undergo the same cutting process. A little more vinegar and oil are added, as well as quality tomato juice. The oil makes the mixture glisten, which Chef Peet likens to diamonds.

The cold soup lives up to the standards Chef sets throughout the Tavern menu. Even the poultry for the Crispy Chicken Sandwich—another fan favorite—is brined and served with a tasty sauce and delectable sides. Many know Chef's motto: "How can we do it differently to add more flavor?" Chef Peet is always looking for ways to capture the diner's attention in one bite.

July is the perfect time for watermelon. So Chef Peet pairs sweet yellow and red watermelon cubes together with sharp feta cheese and a drizzle of reduced golden balsamic vinegar for the Watermelon and Feta Salad. One of the signature dishes at Tavern is the Jumbo Lump Crab Cake. It is quite different from any other crab cake, a mixture of jumbo lump crab meat and chopped sea scallops. Another popular lunch dish is the Yellowfin Tuna Burger with Wasabi Mayonnaise. This dish was created to use the trimmings of tuna from the Tuna Niçoise Salad, but now tuna is purchased just for the burger, as there aren't enough trimmings to keep up with the burger demand. A good problem!

Desserts at this time of year may be meant as a cooling and indulgent ending to the meal, like Chef Peet's Oreo Ice Cream Sandwich, made with an original cookie dough recipe and vanilla ice cream. Dessert might also be inspired by vine-ripened berries, and because of that, Chef Peet says one dessert owns this time of year: Strawberry Shortcake. He seeks out the sweetest strawberries of the season and then crushes them with a little sugar to bring out the best flavor. The berries are spooned over freshly made biscuits that are supremely buttery, flaky, and light. How can it get any better? Add a dollop of freshly whipped cream and dig right in.

CHILLED GARDEN GAZPACHO

This refreshing and hearty chilled soup always took a long time to prepare until Chef Peet realized he didn't need to chop the ingredients by hand. Instead, one beautiful summer weekend, he poured the vegetables into a meat grinder with large holes, creating uniform-sized vegetables in a fraction of the time. Since most home cooks don't have a meat grinder, Chef recommends using a food processor.

To ensure that the soup is properly seasoned, Chef advises adding white wine vinegar a little bit at a time before serving, until you achieve the right balance between acid and olive oil. The soup should have that satisfying and tasty pop of flavor that's the hallmark of a great gazpacho.

SERVES 4

2 plum tomatoes, peeled, seeded, and roughly chopped

1 red bell pepper, split, seeded, and roughly chopped

1 yellow bell pepper, split, seeded, and roughly chopped

1 poblano pepper, split, seeded, and roughly chopped

1 hothouse cucumber, peeled, split, seeded, and roughly chopped

1 small shallot, roughly chopped

1 garlic clove, finely chopped

¼ cup plus 4 teaspoons extra virgin olive oil

2 tablespoons white wine vinegar, plus more for finishing

1 tablespoon cilantro leaves, plus extra leaves for garnish

2 cups good-quality, 100% tomato juice, preferably Sacramento brand

Kosher salt and fresh ground black pepper

In a large bowl, toss the tomatoes, peppers, cucumber, shallot, and garlic with ¼ cup of the olive oil and the vinegar. Refrigerate for at least 2 hours (preferably overnight).

Add the vegetables and cilantro to a food processor, working in batches if necessary, and pulse several times until the vegetables are finely chopped but not puréed, scraping down the side of the bowl a few times.

Pour the mixture into a large bowl and stir in the tomato juice. Season with salt and pepper, and refrigerate until chilled.

Divide the soup into four chilled bowls, being careful to get the same ratio of liquid to solids in each bowl. Drizzle each bowl with 1 teaspoon of olive oil and a touch of vinegar, garnish with the remaining cilantro, and serve.

The gazpacho can be refrigerated for up to 2 days, during which time the flavor will deepen even further.

WATERMELON AND FETA SALAD

When Chef Peet makes this salad in the height of summer, he uses both red and yellow watermelon, which brings vibrancy to the plate. He drizzles the watermelon with a reduction of golden balsamic vinegar from a company called Sparrow Lane. Their golden balsamic is made with lighter-colored grapes than traditional balsamic. Since that product can be hard to source, he suggests using a high-quality Italian balsamic vinegar instead.

SERVES 4

1½ pounds red seedless watermelon, peeled and cut into ½-inch cubes

1½ pounds yellow seedless watermelon, peeled and cut into ½-inch cubes

½ cup upland cress (see note)

¼ pound feta cheese, crumbled (about ¾ cup)

2 tablespoons high-quality aged balsamic vinegar

2 tablespoons extra virgin olive oil

Sea salt flakes, preferably Maldon

Divide the watermelon onto four chilled plates. Top with the cress. Sprinkle the feta over the salads, and then drizzle with the balsamic and olive oil. Finish with a sprinkle of sea salt flakes crushed between your fingers and serve.

NOTE

Upland cress is often called upland watercress, though it's not actually watercress at all. The two are similar in appearance, but upland cress has thinner, more tender leaves. It's often sold with the roots attached. If you can't find it, you can substitute small watercress leaves.

JUMBO LUMP CRAB CAKES

Most crab cakes are prepared with a mixture of crab and a lot of filler, like breadcrumbs and mayonnaise. Chef Peet's are chock full of seafood, as he uses a combination of crab and chopped scallops (which provide a unique texture and help bind the cakes together). This is a variation of a crab cake Chef once made at Lutèce.

SERVES 4

¾ cup panko breadcrumbs

2 tablespoons mayonnaise

1 large egg yolk

Pinch cayenne pepper
(or to taste)

Kosher salt and fresh
ground white pepper

8 ounces jumbo lump crab meat,
picked over for shells

8 ounces dry diver sea scallops,
cut into ¼-inch pieces (see note)

1 tablespoon canola oil

Curried Apple Relish
(recipe follows)

In a medium bowl, mix ¼ cup of the panko with the mayonnaise, egg yolk, and cayenne; season lightly with salt and white pepper. Gently mix in the crab and scallops just to combine.

Place the remaining ½ cup of panko in a shallow bowl and season with salt and white pepper.

To properly season the crab cakes ahead of cooking, dredge 1 tablespoon of the mixture in seasoned panko and pan fry with a bit of oil until cooked through. Taste and adjust seasoning of the raw mixture.

After adjusting the seasoning, form the crab mixture into 4 patties. Dredge each patty in the panko, coating them all over.

Heat the oil in a large nonstick skillet over medium heat. When the oil is shimmering, add the crab cakes and cook for 4 to 5 minutes per side, until golden brown and cooked through. Transfer to a paper-towel-lined plate and serve hot with the relish.

NOTE
Diver sea scallops are hand harvested and shucked directly into a container.
They have a lovely, pure flavor. If they are not available, you can use bay scallops.

CURRIED APPLE RELISH

Crab cakes are frequently served with tartar sauce, but this sweet curry/spiced apple relish is an unexpected way to serve them. A little squeeze of lime juice is a nice complement to both the crab and the relish, if so desired.

MAKES 1½ CUPS

¼ cup white wine

2 teaspoons Madras curry powder

2 Golden Delicious apples, peeled, cored, and cut into ½-inch cubes (about 2 cups)

2 teaspoons mayonnaise

Kosher salt and fresh ground white pepper

Heat a medium nonstick skillet over medium heat. Add the white wine and curry and whisk to combine. Bring to a simmer and add the apples. Cook, stirring, for about 3 minutes (or until the apples are softened but still a bit firm). Remove from the heat, transfer to a bowl, and let cool slightly. Add the mayonnaise to the apples and season with salt and white pepper. Refrigerate for at least 2 hours (or until chilled). Serve cold.

The relish can be refrigerated for 2 days.

YELLOWFIN TUNA BURGERS WITH WASABI MAYONNAISE

In a professional kitchen, every ingredient is cross-utilized to eliminate waste. This burger recipe came about after the kitchen prepared a Yellowfin Tuna Niçoise Salad and had a lot of tuna trimmings remaining. The tuna was used to make tartare as well as this satisfying burger, in which it matches well with the wasabi and seaweed salad.

SERVES 4

2 tablespoons extra virgin
olive oil

2 tablespoons mirin

2 tablespoons sweet soy sauce
(kecap manis)

2 tablespoons unseasoned
rice vinegar

1 tablespoon toasted sesame oil

2 scallions, thinly sliced

Zest and juice from
1 medium lime

Zest and juice from 1 lemon
(1 tablespoon juice)

1 teaspoon finely grated
fresh ginger

¼ teaspoon sambal oelek
chili paste

1 pound ground yellowfin tuna
(see notes)

2 tablespoons canola oil

Wasabi Mayonnaise
(recipe follows)

4 burger buns

¼ cup sesame seaweed salad
(see notes)

YELLOWFIN TUNA BURGERS WITH WASABI MAYONNAISE *continued...*

In a medium bowl, combine the olive oil, mirin, soy sauce, vinegar, sesame oil, scallions, lime zest and juice, lemon zest and juice, ginger, and sambal oelek. Add the ground tuna and gently mix to combine. Form the tuna mixture into four patties and refrigerate for 2 hours to set up.

In a large skillet, heat the canola oil over medium-high heat until it starts to shimmer and smoke. Reduce the heat to medium and cook the burgers until they start to brown (about 4 minutes). Flip and cook until browned on the other side (about 3 minutes).

Spread some of the Wasabi Mayonnaise on the buns and put the burgers on the bottom halves. Divide the sesame seaweed salad between the burgers, cover with the top buns, and serve.

NOTES

- If you don't have a meat grinder, you can ask your fishmonger to grind the tuna for you.
- Seaweed salad can be found in deli section of many grocery stores, as well as in Asian markets and wherever sushi is sold.

WASABI MAYONNAISE

MAKES ½ CUP

½ cup mayonnaise

½ tablespoon wasabi powder

Kosher salt

In a small bowl, mix the mayo with the wasabi and ½ tablespoon of water. Season with salt to taste and add more wasabi powder, if desired.

CRISPY CHICKEN SANDWICHES

This impressive-looking sandwich sells itself as it's carried through the dining room to various tables. It's one of the most popular lunch items, second only to the burger. When serving, it helps to stick a 4-inch bamboo skewer through the bun to keep the crispy towering chicken quarters nice and tall . . . and from toppling over. If you're not a bread kind of person, the chicken and remoulade also make a great meal without the bun!

SERVES 4

½ cup all-purpose flour

2 cups panko breadcrumbs

2 large eggs, beaten

Four 6-ounce boneless skinless chicken breasts, pounded ½-inch thick (see note)

Kosher salt and fresh ground black pepper

½ cup canola oil

½ cup Remoulade Sauce (recipe follows)

4 burger buns

1½ cups finely shredded romaine lettuce

Preheat the oven to 400°F. Separately place the flour, breadcrumbs, and beaten eggs in three small sheet pans or wide, shallow bowls. Lightly season each chicken cutlet with salt and pepper. Working with one piece of chicken at a time, dredge in the flour, being sure to coat well and shake off any excess. Next, dip the breast in the egg, coating it all over and letting any excess drip back into the bowl. Finish by coating in the breadcrumbs. Repeat with the remaining chicken.

CRISPY CHICKEN SANDWICHES

continued...

In a large skillet, heat the oil over medium heat until shimmering and smoking slightly. Cook one cutlet at a time until golden brown on both sides (1 to 1½ minutes per side); the chicken will not be fully cooked. Transfer to a baking sheet and brown the remaining chicken cutlets. Season lightly with salt and pepper and transfer to the oven. Bake for 7 minutes (or until the chicken is cooked through).

Slice each crispy cutlet into four pieces. Spread some remoulade on the top bun. Pile the cut chicken breast on the bottom bun and top with the lettuce. Close the bun and repeat with the remaining sandwiches. Serve immediately.

NOTE

You can buy thinly sliced chicken cutlets, but look for those that weigh around 6 ounces each to make sure the portion size is ample. You can also ask your butcher to pound the breasts for you, if desired.

REMOULADE SAUCE

MAKES ABOUT ½ CUP

½ cup mayonnaise

1 teaspoon Dijon mustard

1 teaspoon fresh lemon juice

1 teaspoon drained capers, finely chopped

1 teaspoon finely chopped shallot

1 teaspoon finely chopped cornichon (1 cornichon)

1 teaspoon finely cut flat-leaf parsley

Kosher salt and fresh ground black pepper

Combine all the ingredients and season with salt and pepper. Refrigerate.

The remoulade can be refrigerated for up to 1 week.

CAUTION - HOT
ATTENTION - CHAUD
CAUTION - HOT
ATTENTION - CHAUD

GRILLED LEG OF LAMB PAILLARD

Chicken, burgers, ribs, and steaks are staples of al fresco dining, but these juicy lamb cutlets should not be forgotten the next time you fire up the grill. They have a simple Mediterranean-inspired marinade and take only a few minutes to cook.

SERVES 4

Four 8-ounce lamb cutlets from the leg or top round

3 tablespoons extra virgin olive oil

1 garlic clove, finely chopped

1 teaspoon chopped oregano

¼ teaspoon crushed black peppercorns

Zest from 1 lemon

1 red bell pepper, cored and sliced lengthwise in thin (½-inch) strips

1 yellow bell pepper, cored and sliced lengthwise in thin (½-inch) strips

2 poblano peppers, cored and sliced lengthwise in thin (½-inch) strips

1 large white onion, halved and sliced lengthwise

1 teaspoon finely cut flat-leaf parsley

Kosher salt and fresh ground black pepper

Canola oil, for grilling

1 bunch watercress, tough stems removed

½ teaspoon fresh lemon juice

½ teaspoon white sesame seeds, toasted

Using the flat side of a meat tenderizer, lightly pound each lamb cutlet between two sheets of plastic wrap until the meat is ½ inch thick. Using the spiked side of the tenderizer, pound to flatten further and tenderize the lamb, being careful not to puncture the plastic wrap. Place the cutlets on a large plate or baking dish.

In a small bowl, combine 2 tablespoons of the olive oil with the garlic, oregano, peppercorns, and lemon zest and rub onto each cutlet, coating both sides. Cover with plastic wrap and refrigerate for about an hour.

In a large skillet, heat 2 teaspoons of the olive oil over medium-high heat. Add the peppers and onion and cook, stirring and tossing, until the peppers have softened slightly (about 8 minutes). Stir in the parsley and season with salt and pepper; keep warm.

Take the lamb out of the fridge. Light an outdoor grill or heat a grill pan over medium-high heat. If using a grill pan, add 2 teaspoons of canola oil and let it heat until almost smoking (3 to 4 minutes). Season the lamb with a little salt and quickly grill for 2 minutes on each side. You may have to do this in 2 batches if using a grill pan.

Place each cutlet in the center of a plate. Mound the peppers and onion on the lamb. In a medium bowl, quickly toss the watercress with the remaining 1 teaspoon of olive oil, the lemon juice, and toasted sesame seeds and season with salt and pepper. Set a small handful on top of the lamb and peppers, and then serve.

SPICED BLACKBERRY BBQ RIBS

While everyone loves eating ribs with their hands—especially sweet and spicy ones like these that fall right off the bone—Chef Peet often pulls the meat off the bones and mixes it into a giant green salad.

SERVES 4

1 tablespoon Cajun spice

1 tablespoon dark brown sugar

2 teaspoons smoked paprika

2 teaspoons onion powder

1 teaspoon cinnamon

½ teaspoon kosher salt

½ teaspoon ground black pepper

4 baby back rib racks (about 1½ pounds each), trimmed of fat

Spicy Blackberry BBQ Sauce (recipe follows)

In a small bowl, mix the Cajun spice, brown sugar, paprika, onion powder, cinnamon, salt, and pepper.

Preheat the oven to 375°F. Rub the spice mixture all over the ribs. Arrange the ribs in a single layer in a shallow pan and cover tightly with aluminum foil. Bake for about 1½ hours (or until tender when pierced with the tip of a knife). Remove from the oven and let cool for 15 minutes. Raise the oven temperature to 425°F.

Pat the ribs dry with paper towels and then baste on both sides with the BBQ sauce. Roast the ribs uncovered for 15 minutes, until the sauce starts to caramelize and brown a little. Baste again liberally and continue to roast for about 10 minutes longer, until the ribs are tacky and slightly browned. Serve hot, with extra BBQ sauce on the side.

SPICY BLACKBERRY BBQ SAUCE

1 cup blackberry purée

1 cup cider vinegar

½ cup molasses

½ cup honey

1 tablespoon tomato paste

1 tablespoon chipotles in adobo sauce, peppers smashed to a purée

2 garlic cloves, finely grated (on a microplane)

½ teaspoon kosher salt

In a medium saucepan, combine all the ingredients and simmer for 10 minutes over moderate heat. Let cool. (The sauce will thicken as it cools.)

The sauce can be refrigerated for 1 month.

OREO ICE CREAM SANDWICHES

If you feel like dressing these up a bit, you can roll the edges in crushed cookie crumbs, mini chips, sprinkles, or cocoa nibs.

MAKES 4 SANDWICHES

3 cups/600g granulated sugar

2⅔ cups/340g all-purpose flour

1⅓ cups/142g unsweetened Dutch-processed cocoa powder

2 teaspoons baking powder

½ teaspoon baking soda

¼ teaspoon kosher salt

2½ sticks/284g unsalted butter, softened

2 large eggs

Vanilla ice cream, for serving

In a large mixing bowl, whisk together the sugar, flour, cocoa, baking powder, baking soda, and salt.

In a stand mixer fitted with the paddle attachment (or in a large bowl using a hand mixer), cream the softened butter and eggs until fluffy and light in color (2 to 3 minutes), scraping down the side of the bowl once or twice. Slowly beat in the dry ingredients until just incorporated.

Split the dough into two equal pieces and wrap each loosely in plastic wrap; flatten each piece out and then refrigerate for 1 to 2 hours.

Preheat oven to 350°F. On a work surface, roll out the dough to a ½-inch thickness. Cut out eight 4-inch rounds. Transfer the rounds to a nonstick baking sheet (or a parchment-paper-lined baking sheet) and bake for 7 to 9 minutes (or until just firm). Let the cookies cool on the baking sheet for 10 minutes, and then carefully transfer them to a wire rack to finish cooling.

Scoop four large scoops (about ½ cup each) of vanilla ice cream and set on a parchment-paper-lined baking sheet. Once soft enough to press down, top with another sheet of paper and use a spatula to flatten the scoops so they fit between the cookies. Freeze for an hour or so to firm up the ice cream.

Insert the ice cream between the cookies and freeze again to set the sandwiches. Serve frozen.

The ice cream sandwiches can be stored in an airtight container and frozen for 2 weeks.

STRAWBERRY SHORTCAKES

The shortcake in this recipe is divine, but if you want to mix things up, feel free to make this dish with a loaf of cornbread instead. Chef Peet says to slice the bread, butter it up, and toss it on a griddle for an entirely different shortcake experience. At home, Chef likes to add 1 tablespoon of Grand Marnier to the strawberries.

SERVES 6

2 pounds ripe strawberries, hulled (6 cups)

4 tablespoons sugar

1¾ cups/227g all-purpose flour, plus more for dusting

¼ cup/50g sugar

2 teaspoons baking powder

½ teaspoon kosher salt

6 tablespoons/84g unsalted butter, cut into ½-inch pieces and chilled

½ cup half-and-half

1 large egg, lightly beaten

2 tablespoons whole milk

1 tablespoon turbinado sugar (Sugar in the Raw)

Whipped cream, for serving

Using a potato masher or a stiff whisk, crush 2 cups of the strawberries in a medium bowl. Slice the remaining strawberries and add to the bowl along with the sugar; stir well. Refrigerate for at least 30 minutes, stirring now and then, to dissolve the sugar and draw out the juices from the strawberries.

Preheat the oven to 400°F. Line a cookie sheet with parchment paper.

In the bowl of a food processor, pulse the flour, sugar, baking powder, and salt until just combined. Drop the butter into the bowl and pulse until a coarse meal forms (about 10 to 12 pulses). Transfer to a bowl.

In another bowl or in a large measuring cup, combine the half-and-half with the egg. Stir this mixture into the dry ingredients until large lumps form.

Lightly dust a work surface with flour. Turn the dough out onto the surface and gently knead until the dough just comes together; don't overwork the dough. Pat the dough to a 1-inch thickness. Use a 2½-inch round cutter to cut out six biscuits; you might need to reroll scraps once.

Transfer the biscuits to the prepared cookie sheet, leaving about 2 inches between them. Brush the tops with the milk and sprinkle with the turbinado sugar. Bake in the middle of the oven until golden brown (about 15 minutes). Let cool.

To serve, split the biscuits and spoon the strawberry mixture over the bottom halves. Top each with a dollop of whipped cream, put the biscuit tops on, and serve.

The biscuits can be kept covered in an airtight container at room temperature for a couple of days, and the strawberries can be refrigerated for the same time. Give them a stir with a fork before spooning onto the biscuits.

AUGUST

*August is one of the quieter months
in New York City.*

This is when many locals take vacations and escape the steamy heat by heading to nearby beaches. Those who opt to stay behind know that it's a great time to take advantage of the emptier restaurants, museums, and theaters that are typically packed—these destinations also offer a chance to get out of the heat and into air conditioning. Despite the temperatures, tourists love New York City in August, and at any given time, the restaurant might have people coming in from all over the globe.

The Tavern's summery menu starts with chunky Maine Lobster Rolls in toasted hot dog buns, as well as a refreshing Watermelon Gazpacho that includes strawberries and raspberries and always hits the spot. For those dreaming of the beaches and ocean, seafood appetizers include White Wine Braised Mussels and Grilled Shrimp with Mango and Papaya Salad. This salad is dressed in an unusual vinaigrette made with passionfruit, making it feel tropical and almost exotic.

Summertime mains are prepared to please. Fan favorite Salmon Burgers (devised when Chef Peet wanted to use up salmon trimmings from butchering) are spread with spicy Chili Aioli. The Grilled Chicken Salad is chock full of crispy almonds and sticky dates, and Pan-Roasted Chilean Sea Bass is served along with melted leeks. As always, desserts are hard to skip and include Caramelized Peach Gratin with Sabayon and Oversized Oatmeal Raisin Cookies (perfect alongside a scoop of ice cream).

Every August, Tavern on the Green participates in the city's Summer Restaurant Week, which brings in people at both lunch and dinner. The specially priced three-course prix fixe menu gives new diners a chance to try the Tavern, and it provides repeat diners with a bit of a bargain. If it's a Friday night, they'll hear the live band performing in the courtyard, or perhaps in the bar, should it be a rainy evening.

Despite the heat, the live music and shady patio (strung with lights for evenings) attract many folks—especially at the bar—and the din that arises makes it feel like an all-day party. While the rest of the city feels a little sleepy in August, the Tavern is going strong.

MAINE LOBSTER ROLLS

The addition of brandy to lobster salad might seem unusual, but trust Chef Peet on this: Along with the mayo, tomatoes, tarragon, and parsley, the brandy brings an utterly alluring pop of flavor to this lobster salad.

SERVES 4

1 pound poached lobster meat, cut in ½-inch chunks

¼ cup plus 2 tablespoons mayonnaise, plus more for brushing

1 tablespoon brandy

Kosher salt and fresh ground black pepper

½ cup diced plum tomatoes (¼ inch)

1 teaspoon finely chopped tarragon

1 teaspoon finely cut flat-leaf parsley

4 top-opening hot dog rolls

In a medium bowl, mix together the lobster, mayonnaise, and brandy and season with salt and pepper. Stir in the tomatoes and herbs, and refrigerate until ready to use.

Lightly brush the outsides of the hot dog rolls with a bit of mayonnaise. Heat a large sauté pan over medium heat. Lightly brown the mayo-painted sides of the rolls. Divide the lobster mixture between the rolls and serve.

The lobster salad can be refrigerated for 2 days.

WATERMELON GAZPACHO

During spring and summer, the restaurant goes through a lot of Watermelon and Feta Salad (page 159). To make that dish, the watermelon is cut into neat squares, so the kitchen uses the trimmings to make cold soups like this gazpacho. While it may seem juice-like, this is a soup and should have a savory edge to it. Don't be shy when it comes to seasoning with salt and white pepper.

SERVES 6

6 cups cubed watermelon, seeded

2 mini cucumbers, peeled and seeded (if necessary)

2 medium shallots, finely chopped

½ cup strawberries, hulled

½ cup raspberries

¼ cup apple cider vinegar

¼ cup extra virgin olive oil

Kosher salt and fresh ground white pepper

1 teaspoon finely cut flat-leaf parsley

In a large bowl, using an immersion blender (or working in batches in a blender), purée the watermelon, cucumbers, shallots, strawberries, and raspberries. Strain through a double mesh strainer into a large bowl.

Stir in the vinegar and olive oil and season with salt and white pepper. Refrigerate for at least an hour. Serve the soup in chilled bowls, garnished with parsley.

The gazpacho can be refrigerated for 2 days. Stir well before serving.

CRISPY CALAMARI SALAD

Instead of serving fried calamari alongside cocktail sauce, Chef Peet mixes the crispy seafood into a tropical-style salad, along with banana, toasted coconut, and chayote, a crisp and mild type of squash. Years ago, Chef Peet was the executive chef of Asia de Cuba, a wildly popular Asian-Latino restaurant concept. This was the number-one salad.

SERVES 4

¼ cup all-purpose flour

¼ cup cornstarch

¼ teaspoon kosher salt, plus more for seasoning

Fresh ground black pepper

14 ounces calamari, tubes cut into ¾-inch rings

1 tablespoon buttermilk

Canola oil, for frying

4 cups thinly sliced kale

1 chayote, peeled and cut into medium dice

1 ripe banana, thinly sliced

2 tablespoons chopped toasted cashews

¼ cup unsweetened coconut flakes, toasted

½ cup Orange Sesame Dressing (recipe follows)

In a medium bowl, mix the flour, cornstarch, and ¼ teaspoon of salt; season with a couple of grinds of fresh pepper. In a separate bowl, mix the calamari with the buttermilk; you want just enough buttermilk to moisten the calamari. Toss the calamari in the flour mixture and then transfer to a mesh strainer and tap to remove any excess flour.

Meanwhile, in a large heavy pot or electric deep fryer, heat the canola oil to 360°F over medium heat. Add the calamari (in batches, if necessary) and deep fry, stirring a couple of times with a slotted spoon, until golden brown and cooked through (3 to 4 minutes). Remove from the pot with a slotted spoon and drain on a paper-towel-lined plate. Season with salt and pepper.

In a medium bowl, combine the kale, chayote, banana, and cashews with half of the coconut flakes. Add the fried calamari, toss with the dressing, and season with salt and pepper. Divide the salad onto four plates, sprinkle with the remaining coconut, and serve immediately.

ORANGE SESAME DRESSING

½ cup frozen concentrated orange juice, not diluted

1 tablespoon honey

1 teaspoon white miso paste

½ teaspoon toasted sesame oil

½ teaspoon minced ginger

½ teaspoon minced garlic

½ teaspoon sriracha

½ cup canola oil

Kosher salt

In a blender, pulse all the ingredients except the canola oil and salt. With the blender on high speed, add the canola oil slowly in a steady stream and blend until emulsified. Season with salt, if needed.

The dressing can be refrigerated for 3 weeks.

WHITE WINE BRAISED MUSSELS

Back in his day, Chef Peet opened a Belgian restaurant where he cooked many different mussel dishes; this one was his favorite. It's simple and very satisfying and perfect accompanied by crusty bread and a glass of wine for a stellar meal. Take note that the recipe comes together quickly, so it's key to have all the ingredients prepped and ready to go.

SERVES 4 TO 6

6 tablespoons unsalted butter, 4 tablespoons at room temperature

2 large shallots, minced

1 garlic clove, minced

2 fresh thyme sprigs

2 cups dry white wine

6 pounds mussels, scrubbed

1 teaspoon fresh lemon juice

1 tablespoon finely cut flat-leaf parsley

Kosher salt and fresh ground black pepper

1 baguette, warmed

In a large stockpot or Dutch oven, melt 2 tablespoons of the butter over medium heat. Add the shallots, garlic, and thyme and cook until softened (about 5 minutes). Add the wine and bring to a boil over medium-high heat. Add the mussels and stir to combine, and then cover and cook for 5 to 6 minutes, until all the mussels open; discard any unopened mussels.

Using a slotted spoon, transfer the mussels to a large bowl. Cover and keep warm.

Slowly pour the mussel-cooking liquid into a medium saucepan, pouring just until you start to see debris in the liquid. Discard the remaining liquid.

Bring the mussel broth to a simmer and then whisk in the softened butter a bit at a time, until melted and emulsified. Add the lemon juice and parsley and season with salt and pepper. Ladle the liquid over the mussels; then transfer to bowls and ladle the broth over the top. Serve with warm, crusty bread.

GRILLED SHRIMP WITH MANGO AND PAPAYA SALAD

Shrimp is very easy to cook; once the color changes, it's pretty much done. This simple recipe can be served on a platter for a family-style meal, and it's also easily multiplied to feed more than four people. Not only does it look great, but it can also sit on a table (or buffet) for a good amount of time without suffering.

SERVES 4

12 jumbo shrimp, peeled and deveined, tails left on (see note)

¼ cup extra virgin olive oil

1 tablespoon grated lemon zest

1 garlic clove, smashed to a paste with a pinch of salt

⅛ teaspoon cayenne

⅛ teaspoon smoked paprika

Twelve 6–8-inch bamboo skewers, soaked in cold water

1 fresh ripe mango, peeled and cut into ½-inch pieces (about 1 cup)

1 fresh ripe papaya, peeled, seeded, and cut into ½-inch pieces (about 1 cup)

2 tablespoons minced red onion

2 teaspoons finely chopped cilantro

2 teaspoons fresh lime juice

½ teaspoon honey

½ teaspoon minced seeded jalapeño, rinsed in cold water

2 cups frisée, cleaned and cut into 2-inch pieces

Kosher salt and fresh ground black pepper

Passionfruit Vinaigrette (recipe follows)

In a large resealable plastic bag, combine the shrimp with the olive oil, lemon zest, garlic, cayenne, and paprika. Seal and massage the outside of the bag to mix everything. Refrigerate for at least an hour or up to 12 hours.

Just before grilling the shrimp, prepare the salad. In a medium bowl, combine the mango and papaya with the onion, cilantro, lime juice, honey, jalapeño, and frisée.

Preheat a grill pan over a medium-high heat. Skewer each shrimp from tail to head and season with salt and pepper. Grill, turning once or twice, until browned (5 to 6 minutes).

Toss the salad with half the vinaigrette and season with salt and pepper. Divide the salad onto four plates, off to one side of each plate. Lay three skewered shrimp across the salad. Drizzle with the remaining vinaigrette and serve immediately.

NOTE

To prevent the shrimp from curling while they're cooking, make 5 to 6 shallow slices widthwise on the bottom of the shrimp (the opposite side from where the shrimp is deveined), slicing along the length of the shrimp.

PASSIONFRUIT VINAIGRETTE

MAKES ½ CUP

¼ cup passionfruit purée
(see note)

1 tablespoon sherry vinegar

1 tablespoon fresh lime juice

¼ cup extra virgin olive oil

Pinch cayenne pepper

Kosher salt and fresh
ground white pepper

In a small bowl or in a jar, whisk (or cover and shake the jar) to combine the passionfruit purée with the vinegar and lime juice. While whisking constantly, drizzle the olive oil until emulsified. Stir in the cayenne and season with salt and pepper.

The vinaigrette can be refrigerated for 2 weeks.

NOTE

If you can't buy passionfruit purée, you can make your own. Slice and scoop about 4 passionfruit in half and purée in a blender until smooth. Strain through a fine-mesh strainer to remove seeds.

SALMON BURGERS

This is a great example of how some of the most popular restaurant dishes are born from practicality: Chef Peet devised these burgers when he wanted to use up salmon trimmings from butchering. They were so delicious that he added them to the regular menu rotation. The burgers are served with sweet potato fries at the restaurant, but Chef says sweet potato chips are a great substitute at home.

MAKES 4 BURGERS

2 pounds skinless salmon fillet, finely chopped

¼ cup finely chopped red onion

2 teaspoons finely chopped fresh tarragon

1 teaspoon finely chopped fresh chives

Kosher salt and fresh ground black pepper

1 fennel bulb, cored and thinly shaved

¼ cup cilantro leaves

1 small radish, thinly shaved

1 tablespoon fresh lemon juice

1 tablespoon canola oil

Chili Aioli (recipe follows)

4 burger buns, toasted

SALMON BURGERS *contiued . . .*

In a large bowl, combine the salmon, onion, tarragon, and chives and season with salt and pepper. Pat into four patties and refrigerate for an hour.

In a medium bowl, combine the fennel, cilantro, and radish with the lemon juice and season lightly with salt and pepper. Refrigerate until ready to use.

Rub the canola oil on the outside of the burgers and season liberally with salt and pepper. Heat a large nonstick skillet over medium-high heat, add the burgers, and cook for 5 minutes. Flip and cook for 5 minutes longer (or until medium/medium-well); do not press out the juices while the burgers are cooking, or they will dry out.

Meanwhile, spread some aioli on the bottoms and tops of the buns. Top with the burgers and the fennel salad, using skewers to keep everything in place. Serve immediately.

CHILI AIOLI

MAKES 1 CUP

¾ cup mayonnaise

2 tablespoons sweet chili sauce (Mae Ploy is a popular brand)

1 teaspoon sriracha

½ garlic clove, minced

1 teaspoon fresh lime juice

In a small bowl, combine all the ingredients. Cover and refrigerate.

The aioli can be refrigerated for 3 weeks.

GRILLED CHICKEN SALAD

Not all grilled chicken salads are special, but this one is because it's light and crunchy with a perfect blend of flavors and texture. Don't skip the sweet, sticky dates and lightly toasted almonds, which make this version exceptionally good.

SERVES 4

1 tablespoon extra virgin olive oil

1 large garlic clove, minced or grated

1 teaspoon chopped fresh thyme

1 teaspoon finely grated lemon zest

1 teaspoon fresh lemon juice

Kosher salt and fresh ground black pepper

4 boneless, skinless chicken breasts (about 6 ounces each), pounded ¼ inch thick

14 ounces romaine, chopped (about 7 cups)

1 cup frisée, trimmed and cleaned

½ cup very finely sliced radicchio leaves

⅓ cup Pear D'Anjou Vinaigrette (recipe follows)

¼ cup pitted dried dates, cut into ¼-inch rounds

¼ cup sliced blanched almonds, lightly toasted

1 teaspoon finely cut flat-leaf parsley

In a large resealable plastic bag, mix the olive oil, garlic, thyme, lemon zest, and lemon juice and season with black pepper. Add the chicken, massaging and turning it around to coat in the marinade. Refrigerate for an hour.

In a large bowl, toss the romaine with the frisée and radicchio, toss with half the vinaigrette, and season with salt and pepper. Transfer to four shallow bowls.

Preheat a grill pan over medium-high heat. Season the chicken with salt and grill for 2 to 3 minutes on each side, until cooked through. Cut into ½-inch strips and lay over the salads. Drizzle the remaining vinaigrette over the chicken. Sprinkle with the dates and toasted almonds, garnish with parsley, and serve.

PEAR D'ANJOU VINAIGRETTE

MAKES 1½ CUPS

¼ cup pear D'Anjou vinegar
(or other quality fruit vinegar)

½ tablespoon Dijon mustard

¾ cup extra virgin olive oil

Kosher salt and fresh
ground black pepper

In a small bowl or in a jar, whisk (or cover and shake the jar) to combine the vinegar, mustard, and oil. Season with salt and pepper.

TIP An easy way to pick thyme leaves off the stems is to place the thyme sprigs in a resealable plastic bag and freeze for 2 hours. Remove the bag from the freezer and clap the bag lightly between your hands a couple of times. The leaves will pop right off the stems. They do this at the restaurant, but by the kilo!

NOTE
Pickled Wild Ramps (recipe in the "Pantry" section) can be chopped up and added to the salad for an extra flavor surprise.

PAN-ROASTED CHILEAN SEA BASS WITH MELTED LEEKS

Chef Peet is a big fan of Chilean sea bass for its clean taste and the fact that the thick fillets are like steaks. He dredges the fish in heavy cream before it goes in the pan, adding both flavor and color to the finished dish.

SERVES 4

FOR THE LEEKS AND COULIS:

1 teaspoon unsalted butter

1 medium leek, split lengthwise and thinly sliced crosswise, cleaned in a bowl of cold water

Kosher salt and fresh ground white pepper

1 medium red bell pepper, seeded and cut into 2-inch pieces

1 medium shallot, sliced

1 tablespoon white wine vinegar

FOR THE FISH:

Four 8-ounce skinless Chilean sea bass fillets

Kosher salt and fresh ground white pepper

2 tablespoons heavy cream

1 tablespoon canola oil

2 teaspoons finely cut flat-leaf parsley

Make the leeks and coulis. In a small saucepan, bring ¼ cup of water to a boil with the butter. Add the leeks, season with salt and pepper, and stir to coat. Cover and cook for 1 minute (or until the leeks lose their crunch but retain their color). With a slotted spoon, transfer the leeks to a bowl and set aside; keep the liquid in the saucepan.

Add the red pepper and shallot to the saucepan, cover, and cook over medium heat for 5 to 7 minutes (or until the peppers are very soft). Transfer to a blender, add the vinegar, and blend until very smooth. Strain through a fine-mesh strainer and season with salt and pepper. Keep warm.

Make the fish. Preheat the oven to 425°F. Season the fillets with salt and pepper, and dredge one side of each fillet in the heavy cream.

Heat a large heatproof skillet over medium heat. Add the oil to the pan (it should smoke slightly) and add the fillets, creamed side down. Cook for 3 minutes, and then flip the fillets. Transfer the skillet to the oven and cook for 3 minutes longer (or until the fish is cooked through).

Spoon the warm leeks onto four plates and top with the fillets. Spoon the warm red pepper coulis around each plate. Garnish with parsley and serve immediately.

CARAMELIZED PEACH GRATIN
WITH SABAYON

This sabayon takes on even more flavor when it's browned, but you can feel free to skip the browning—the dessert will still taste great.

SERVES 4

½ cup granulated sugar

¼ cup Kirschwasser (cherry brandy)

Juice of 1 lemon

1 vanilla bean, split, seeds scraped

4 ripe peaches, peeled

½ cup Sabayon Sauce (page 32)

6 mint leaves, very thinly sliced

In a medium saucepan, combine 2 quarts of water with the sugar, Kirschwasser, lemon juice, and vanilla bean and bring to a boil. Add the peeled peaches and cover with a lid slightly smaller than the saucepan to keep the peaches submerged. Simmer until almost softened (about 7 minutes, depending on how ripe the peaches are). Remove from the heat and cool the peaches in the liquid.

Once cooled, drain the peaches and split them in half. Cut the halves into crescent moon–shaped segments.

Preheat the broiler. On a baking sheet, arrange the peaches in four separate sunburst shapes on four heatproof plates. Drizzle the sabayon over the segments and broil (or use a torch), watching carefully, until the sabayon is golden brown (1 to 1½ minutes). Let rest for 1 minute, and then sprinkle with mint and serve, noting that the plates will be hot to the touch.

OVERSIZED OATMEAL RAISIN COOKIES

These are classic, old-fashioned oatmeal cookies made special by their super size. While they look and taste fantastic, they are easy to make and come together using basic pantry staples.

MAKES 9 LARGE COOKIES

2½ cups/325g all-purpose flour

1½ teaspoons baking soda

1 teaspoon kosher salt

1 cup/226g unsalted butter, melted and cooled

1 cup/200g light brown sugar

¾ cup/150g granulated sugar

1 teaspoon ground cinnamon

2 large eggs, lightly beaten

2 teaspoons pure vanilla extract

3 cups/300g rolled oats

1 cup/165g golden raisins

In a medium bowl, whisk the flour with the baking soda and salt. In a large bowl, whisk the cooled butter with both sugars and the cinnamon. Stir in the eggs and vanilla, and then gradually stir in the dry ingredients until thoroughly combined.

Sprinkle the oats and raisins over the mixture and then stir to evenly distribute. Cover and refrigerate for an hour.

Preheat the oven 375°F. Line a baking sheet with parchment paper or a silicone mat. Divide the dough into nine balls (6 ounces/170g each) and press them out on the baking sheet to ½ inch thickness (roughly 4½ inches round); leave 2 inches between cookies.

Bake for 12 to 15 minutes, until the centers are still a little soft; the cookies will continue to bake after they are out of the oven. Cool completely on the baking sheet.

The cookies can be stored in an airtight container for 3 days.

MONTH OF
SEPTEMBER
After the quiet of August, New York
feels alive again in September.

New Yorkers flock back to the city from summer houses, kids return from sleepaway camps and get back to school, and New York City's myriad street festivals start up again in earnest. The city and the park are buzzing. It's also one of the most abundant times of year at farmers markets, which overflow with summer's colorful bounty.

Every September, the city welcomes the New York Film Festival, hosted just steps from the Tavern at Lincoln Center. Part of the annual event is a big party at the Tavern, when the whole space is cleared out for an abundance of food stations, stocked bars, and hundreds of people. Years ago, Jim Caiola said he wanted to one day own the Tavern simply so he could host the New York Film Festival! From Broadway and movie premieres to weddings and corporate gatherings, all sorts of parties have a home at Tavern on the Green.

September is that time of year when diners might opt to bask in the warmth of Tavern's courtyard, listening to live music and enjoying a cold beer or chilled glass of rosé, or they may want to dine inside in the cool of the air conditioning. The Tavern's menu begins with Grilled Corn Chowder, a play on New England clam chowder and one Chef Peet's favorite soups. Diners can dig into Heirloom Tomato Salad dressed in a sherry vinaigrette, which is all about colorful and juicy seasonal tomatoes highlighted by the crunch of pickled red onions. The sultry September heat demands cold appetizers, and Jumbo Shrimp Cocktail and Smoked Salmon Mousse with brioche toast-point soldiers are must-haves.

Enticing main dishes include Maine Lobster Mac 'n' Cheese, which is a perfect example of how Chef Peet looks for interesting ways to ramp up beloved dishes. Lobster in mac 'n' cheese? But of course! The Caramelized Diver Sea Scallops dish is a deceptively rich option that includes simple and healthy ingredients. The plate is schmeared with a vibrant green arugula pesto that screams "restaurant" but is way easier to make at home than it looks.

September is prime apple month, and Chef Peet's Warm Apple Strudel is a delicious way to showcase the bounty of local apples. After sautéing Golden Delicious apples with butter, honey, and vanilla, Chef spoons them into layers of phyllo dough and bakes his strudel until it's golden and crisp. A warm vanilla custard sauce finishes the dish and eases diners into this magical season of changing light and colors.

HEIRLOOM TOMATO SALAD

In early fall, Chef Peet loves to go to New York City's Union Square Greenmarket, which abounds with fresh produce from all over the region. He seeks out heirloom tomatoes in all different sizes, shapes, and colors with fun names like Green Zebra, Pineapple, Brandywine, and Purple Calabash, just to name a few. These tomatoes are older varieties that have not been crossbred and are open pollinated, meaning they are fertilized by nature. Chef likes using them in dishes that highlight their beautiful colors and pure tomato flavor, like this super simple salad, which showcases the very best of the season.

SERVES 4

4 ripe heirloom tomatoes of different varieties and colors, each cut into 6 slices

Flaky sea salt, preferably Maldon

2 tablespoons Pickled Red Onions (recipe follows)

Extra virgin olive oil, for drizzling

2 tablespoons micro arugula sprouts or other sprouts

Arrange the sliced tomatoes on four plates, mixing up the colors. Crush a sprinkle of flaky salt over each plate and arrange some pickled red onions over the tomatoes. Drizzle with olive oil and top with the greens to serve.

PICKLED RED ONIONS

These onions are perfectly wilted but still crunchy and can completely transform a dish. They are excellent on greens and in sandwiches, among other things.

MAKES 1 CUP

1 cup sugar

1 cup water

2 cups thinly sliced red onions (cut into rings)

½ cup kosher salt

¼ cup sherry vinegar

In a small saucepan, make a basic simple syrup: Bring the sugar and water to a boil to dissolve the sugar; remove from the heat. At the same time, in a small bowl, cover the sliced red onions with the salt and let sit for 10 minutes.

Submerge the red onions in a bowl of cold water three separate times, discarding the water and using fresh cold water each time; you want to purge the onions of the salt. Drain well and pat dry. Transfer the onions to a plastic or glass container. Add the sherry vinegar to the simple syrup and pour over the red onions. Refrigerate the onions for at least 2 hours (preferably overnight).

The pickled onions can be refrigerated in their liquid for a month.

BABY BLT WEDGE SALAD

Chef Peet loves a great BLT sandwich, and this salad is a fun twist on that. He says that many wedge salads include blue cheese, but this one gets its creamy texture and tang from a combination of buttermilk and mayo.

SERVES 4

1 cup mayonnaise

¾ cup buttermilk

1 medium plum tomato,
cut into small dice (½ cup)

4 slices cooked bacon,
chopped into small dice (½ cup)

2 tablespoons finely cut
flat-leaf parsley

Kosher salt and fresh
 ground black pepper

3 heads baby iceberg lettuce,
each cut into quarters

In a small bowl, whisk the mayonnaise with the buttermilk. Stir in half each of the tomato, bacon, and parsley and season with salt and pepper.

Arrange three iceberg wedges each on four plates. Spoon the dressing over the lettuce and sprinkle with the remaining tomato, bacon, and parsley. Serve.

GRILLED CORN CHOWDER

During the late summer, the Tavern gets a lot of fresh corn, which gets used in salads, fritters, cold soups, succotash, and more. This is a corny twist on New England clam chowder, one of Chef Peet's favorite soups. Instead of clams, he makes grilled corn the star.

SERVES 4 TO 6

2 tablespoons extra virgin olive oil

One 5-ounce piece of slab bacon

5 ears grilled corn, kernels cut off the cobs

1 small white onion, finely chopped

1 celery stalk, diced small

1 garlic clove, finely chopped

Kosher salt and fresh ground black pepper

1 Idaho potato, peeled and cut into small dice (1 cup)

3 cups Vegetable Stock (page 341) or low-sodium broth

½ cup whole milk

2 tablespoons cornstarch

¼ cup snipped chives

In a heavy-bottomed saucepot, heat the olive oil until shimmering. Add the bacon and cook over medium-high heat until browned all over. Add the corn, onion, celery, and garlic, and season lightly with salt and pepper. Reduce heat to medium and cook, stirring frequently, until the onions are transparent.

Add the potato and stock and bring to a boil over high heat; then reduce heat to medium-low and simmer until the potatoes are just cooked (about 15 minutes).

In a small bowl, mix the milk with the cornstarch, and then stir this mixture into the soup. Bring back up to boil, and then remove from the heat. Remove the slab bacon and cut it into small dice.

In a blender or food processor (or in a separate bowl using an immersion blender), carefully purée half of the soup. Add this back to the soup along with the bacon. Season with salt and pepper. Garnish the soup with chives when serving.

The soup can be refrigerated for 5 days.

JUMBO SHRIMP COCKTAIL

The key to making shrimp that isn't rubbery is being careful not to boil it. The easiest way to avoid that result is this simple method of bringing the water up to a simmer with the shrimp and then turning off the heat and letting the shrimp cook in the residual heat in the water.

SERVES 4

2 tablespoons kosher salt

1 sprig tarragon

1 bay leaf

8 black peppercorns

1 lemon, halved

16 unpeeled jumbo shrimp (U/12 size; under 12 shrimp per pound)

1 cup ketchup

1 tablespoon prepared white horseradish, drained

⅛ teaspoon Worcestershire sauce

⅛ teaspoon hot sauce, preferably Tabasco

In a medium pot, combine 2 quarts of water with the salt, tarragon, bay leaf, peppercorns, and the juice from half a lemon; add the squeezed lemon half to the pot. Bring to a boil for 1 minute.

Add the shrimp and stir to separate them. Bring the liquid to a simmer, and then turn off the heat and let stand for 10 minutes. Transfer the shrimp to a strainer and let cool.

Peel the shrimp, and then cut along the back of the shrimp and remove any dark matter. Rinse the shrimp under cold water. Refrigerate for at least an hour.

Meanwhile, in a small bowl, combine the ketchup, horseradish, Worcestershire, hot sauce, and the juice of the remaining lemon half. Stir well and refrigerate until serving. Serve the shrimp with cocktail sauce.

The cooked and chilled shrimp can be refrigerated for 2 days. The cocktail sauce can be refrigerated for 5 days.

SMOKED SALMON MOUSSE

This silky, velvety mousse is a bit of a chameleon. Chef Peet has served it many ways: layered between crisp sheets of puff pastry, as a simple quenelle on a plate topped with caviar, and wrapped in smoked salmon and served with pickled cucumbers. This is the mousse in its simplest form, served with buttery brioche toasts.

SERVES 4

½ cup crème fraîche

½ cup heavy cream

½ pound Nova smoked salmon (see note)

1 teaspoon fresh lemon juice

Kosher salt and fresh ground white pepper

1 teaspoon chopped fresh tarragon

1 teaspoon chopped flat-leaf parsley

Toasted brioche and caviar (optional), for serving

In a small bowl, lightly whip the crème fraîche with the cream.

In the bowl of a food processor, purée the salmon. Add the crème fraîche mixture and process until very smooth; do not overmix. Add the lemon juice, and season with salt and pepper only if necessary.

Pass the mousse through a fine-mesh sieve into a bowl and fold in the herbs. Cover and refrigerate until fully chilled (at least 2 hours). Serve with toasted brioche and caviar, if desired.

The mousse can be refrigerated for 3 days.

NOTE

Nova is a type of smoked salmon from the Canadian province of Nova Scotia. It's cured and lightly smoked, yielding a silky texture and rich flavor. Nova is a little drier than other smoked salmon, but any plain smoked salmon can be substituted.

MAINE LOBSTER MAC 'N' CHEESE

Chef Peet looks for interesting ways to ramp up classic dishes, like this mac 'n' cheese. Lobster is a great way to add elegance to anything, from mashed potatoes and pasta to risotto. Other accent ingredients he likes to use in mac 'n' cheese include bacon, truffles, caviar, and sea urchin.

SERVES 4

1½ cups (5 ounces) cavatappi pasta

1 cup Bechamel Sauce (recipe follows)

½ cup heavy cream

1 cup cheddar cheese, grated

⅓ cup Parmesan cheese, grated

Kosher salt and fresh ground black pepper

¾ pound cooked lobster meat, cut into 1-inch pieces

2 tablespoons snipped chives

Preheat the oven to 425°F. In a large pot of boiling salted water, cook the pasta until al dente.

In a large ovenproof sauté pan, bring the bechamel and heavy cream just to a boil over medium-high heat, and then reduce heat and simmer for 2 minutes, stirring occasionally with a rubber spatula. Add the cheddar and half the Parmesan, and bring back to a boil. Season with salt and pepper and remove from the heat.

Fold in the lobster and cooked pasta. Spread the remaining Parmesan over the surface. Bake for 18 to 20 minutes (or until brown and bubbling). Remove from the oven and let stand for 5 minutes. Serve warm, sprinkled with chives.

BECHAMEL SAUCE

2 tablespoons unsalted butter

2 tablespoons all-purpose flour

1¼ cups whole milk, warmed

Pinch ground nutmeg

Kosher salt and fresh
ground white pepper

In a medium saucepot over medium heat, melt the butter. Add the flour and stir with a wooden spoon or whisk to combine. Cook the mixture, stirring frequently, until it starts to brown slightly (about 6 minutes). Add the warm milk, whisking constantly until smooth. Bring to a simmer and cook over medium heat, whisking, until thickened (about 6 minutes). Season with ground nutmeg, salt, and pepper. Remove from the heat and pass through a fine-mesh strainer into a clean bowl. Set aside until you are ready to make the pasta.

CARAMELIZED DIVER SEA SCALLOPS with ASPARAGUS AND ARUGULA PESTO

Diver sea scallops are hand harvested and shucked directly into a container. They have a lovely, pure flavor. When Chef Peet gets them delivered, they are often still alive and will cringe a bit when salted—that's how fresh they are. He aims for a U/10 size, which indicates that there are fewer than 10 scallops in a pound.

SERVES 4

5 ounces white asparagus, trimmed and stems peeled

5 ounces jumbo green asparagus, trimmed and stems peeled

2 tablespoons canola oil

1½ pounds dry diver sea scallops (about 20), patted dry (see notes)

Kosher salt and fresh ground black pepper

2 tablespoons unsalted butter

1 garlic clove, smashed

1 sprig fresh thyme

3 cups sweet pea shoots (about 2 ounces)

1 tablespoon extra virgin olive oil

1 tablespoon fresh lemon juice

2 tablespoons Arugula Pesto (recipe follows)

In a steamer basket set over a pot of boiling water, steam the asparagus for 3 to 4 minutes, until barely crisp-tender. Transfer the asparagus to a plate to cool. Cut on the bias into 2-inch-long pieces.

In a large skillet, heat 1 tablespoon of the canola oil over medium-high heat until shimmering. Add half the scallops, season with salt and pepper, and cook, undisturbed, until golden brown (2 to 3 minutes). Turn the scallops over, season again, and cook until just cooked through (1 to 2 minutes). Transfer to a plate and cover loosely with foil. Add the remaining 1 tablespoon of canola oil to the skillet and cook the remaining scallops. Transfer to the plate and keep warm.

Add the butter, garlic, and thyme sprig to the skillet, and then add the scallops and quickly baste with the butter to warm through. Transfer to the plate. Add the asparagus and cook in the butter until warmed through crisp-tender (2 minutes).

In a medium bowl, quickly toss the pea shoots with the olive oil and lemon juice; season with a little salt and pepper. Using a spoon, drag some of the pesto across four plates and spoon the asparagus on top. Arrange the scallops around the asparagus and top with the pea shoots. Serve hot.

ARUGULA PESTO

MAKES 1 CUP

1 packed cup arugula,
stems removed

1 packed cup spinach,
stems removed

1 cup extra virgin olive oil

Kosher salt and fresh
ground black pepper

In a medium pot of boiling water, blanch the arugula and spinach for 20 seconds, and then drain and immediately plunge the leaves into a bowl of ice water. (This method will help preserve the color.) After a minute or two, remove the arugula and spinach and squeeze dry.

Add the arugula, spinach, and olive oil to a blender or food processor and purée until blended. Season with salt and pepper to taste. If the pesto seems too thick, add a little cold water.

The pesto can be refrigerated for up to 2 days.

NOTES

- Dry scallops have not been treated with phosphates; as a result, they have better flavor and texture. They sear exceptionally well.
- If you are unable to find white asparagus, you can use all green.

ROASTED VEAL TENDERLOIN
WITH WILD MUSHROOMS

This is a perfect "restaurant" dish that can be made at home. It's elegant and special enough for a dinner party but easy enough to put together any night of the week. Chef Peet serves it alongside mashed potatoes or polenta.

SERVES 4

3 veal tenderloins (about 1 pound each), trimmed of excess fat and silver skin

Kosher salt and fresh ground black pepper

2 tablespoons canola oil

1 tablespoon unsalted butter

½ cup oyster mushrooms, stemmed and sliced about ¼ inch thick

½ cup shiitake mushrooms, stemmed and sliced about ¼ inch thick

½ cup cremini mushrooms, cleaned and sliced about ¼ inch thick

1 fresh thyme sprig

1 tablespoon minced shallot

1 teaspoon all-purpose flour

2 tablespoons brandy

2 cups Veal Stock (page 344)

1 teaspoon finely cut flat-leaf parsley

Preheat the oven to 425°F. Season the veal tenderloins all over with salt and pepper. In a large overproof skillet, heat the oil over medium-high heat. Add the tenderloins and cook until browned all over (3 to 4 minutes per side). Transfer the skillet to the oven and roast until a meat thermometer inserted in the thickest part of the tenderloins reaches 135°F to 140°F for medium-rare (about 8 minutes). Transfer the tenderloins to a platter and tent with foil to keep warm.

Add the butter, mushrooms, and thyme to the skillet and cook over medium heat, stirring occasionally, until the mushrooms are lightly browned (about 3 minutes). Add the shallot and cook until softened (1 to 2 minutes), and then stir in the flour to coat. Take the pan off the heat and stir in the brandy. Return the pan to the heat and cook, scraping up the bottom of the skillet with a wooden spoon, until the brandy is slightly reduced (about 1 minute). Add the veal stock and bring to a boil, and then simmer for about 5 minutes, until slightly reduced. Season with salt and pepper. Discard the thyme sprig.

Pour any juices from the resting meat into the mushroom mixture and stir in the parsley. Slice the tenderloins into ¼-inch-thick slices and serve with the warm mushrooms and sauce spooned on top.

WARM APPLE STRUDEL WITH VANILLA CUSTARD SAUCE

These apples are delicious on their own and would make a great gluten-free dessert served over vanilla ice cream or with the custard sauce. Chef Peet often serves this dish with schlag, a lightly sweetened whipped cream, too. This recipe is a strudel made with phyllo pastry, not regular strudel dough. It is a little easier to work with.

SERVES 4

1 stick unsalted butter

6 Golden Delicious apples, peeled and cut into ½-inch dice (6 cups)

2 tablespoons vanilla sugar (see notes)

2 tablespoons apple brandy

2 tablespoons honey

1 tablespoon golden raisins

Finely grated zest of 1 lemon

Three 14-by-18-inch phyllo sheets, defrosted (see notes)

1 teaspoon panko breadcrumbs (see notes)

1 teaspoons confectioners' sugar

1 cup Custard Sauce (recipe follows)

Preheat the oven to 400°F. In a large nonstick skillet, melt 6 tablespoons of the butter over medium-high heat. When the butter starts to brown slightly, add the apples and vanilla sugar. Cook, stirring occasionally, until the apples turn a light golden color (about 15 minutes). Add the brandy and cook until it evaporates (1 to 2 minutes). Drizzle the honey over the apples and add the raisins. Bring the mixture to a simmer and stir thoroughly. Remove from the heat and cool for about 15 minutes. Stir in the lemon zest.

Melt the remaining 2 tablespoons of butter. Lay a sheet of phyllo on a work surface and brush with the butter. Sprinkle with half of the panko. Top with another phyllo sheet and brush with butter; sprinkle with the remaining panko. Lay the third sheet of phyllo on top and brush with melted butter.

Spoon the apple mixture along the length of the phyllo in an 8-inch-long mound. Roll the phyllo up and around the apple mixture, tucking in the sides in as you roll. Finish the wrapping with the seam on the bottom and brush with the remaining butter. Transfer the roll to a parchment-paper-lined baking sheet. Bake for about 25 minutes (or until the phyllo is

WARM APPLE STRUDEL WITH VANILLA CUSTARD SAUCE

continued . . .

golden brown). Let stand for 10 minutes before slicing into four portions and dusting with confectioners' sugar. Serve with the warm custard sauce.

The strudel can be refrigerated for 2 days. Reheat gently to serve.

NOTES

- You can buy premade vanilla sugar at many markets, but if it's unavailable, you can tuck a used vanilla pod into a bowl of sugar and let it infuse for a couple of days. You can also substitute 2 tablespoons of plain granulated sugar and add 2 teaspoons of vanilla extract for this recipe.
- Defrost the phyllo sheets and keep in the package until you're ready to use them, or else they will dry out.
- Chef uses white cake crumbs at the Tavern, but any sweet crumbs or breadcrumbs can be substituted, as they are there to create airflow between the layers of phyllo.

CUSTARD SAUCE

MAKES ABOUT 1 CUP

1 cup whole milk

¼ cup/50g granulated sugar

3 large egg yolks

½ teaspoon Grand Marnier

½ teaspoon pure vanilla extract

In a small saucepan, bring the milk and half of the sugar just to a simmer over medium-high heat; do not let it boil. Meanwhile, in a medium bowl, whisk the egg yolks with the remaining sugar. Carefully whisk the hot milk into the yolks, whisking constantly until combined. Pour the mixture back into the saucepan and simmer over medium heat until the custard starts to thicken and coats the back of a spoon (about 5 minutes). Strain the custard through a fine-mesh sieve into a medium bowl and stir in the Grand Marnier and vanilla. Serve warm.

The custard sauce can be refrigerated for 3 days. Reheat gently to serve.

VENS

MAPLE FINANCIERS WITH CARAMELIZED BANANAS

When these maple cakes come on the menu, it's a sign that fall is in the air. The moist, deeply flavorful financiers are irresistible, but when there are any left over, Chef likes snacking on them with a cup of hot tea. Note that you will need silicone financier molds to make this recipe.

SERVES 8

FOR THE FINANCIERS:

1½ sticks/170g unsalted
butter, cubed

1 teaspoon pure vanilla extract

1 cup/110g pastry flour (see note)

½ cup/56g almond flour

½ cup/100g sugar

1½ teaspoons baking powder

¼ cup/56ml maple syrup

4 large egg whites,
whipped to soft peaks

FOR THE CARAMELIZED BANANAS:

2 ripe bananas,
cut into 12 slices each

¼ cup/50g turbinado sugar
(Sugar in the Raw)

Caramel Sauce, for serving
(recipe follows)

Whipped cream, for serving

Make the financiers. Preheat the oven to 400°F. Place a medium sauté pan over medium heat. Add 1 stick of the butter and melt, swirling the pan occasionally, until foamy and popping. Keep cooking, stirring now and then, until the butter smells nutty and brown bits form on the bottom (about 8 to 10 minutes total). Add the remaining 4 tablespoons of butter to melt and stop the browning. Transfer to a small bowl, add the vanilla, and set aside.

In a medium bowl, whisk the pastry flour, almond flour, sugar, baking powder, and maple syrup to combine. Fold in the whipped egg whites. Slowly add the butter mixture to the flour mixture, folding until combined.

Fill each financier mold with 3 to 4 tablespoons of the batter, filling almost to the rim. (You may have to do this in batches depending on how many rounds are in your mold.) Bake 10 to 12 minutes (or until golden brown).

Invert the molds onto a sheet pan and release the cakes. When cool enough to handle, invert them to cool right side up.

MAPLE FINANCIERS WITH CARAMELIZED BANANAS *continued...*

To serve, preheat the broiler. On a sturdy baking sheet, arrange the banana slices in sets of three, overlapping them slightly. Generously sprinkle the turbinado sugar over the bananas. Broil for about 3 minutes, or until the sugar is caramelized, watching carefully (it can happen fast). Let cool slightly.

Place the cakes on plates and top each with a set of bananas. Drizzle with caramel and serve with a dollop of whipped cream.

Any leftover cakes are perfect for snacking. The financiers will keep for 3 days stored in an airtight container at room temperature.

NOTE

Pastry flour has less protein than all-purpose flour, creating a lighter texture in cakes like these. You can substitute a 50/50 mix of all-purpose flour and cake flour, or just use all-purpose flour, which will make a denser (but equally tasty) cake.

CARAMEL SAUCE

MAKES 1⅓ CUPS

1 cup granulated sugar

6 tablespoons unsalted butter, cut into 1-inch pieces

½ cup heavy cream

Pinch kosher salt

In a medium heavy-bottomed saucepan, combine the sugar with ¼ cup of water. Simmer over medium heat until the sugar dissolves, turns clear, and starts to bubble (5 to 7 minutes). Continue to simmer, swirling the saucepan occasionally and brushing down the side of the pan with a wet pastry brush if the sugar starts to crystalize, until the mixture thickens and turns an amber color (15 to 20 minutes); watch carefully as the syrup starts to color, as you don't want it to burn. Carefully whisk in the butter, a little at a time (the mixture may bubble up a bit) until the butter is completely melted and smooth.

Remove the saucepan from the heat, and slowly and carefully whisk in the heavy cream until it is completely incorporated; it might bubble and steam. Stir in a pinch of salt. Let the sauce cool completely; it will continue to thicken as it cools. Serve cool.

The sauce can be refrigerated for 3 weeks.

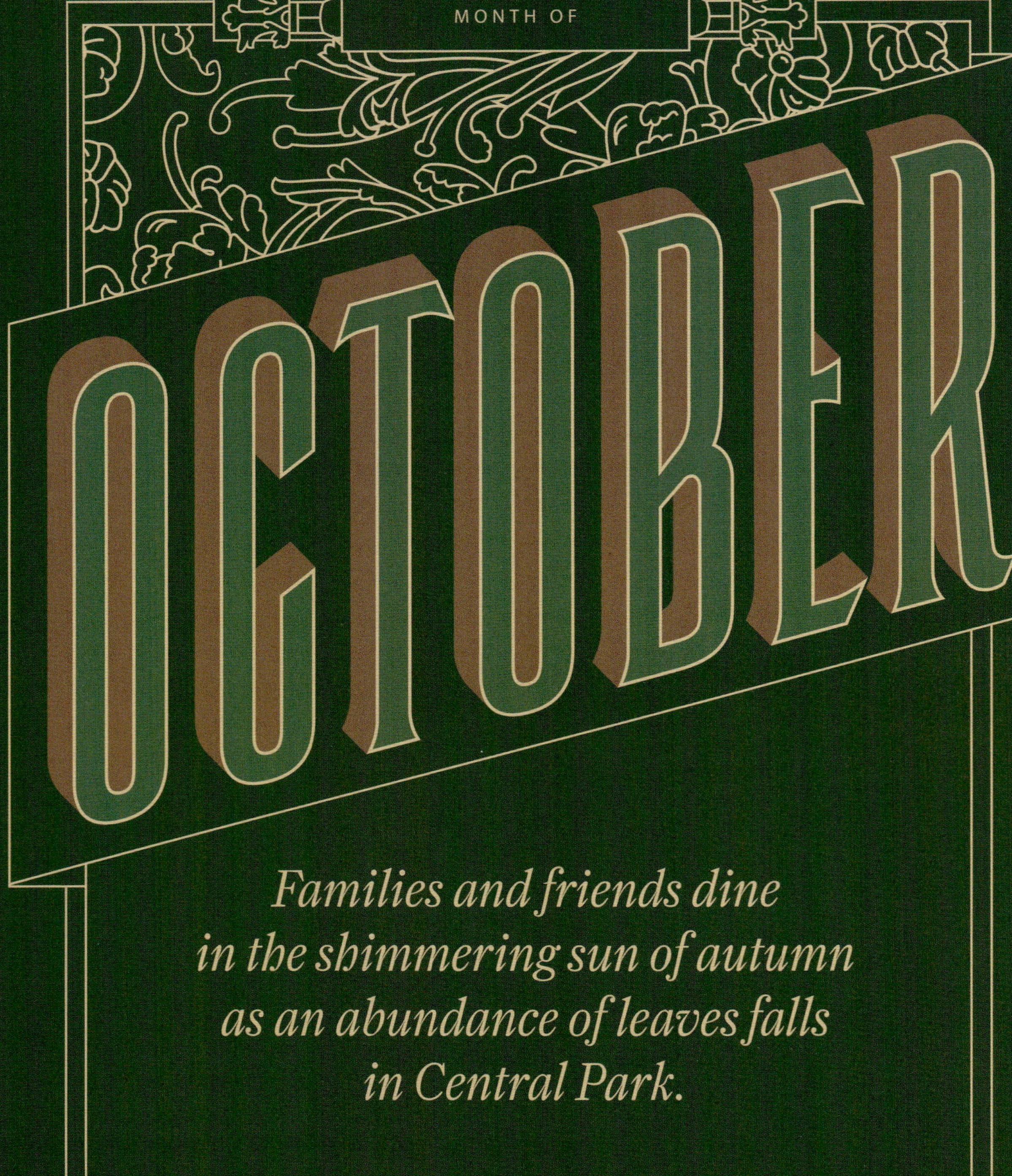

MONTH OF
OCTOBER
Families and friends dine
in the shimmering sun of autumn
as an abundance of leaves falls
in Central Park.

This is a magical time to be in New York City, as the weather is cool and comfortable and the holiday crowds have yet to descend on the city. It's also harvest season, and the profusion of fruits and vegetables is a boon to any restaurant, including the Tavern. From end-of-summer tomatoes and corn to fruits like apples, pears, melons, grapes, and figs and vegetables such as broccoli, cauliflower, Brussels sprouts, beets, carrots, kale, and so much more, fall is a gift to any eater.

With a final nod to summer, diners begin with Roasted Plum Tomato Soup, which sometimes comes with a small grilled cheese sandwich on the side. Other quintessential autumn appetizers include Salt Roasted Golden Beet Salad and Duck Confit and Grilled Melon Salad adorned with crackling duck skin "croutons." Some diners may opt to start with Miso and Mustard Glazed Marrow Bones, which feel straight out of a Parisian bistro.

The mains are varied. Fluffy Ricotta Gnocchi with Mushroom Ragout is a delightful vegetarian meal, while lobster fans can enjoy Grilled Lobster Risotto, which gets a Latin spin with mango, jalapeño, and cilantro. At brunch, Eggs Benedict Florentine is the number-one ordered item: The Tavern can go through as many as twenty-one hundred eggs in a single weekend for this dish alone!

October is a delightful month for dessert. Chef Peet gets freshly picked apples from upstate New York and uses them in a Golden Delicious Apple Crisp topped with a coconut streusel. In keeping with his French training in the kitchen, Chef features Honey Cinnamon Crème Brulée on the menu, a creamy indulgence that tastes like an upscale version of Cinnamon Toast Crunch.

As seasons change, the Tavern menu responds with a mixture of chilled and grilled dishes. Chef Peet teaches the servers to respect the range of food temperatures. Plates must enhance whatever appetizer or main dish is being served: warm for hot, cool for chilled. A cold plate under a sizzling 28-Day Aged New York Sirloin is unacceptable. Chef believes that the dining experience encompasses far more than just the ingredients on the plate, and the servers are taught every little detail so they can help provide the best experience for the diner. So as the weather starts to take on a chill, be sure your plates are the appropriate temperature.

ROASTED PLUM TOMATO SOUP

This is a very popular soup at the restaurant on cold, rainy days. Sometimes it's served with a small grilled cheese sandwich on the rim of the bowl. This soup—like all the soups served at the Tavern—is made by Benito Martinez, who has worked with Chef Peet since 1996.

SERVES 6

10 ripe plum tomatoes, halved

½ cup olive oil

1 medium onion, chopped

1 medium carrot, chopped

1 large celery stalk, chopped

1 garlic clove, crushed

Bundle of herbs: 3 parsley stems, 1 bay leaf, and 1 sprig of oregano tied together

1½ cups Vegetable Stock (page 341) or low-sodium broth

1½ cups prepared tomato juice

Kosher salt and fresh ground black pepper

3 to 4 basil leaves, very thinly sliced

Preheat the oven to 400°F. Working over a medium bowl, squeeze the juice from the tomatoes and set aside.

Arrange the cut tomatoes on a baking sheet and roast for about 35 minutes (or until softened and starting to collapse a little).

In a medium stockpot, heat the olive oil over medium heat. Add the onion, carrot, celery, garlic, and herb bundle and cook until softened (8 to 10 minutes). Add the roasted tomatoes, reserved tomato juice, stock, and prepared tomato juice. Bring to a boil, and then simmer, stirring occasionally, until everything is softened (25 to 30 minutes). Discard the herb bundle.

Using an immersion blender (or in batches using a blender), carefully purée the soup. Strain through a double mesh strainer, using a rubber spatula to help push the liquid through and discarding the solids as necessary. Season with salt and pepper.

Serve the hot soup in warm bowls, garnished with basil.

NOTE

To make a creamy tomato soup, add ½ cup of heavy cream after puréeing the soup and reheat to serve.

SALT-ROASTED GOLDEN BEET SALAD

This is a fun riff on the classic combination of beets and goat cheese. Instead of crumbling the goat cheese into the salad, Chef Peet rolls it into tasty little balls covered with chopped pistachios.

SERVES 4

1½ cups kosher salt,
plus more for seasoning

4 medium golden beets, trimmed

1¾ cups fresh goat cheese

½ cup shelled unsalted
pistachios, finely chopped

Fresh ground black pepper

2 bunches watercress,
stemmed and washed

1 Belgian endive, sliced crosswise
into ½-inch pieces

White Wine Vinaigrette
(recipe follows)

½ teaspoon finely cut
flat-leaf parsley

Preheat the oven to 425°F. Spread the salt on a rimmed baking sheet and arrange the beets on the salt, leaving room between each beet. Roast for 30 to 40 minutes (or until the beets are soft when pierced with the tip of a knife). Transfer the beets to a work surface to cool.

Meanwhile, roll the goat cheese into 24 balls, each about 1 teaspoon. Roll each ball in the chopped pistachios.

Peel the beets and cut into ½-inch-thick slices. (Keep each beet separate, as you will use one beet per plate.) Arrange each sliced beet in an overlapping round on a plate and season lightly with salt and pepper.

In a medium bowl, toss the watercress and endive with 2 tablespoons of the vinaigrette and season lightly with salt and pepper. Mound the salad up in the center of the beets on each plate. Drizzle the remaining vinaigrette over the beets and salad and around the perimeter of each plate. Place six goat cheese balls around the beets, evenly spaced. Sprinkle with parsley and serve immediately.

WHITE WINE VINAIGRETTE

MAKES ABOUT ⅓ CUP

2 tablespoons white wine vinegar

1 teaspoon Dijon mustard

¼ cup extra virgin olive oil

Kosher salt and fresh ground
black pepper

In a small bowl or in a jar, whisk (or cover and shake the jar) to combine the vinegar, mustard, and oil. Season with salt and pepper.

The vinaigrette can be refrigerated for 1 month.

NOTE

The White Wine Vinaigrette can be switched out with Balsamic Vinaigrette (recipe in the "Pantry" section) if desired.

DUCK CONFIT AND GRILLED MELON SALAD

This recipe will wow guests and friends, but it's quite easy to prepare because you can make the confit ahead or even just buy it and skip making it yourself. The saltiness of the confit melds perfectly with the sweetness of the melon and the bitterness of the frisée, and the crackling duck skin "croutons" give the whole dish an appealing crunch.

SERVES 4

Duck Leg Confit (page 245) or 6 store-bought duck legs in confit, heated (see note)

2 teaspoons extra virgin olive oil

Eight ½-inch-thick slices ripe melon (such as cantaloupe, Charentais, or honeydew), rinds removed

3 cups frisée, dark green leaves discarded, leaves torn into 3-inch pieces

Kosher salt and fresh ground black pepper

½ cup Whole Grain Mustard Vinaigrette (recipe follows)

1 tablespoon finely cut flat-leaf parsley

Preheat the broiler and heat a grill pan. Line a broiler pan or rimmed baking sheet with foil. Place 4 of the duck legs on the pan, skin side up, and blot off any excess duck fat on the skin with a paper towel. Remove the skin from the other 2 duck legs and lay the skin flat on the pan; add the skinless legs to the pan as well. Broil for 3 to 3½ minutes (or until the skin is lightly browned and crisp). Remove the meat from the skinless duck legs, shred, and set aside. Once cool, cut up the extra duck skins.

Rub the olive oil all over the melon and grill (in batches, if necessary) over medium-high heat, turning once (about 2 minutes per side). Transfer to four plates.

In a bowl, toss the frisée with the shredded duck and season with salt and pepper. Add about ¼ cup of the vinaigrette and lightly toss to coat. Mound the salad onto the plates and lay a crispy duck leg on each plate close to the mound of salad. Top with the extra duck skins.

Drizzle the remaining vinaigrette over and around each plate, sprinkle with parsley, and serve.

NOTE

To heat the duck confit, place the duck legs and solidified fat in a large pot and heat slowly over medium-to-medium-low heat until the fat is melted and the legs are heated through and falling off the bone (about 30 minutes).

WHOLE GRAIN MUSTARD VINAIGRETTE

MAKES ABOUT 1½ CUPS

¼ cup white wine vinegar

1 tablespoon Dijon mustard

1 cup canola oil

Kosher salt and fresh ground
black pepper

2 tablespoons whole
grain mustard

In a medium bowl or tall container, whisk (or cover and shake the container) to combine the vinegar, Dijon mustard, and oil. Season with salt and pepper and stir in the whole grain mustard.

The vinaigrette can be refrigerated for 3 weeks.

DUCK LEG CONFIT

MAKES 6 DUCK LEGS

6 large whole duck legs, preferably Moulard duck

¼ cup Confit Spice (page 97)

2 quarts rendered duck fat

6 garlic cloves

2 fresh thyme sprigs

Trim the duck legs of extra big pieces of fat and reserve. Do not split the drumsticks and thighs. Using a roasting fork or a regular fork with sharp tines, poke holes over the entire surface of each leg. Season with the confit spice on all sides.

Line a rimmed baking sheet with plastic wrap. Place the duck on the plastic wrap, skin side down, and cover with another sheet of plastic wrap. Top with another baking sheet and weigh down with cans or filled bottles weighing roughly 2 to 3 pounds total. Refrigerate overnight.

Preheat the oven to 300°F. In a heavy-bottomed Dutch oven or large ovenproof pot, heat the duck fat over low heat. Stir in the garlic and thyme. Wipe any moisture and spices off the duck legs and add to the pot. Cook over low heat until the fat reaches a temperature of 125°F or until you start to see a few little bubbles in the fat (20 to 25 minutes); do not let boil. The duck should be submerged under the duck fat. Add the reserved duck fat to the pot.

Transfer the pot to the oven and cook uncovered until the duck is falling off the bone (about 3 hours). Check from time to time to make sure the fat isn't too hot (see note), or the duck will fry and dry out.

When the duck is done, remove the pot from the oven and let cool (about an hour).

Transfer the duck legs to a container that will fit them in 2 layers and cover tightly with plastic wrap. Put the duck fat back on the heat and bring back to a low simmer over medium heat; skim the impurities that rise to the surface, and do not let the fat boil. When the bubbles stop and the fat is clear, it is clarified. Let cool (about an hour).

Ladle the cooled fat over the duck legs; they need to be completely submerged in the fat. Add the garlic confit to the container. Cover and refrigerate.

The duck will keep refrigerated under the fat for years as long as it is submerged and not poking out anywhere. The remaining fat can be refrigerated and used for frying or sautéing in dishes like Lyonnaise Potatoes (page 329) or the Pork Confit and Broccoli Rabe Sandwich (page 95).

> **NOTE**
>
> You can tell the fat is too hot if it starts to bubble; if that occurs, add more cold fat to bring the temperature down and lower the oven to 275°F.

MISO AND MUSTARD GLAZED MARROW BONES

During his time working in French restaurants, Chef Peet developed a love for variety meats like offal, as well as other delicacies like bone marrow. He has used it in dumplings, stuffing, soups, and sauces. But one of his favorite ways to enjoy marrow is roasting the bones with a honey-miso glaze and eating it with crusty toasted garlic bread, parsley salad, and sweet and sour shallot marmalade. It's a very simple dish, but he says it doesn't get any better than this.

SERVES 4

Six 4-inch veal or beef marrow bones, split lengthwise

2 tablespoons honey

1 teaspoon light miso paste

1 teaspoon Dijon mustard

½ teaspoon chopped fresh thyme

2 teaspoons extra virgin olive oil

6 sourdough slices, toasted

1 large garlic clove

1 cup roughly chopped flat-leaf parsley leaves

1 small shallot, thinly shaved

2 tablespoons Sherry Vinaigrette (page 70)

Sea salt, preferably Maldon

Sweet and Sour Shallot Marmalade (recipe follows)

Set racks in the middle and lower third of the oven and preheat the broiler. Line a baking sheet with foil and arrange the marrow bones on it, cut side up. Cover with a sheet of foil and crimp the foil to enclose the bones. Broil on the lower rack of the oven for 15 minutes.

Meanwhile, in a small bowl, mix the honey, miso, mustard, and thyme. Remove the bones from the broiler and remove the top sheet of foil. Brush or spoon the honey mixture over the bones. Return to the middle rack and broil for 4 to 5 minutes, until the tops of the bones begin to bubble and brown and the marrow is soft but not melted away. Keep warm.

Drizzle the olive oil over the toast and rub with the raw garlic clove. Cut each piece of toast on the bias into three slices.

In a small bowl, mix the parsley and shaved shallot. Toss with 1 tablespoon of the vinaigrette and season lightly with sea salt. Place the warm bones on four plates and divide the toast, parsley salad, and marmalade between the plates. Drizzle the vinaigrette over the salad and bones and serve.

SWEET AND SOUR SHALLOT MARMALADE

MAKES ½ CUP

1 tablespoon extra virgin olive oil

6 medium shallots,
thinly sliced into rings

½ cup dry red wine

2 tablespoons honey

1 tablespoon balsamic vinegar

Kosher salt and fresh
ground black pepper

In a small saucepan, heat the olive oil. Add the shallots and cook over medium-low heat, stirring occasionally, until softened and transparent (about 15 minutes). Add the wine, honey, and balsamic vinegar and cook over low heat until the liquid is almost completely reduced and the shallots are soft and caramelized (30 to 40 minutes). Transfer to a small container and refrigerate.

The marmalade can be refrigerated in an airtight container for 1 week.

RICOTTA GNOCCHI WITH MUSHROOM RAGOUT

Ricotta gnocchi can be easier to make than potato gnocchi because there's less work involved, but the key is not to overwork the dough—you want to just combine it. You can roll the gnocchi off a gnocchi board or along the back of a fork to create ridges, but you can also skip that part and leave your gnocchi unridged so they look like little pillows.

SERVES 6

FOR THE GNOCCHI:

1 pound whole milk ricotta cheese

2 large eggs, lightly beaten

3 ounces Parmesan cheese, finely grated (1 cup)

¼ teaspoon kosher salt

⅛ teaspoon fresh ground black pepper

1¼ cups all-purpose flour, sifted

FOR THE MUSHROOM RAGOUT:

2 tablespoons unsalted butter

2 pounds medium cremini mushrooms, cleaned and sliced

1 pound medium white button mushrooms, cleaned and sliced

1 pound oyster mushrooms, stemmed and cleaned

Kosher salt and fresh ground black pepper

1 cup dry white wine

2 teaspoons arrowroot

Freshly grated Parmesan cheese, for serving

1 tablespoon finely cut flat-leaf parsley

To make the gnocchi, line a strainer with cheesecloth and set it in a bowl. Add the ricotta and drain for at least an hour or overnight in the fridge.

In a medium bowl, lightly stir the drained ricotta with the eggs, Parmesan, salt, and pepper. Add the flour a little at a time, kneading with floured hands, until just incorporated and not sticky; if the dough still seems too sticky, add a bit more flour.

On a lightly floured work surface, pat the dough into a disk and cut it into six equal pieces. With both hands, roll each piece into a 1-inch-thick rope about 12 inches long. Cut the gnocchi into 1-inch pieces. Roll each piece off a gnocchi board or along the back tines of a fork onto a parchment-paper-lined sheet pan.

Meanwhile, bring a large pot of salted water to a simmer. Add half the gnocchi and cook until they start to float (2 to 3 minutes). With a slotted spoon, transfer to a baking sheet and repeat with the remaining gnocchi.

Drain any excess water from the gnocchi and use right away or cover with plastic wrap and refrigerate until ready to use.

RICOTTA GNOCCHI WITH MUSHROOM RAGOUT *continued...*

Make the ragout. In a large pot, melt the butter over medium-high heat. Add the mushrooms, season with salt and pepper, and cook, stirring frequently, until the mushrooms have released much of their liquid (about 7 minutes). Strain the mushrooms and reserve the cooking liquid.

Return the mushrooms to the pot and continue to cook, stirring now and then, until the mushrooms start to brown. Add the white wine and continue to cook until the wine is reduced by half (about 3 minutes).

Meanwhile, using a fork, mix the arrowroot into the reserved mushroom liquid. Add to the mushrooms and bring to a boil, and then simmer for about 5 minutes, until the liquid thickens. Season with salt and pepper.

Add the gnocchi to the pot and gently stir to combine with the ragout. Cook over medium heat until everything is heated through (3 to 5 minutes). Divide the gnocchi into six bowls, top with Parmesan and parsley, and serve immediately.

GRILLED LOBSTER RISOTTO

At the Tavern, this lobster risotto, with the addition of mango, cilantro, and jalapeño, is very popular. The jalapeño adds a lot of flavor, but blanching it eliminates most of the heat, leaving behind the pure pepper taste.

SERVES 4

4 cups Vegetable Stock (page 341) or low-sodium broth

1 tablespoon canola oil

3 tablespoon unsalted butter

½ white onion, finely chopped (½ cup)

1 cup arborio rice

½ cup dry white wine

½ cup diced mango

2 tablespoons finely chopped jalapeño (see notes)

1 tablespoon finely chopped cilantro, plus sprigs for garnish

Kosher salt and fresh ground white pepper

8 ounces cooked lobster meat, cut into ½-inch pieces (see notes)

½ cup Mango Vinaigrette (recipe follows)

In a medium saucepan, bring the stock to a low simmer. In a heavy-bottomed pot, heat the oil and 1 tablespoon of the butter over medium heat. Add the onion and cook until softened (about 4 minutes). Add the rice and stir until well coated with the oil and butter (about 2 minutes). Add the wine and cook, stirring constantly, until evaporated (about 2 minutes).

Add 1 cup of the stock and cook, stirring, until absorbed (about 4 minutes). Keep adding the stock about ¾ cup at a time and cook, stirring well, until the stock is absorbed before adding more. When the rice is just cooked through, remove from the heat.

Add the remaining 2 tablespoons of butter, along with the mango, jalapeño, and chopped cilantro; season with salt and pepper. Fold in the lobster meat and add little more stock if the risotto seems too thick. Divide into four bowls, drizzle with the vinaigrette, and top with cilantro sprigs. Serve right away.

NOTES
- To remove the heat from the jalapeño, place the chopped jalapeño in a pot of cold water and bring to a boil, and then drain.
- Chef Peet often grills the lobster to add a smoky dimension to the dish, but this step is optional. If you want to do so, quickly brown the lobster in a grill pan over high heat.

MANGO VINAIGRETTE

½ cup mango purée (see note)

2 tablespoons sherry vinegar

1 tablespoon fresh lime juice

½ cup extra virgin olive oil

Pinch cayenne pepper

Kosher salt and fresh
ground white pepper

In a small bowl or in a jar, whisk (or cover and shake the jar) to combine the mango purée, vinegar, lime juice, and oil. Stir in the cayenne, and season with salt and pepper.

The vinaigrette can be refrigerated for 2 weeks.

NOTE

You can purchase mango purée or make your own: Place the flesh of one small, ripe mango into the bowl of a food processor and purée until smooth.

EGGS BENEDICT FLORENTINE

This eggs Benedict dish is the number-one item sold during brunch, with as many as six hundred orders placed on some weekends. As a result, the kitchen poaches off about six cases of eggs each weekend, which is more than twenty-one hundred eggs! The Tavern also mixes the dish up now and then, offering the classic made with lobster, smoked salmon, crab, or creamed spinach, and sometimes swapping the Canadian bacon with country ham.

SERVES 4

1 tablespoon white vinegar

8 large eggs

1 tablespoon unsalted butter

1 pound fresh spinach, stemmed

Kosher salt and fresh ground black pepper

8 slices Canadian bacon, cut ¼ inch thick

4 English muffins, split and toasted

Hollandaise Sauce (recipe follows)

In a medium rondeau (a wide, shallow pan with straight sides), add enough water to fill halfway; bring to a simmer and add the vinegar. With a slotted spoon, stir the water in a circular motion. One at a time, crack the eggs into the moving water. Cook gently for about 6 minutes for a medium poach. Using the slotted spoon, transfer the eggs to a paper-towel-lined plate and keep warm.

EGGS BENEDICT FLORENTINE

continued . . .

Meanwhile, in a large sauté pan with a lid, melt the butter over medium heat. Add the spinach (the pan will be very full), season with salt and pepper, cover, and cook until it starts to wilt (about 1 minute). Remove the lid and cook, stirring the spinach until just wilted. Transfer to a colander and use the back of a spoon to press the spinach, draining the excess liquid. Keep the spinach hot.

Add the Canadian bacon to the same pan and cook just to heat through.

Place the toasted English muffins open-faced on four plates. Top each half with warm bacon and a mound of spinach. Top with the poached eggs, spoon the hollandaise on top, and serve immediately.

The poached eggs can be refrigerated in ice water overnight. When ready to assemble, reheat the eggs briefly in warm water. Pat dry with a paper towel before serving.

HOLLANDAISE SAUCE

MAKES 1 CUP

3 large egg yolks

1½ sticks unsalted butter, melted and at room temperature

1 teaspoon fresh lemon juice

4 drops hot sauce, preferably Tabasco

Kosher salt and fresh ground white pepper

Bring a small saucepan of water to a low simmer. Place the egg yolks and 2 tablespoons of water in a heatproof bowl that fits over (not in) the simmering water in the pot. Cook, whisking the egg yolks, until they hold a ribbon trail when the whisk is dragged through (about 5 minutes). If the bowl gets too hot, remove it from the heat briefly and then return it to continue cooking.

Remove the bowl from the heat. While still whisking, very slowly drizzle in the melted butter. Patience is key here, as you want to fully incorporate each addition of butter before adding more. It should slowly thicken up (about 5 minutes). Stir in the lemon juice and hot sauce, and season with salt and pepper. The sauce can be kept warm in the bowl set into another bowl of warm water for up to an hour.

TAVERN TU GO
TAVERN ON THE GREEN

GOLDEN DELICIOUS APPLE CRISP

One of Chef Peet's favorite desserts is a simple apple crisp prepared with apples picked from Upstate New York, where he grew up. In this version, he adds coconut to the topping for a tasty twist on a classic streusel. Be sure to have plenty of vanilla ice cream handy to melt over the warm apples.

SERVES 4 TO 6

FOR THE FILLING:

4 tablespoons/56g unsalted butter

6 Golden Delicious apples, peeled and cut in ½-inch dice

3 tablespoons/45g granulated sugar

2 tablespoons/30g dark brown sugar

1 teaspoon finely grated lemon zest

2 tablespoons/42g honey

FOR THE STREUSEL:

6 tablespoons/85g unsalted butter, cubed, at room temperature

6 tablespoons/90g granulated sugar

5 tablespoons/50g all-purpose flour

5 tablespoons/25g unsweetened coconut flakes

1 tablespoon dark rum

Vanilla ice cream, for serving

Make the filling. Preheat the oven to 375°F. In a large skillet, melt the butter over medium-high heat. Add the apples and cook, tossing and stirring often, until the apples begin to take on some color (5 to 7 minutes). Sprinkle the granulated sugar, brown sugar, and zest over the apples and cook until the apples soften and turn golden brown (about 5 minutes). Drizzle in the honey and continue cooking for 2 more minutes to meld the flavors. Transfer the apple mixture to a 1-quart gratin dish or casserole.

Make the streusel. In a medium bowl, combine all the ingredients. Using your fingers, rub and smear all the ingredients together with the butter. Spread the streusel over the top of the apple mixture; lumps are fine.

Bake for 20 to 25 minutes (or until the streusel is golden brown and the apple mixture is bubbling at the edges). Remove from the oven and let cool slightly before serving with vanilla ice cream.

The crisp can be baked up to 3 days ahead and rewarmed before serving.

HONEY CINNAMON CRÈME BRÛLÉE

Years ago at the Tavern, a pastry chef named Yefrii Matos created this unique take on crème brûlée. For diners who love breakfast cereal, this tastes just like Cinnamon Toast Crunch. Even for those who might not love cereal, the warming cinnamon flavor coupled with the honey makes this creamy indulgence hard to not love.

SERVES 6

2 cups heavy cream

½ cup milk

4 cinnamon sticks, cracked (see note)

½ cup granulated sugar

3 tablespoons honey

6 large egg yolks

⅛ teaspoon kosher salt

½ cup turbinado sugar (Sugar in the Raw)

Small pinch ground cinnamon

Preheat the oven to 300°F. In a small saucepan, bring the heavy cream, milk, and cracked cinnamon sticks just to a simmer over medium heat, stirring occasionally with a rubber spatula to keep the bottom from scorching (about 13 minutes). Remove from the heat and let stand for 5 minutes. Remove and discard the cinnamon sticks.

Meanwhile, in a medium bowl, whisk the granulated sugar, honey, egg yolks, and salt until the eggs are pale (1 to 2 minutes).

While whisking constantly, gradually pour the hot cream into the egg mixture. Continue whisking until completely combined. Strain the custard through a fine-mesh strainer into a clean bowl.

Set six crème brûlée dishes in a roasting pan. Pour the custard into the dishes. Pour hot water into the pan to reach halfway up the sides of the dishes. Carefully slide the pan into the oven and bake for 35 to 40 minutes, until the crème brûlées no longer jiggle when gently shaken.

Gently remove the crème brûlées from the water bath and let cool for an hour, and then refrigerate for at least an hour (or until fully chilled).

Combine the turbinado sugar with the ground cinnamon. Sprinkle the sugar mixture in a thin layer over the surface of each crème brûlée. Using a torch, brown each dish until the sugar melts and browns evenly; alternately, broil the custards as close to the heat source just until the sugar is browned. Serve immediately.

The baked crème brûlées can be covered and refrigerated for 3 days. Brûlée the tops just before serving.

NOTE

To crack the cinnamon sticks, a soft whack with a rolling pin does the trick.

ALMOND BISCOTTI

Using a food processor makes these sweet, crispy biscotti a cinch to prepare. If almonds aren't your thing, feel free to swap in walnuts, pecans, pine nuts, pistachios, or any other nut you like. These are perfect with crème brûlée but also just right alongside a good cup of coffee.

MAKES 30 BISCOTTI

1 scant cup/100g whole blanched almonds

2 cups/250g all-purpose flour, plus more for dusting

1¼ cups/250g superfine sugar

1 teaspoon baking powder

¼ teaspoon kosher salt

2 large eggs

1 large egg yolk

¾ teaspoon pure vanilla extract

Preheat the oven to 350°F. Place the almonds on a small baking sheet and toast until nutty smelling (about 6 minutes). Cool, and then chop.

In the bowl of a food processor, combine the remaining ingredients and blend, stopping to scrape down the side of the bowl once or twice, until a ball of dough forms (1 to 2 minutes). Turn the dough out onto a lightly floured work surface. Press the dough flat and sprinkle the almonds on top. Lightly knead the dough with the almonds to mix them in. Divide the dough into two equal pieces and roll each into an 8–10-inch-long log about 2 inches thick.

Line a baking sheet with a silicone liner or parchment paper. Place the logs on the sheet, leaving 4 inches between them. Bake for 25 to 30 minutes (or until firm and the logs start to color lightly). Let cool on the baking sheet for 15 minutes. Lower the oven temperature to 275°F.

Using a large spatula, carefully transfer the biscotti to a cutting board (the biscotti will still be soft in the center). Cut the logs on a bias into ¾-inch-thick slices.

Lay the slices cut side down on the baking sheet and bake for 30 minutes longer, until dry but not browned. Let cool before serving.

The biscotti can be stored in an airtight container at room temperature for 3 weeks.

November is an especially busy month at the Tavern, as two huge events happen in and around Central Park: the annual New York City Marathon and the Macy's Thanksgiving Day Parade.

The marathon is an international event that passes through all five boroughs of New York City, and the finish line is adjacent to the entrance to Tavern on the Green. The race is the first Sunday of the month, but preparation at the Tavern starts in the last week of October.

At 3:00 a.m. on the day of the race, Chef Peet and the Tavern team show up to get ready for the day. The kitchen is bustling with activity while most of the city sleeps; they have to be ready to feed more than fifteen hundred people in the coming hours. The first meals start at 5:00 a.m., when staff of New York Road Runners come in for coffee and bites, and the Tavern team ships out dozens of boxed lunches for NYRR staff working in other boroughs.

Just outside the Tavern's doors, a huge tent called the Blueline Lounge (named for the color of the marathon's finish line) is set up for athletes, friends, family, and VIPs. Television screens are stationed throughout to watch the excitement of the race. By 9:00 a.m., the tent starts to fill. Breakfast hors d'oeuvres are passed: mini waffles, little French toast bites, and more. The buffet is a breakfast lover's dream, with plenty of eggs, sausage, bacon, oatmeal, and other staples. Outside, a trailer right at the finish line feeds super VIPs, like Bill and Hillary Clinton and famed New York Yankee Aaron Judge.

The restaurant opens at 11:00 a.m. for another group of VIPs, including elite runners. Lunch includes a smoothie station, carving stations, plenty of fried chicken, and even a kids' station. At 3:00 p.m., the kitchen shifts and sets out a whole new menu with more hearty food: beef sliders and an array of different skewers are just a sample. No one goes hungry at the Tavern. While the restaurant will be buzzing until after 9:00 p.m., Chef Peet begs off by 5:00 p.m. and the police escort him out of the park, which is still teeming with exhilarated (if exhausted) runners finishing the race.

While November may be overshadowed by the marathon and Thanksgiving, the menu for the month is a perfect expression of fall, starting with Cream of Pumpkin Soup made with fresh sugar pumpkins and sometimes served right in the mini gourds. Fresh and Smoked Salmon Rillettes (a creamy spread made with both fresh and smoked salmon) comes to be table with little toasted pumpernickel soldiers for spreading.

Mains include delicious considerations such as Grilled Whole Fish with a Rustic Vinaigrette: a beautifully grilled branzino bathed in a tangy dressing of onions, capers, and olives. The Caramelized Rack of Lamb, with its sticky honey, mustard, and thyme glaze, is not to be missed. For vegetarians, Chef Peet's Roasted Beet Risotto is simple, creamy, warming, and a stunning pink color.

For dessert, Bittersweet Chocolate Mousse is silky and decadent, but for the kid in all of us, it's also a little reminiscent of a Fudgsicle and a must-have.

Not to be outdone, at the end of the month, Thanksgiving Day dinner begins with a vegan and gluten-free Mushroom and Black Lentil Soup, accompanied by generous slabs of Cornbread with Whipped Honey Butter and Sun-Dried Cranberry Conserves. Turkey with pan gravy is served with sides such as Rustic Sage and Sausage Stuffing, Mashed Potatoes, Glazed Carrots, and Maple-Infused Sweet Potato Mash. All this is a hard act to follow, until the Pumpkin Pots de Crème and Sticky Pecan Tarts are served. For more on Thanksgiving Day, see page 290.

HOUSE-MADE RICOTTA DIP

This dip starts as homemade ricotta cheese that Chef Peet uses to make fresh gnocchi. Adding garlic, lemon zest, and reduced cream turns it into a very smooth and irresistible way to start any meal.

MAKES ABOUT 3 CUPS; SERVES 4

2 quarts whole milk

1 cup buttermilk

2 teaspoons kosher salt

2½ tablespoons white vinegar

1¾ cups heavy cream

2 garlic cloves, 1 minced

1¼ teaspoons flakey sea salt, such as Maldon

½ teaspoon extra virgin olive oil

½ teaspoon finely grated lemon zest

Fresh ground black pepper

½ teaspoon finely cut flat-leaf parsley

12 slices toasted baguette slices, for serving

In a large pot or Dutch oven fitted with a thermometer, heat the whole milk, buttermilk, and salt over medium-high heat to 185°F to 190°F, stirring often with a rubber spatula to keep the bottom from scorching (10 to 12 minutes). Remove from the heat and stir in the vinegar. Let stand for 5 minutes.

Line a strainer with cheesecloth and set it over a medium bowl. Using a slotted spoon, transfer the curds to the strainer and drain for 3 minutes.

Meanwhile, in a small pot, bring the heavy cream and minced garlic just to a boil over medium heat, and then lower the heat and simmer for 8 minutes, stirring occasionally.

Transfer the drained curds to a medium bowl and thoroughly stir in the infused cream; the mixture will still look very loose but will firm up a bit after sitting for 10 minutes or so. Stir the sea salt, olive oil, lemon zest, and a few grinds of pepper. Garnish with a sprinkling of the cut parsley.

Rub the whole garlic clove over the toasted baguette slices and serve with the warm dip.

TIP This dip is excellent served warm but is also great when it's served at room temperature. For a boost of flavor, drizzle the dip with a good finishing olive oil, extra lemon zest and sea salt, and a mix of fresh herbs.

CREAM OF PUMPKIN SOUP

This warming soup is very tasty and comforting; it really tastes and looks like fall! Cooking the croutons in the soup is an interesting technique that Chef Peet learned from the legendary Chef André Soltner. It's also reminiscent of pappa al pomodoro, the Tuscan tomato soup simmered with stale or leftover bread.

SERVES 6 TO 8

1 stick plus 2 tablespoons unsalted butter

1 small, thin baguette, cut into ½-inch cubes (about 3 cups)

1 medium white onion, cut into 1½-inch pieces

1 medium garlic clove, peeled and smashed

One 4-pound sugar pumpkin, peeled, seeded, and cut into 1½-inch pieces (about 5 cups)

1 large Yukon Gold potato, peeled and cut into 1½-inch pieces

1 medium white turnip, peeled and cut into 1½-inch pieces

1 medium carrot, peeled and cut into 1½-inch pieces

4 cups Chicken Stock (page 342), Vegetable Stock (page 341), or low-sodium broth

Kosher salt and fresh ground black pepper

½ cup heavy cream

Preheat the oven to 400°F. In a medium heatproof skillet, melt 4 tablespoons of butter over medium heat. Add the bread cubes and cook, stirring occasionally, until light golden (about 5 minutes). Transfer the skillet to the oven and toast the croutons until they are a rich, golden-brown color. Set aside half of the croutons for the garnish.

In a large saucepot over medium heat, melt the remaining 6 tablespoons of butter. Add the onion and garlic and cook until the onion is softened and translucent (8 to 10 minutes). Add the pumpkin, potato, turnip, carrot, and stock; season lightly with salt and pepper and bring to a boil. Add the remaining croutons to the soup, cover, and simmer for about an hour, stirring occasionally, until the vegetables are very tender and the croutons have broken apart.

Using an immersion blender (or in batches in a standard blender), purée the soup. Add the heavy cream to the pot and bring the soup back up to a simmer. Season with salt and pepper as needed. Serve the soup in warm bowls or in small, hollowed pumpkins with the reserved croutons floating in the center of each.

The soup can be refrigerated for 3 days.

FRESH AND SMOKED SALMON RILLETTES

Rillettes are slow-cooked meats (typically duck, pork, and chicken) that are seasoned and cooked in their own fat for hours until the meat falls off the bone. Then the meat is shredded, and the cooking liquid and fat are incorporated back into the meat, which is packed in little pots or containers and covered in fat. To achieve exquisite flavor for his salmon rillettes, Chef Peet prepares the fish in much the same way, using mayonnaise as the fat. This is a perfect Thanksgiving Day hors-d'oeuvre, as it's light and perfect to prepare in advance.

SERVES 4

2 cups dry white wine

1 large shallot, minced

2 sprigs thyme

8 ounces fresh salmon fillet, trimmed of skin and bone and cut into large cubes

6 ounces smoked salmon, finely chopped

¼ cup mayonnaise

Kosher salt and fresh ground white pepper

1 tablespoon finely cut flat-leaf parsley

Small pieces of toast, for serving

In a medium saucepan set over medium-high heat, bring the white wine, shallot, and thyme to a boil. Add the fresh salmon and reduce the heat to a simmer. Cook the salmon until it is medium-rare (5 to 8 minutes, depending on the size and thickness of salmon).

Using a slotted spoon, transfer the salmon to a plate. Lightly cover the salmon with plastic wrap and refrigerate for at least an hour (or until the salmon is cold).

Bring the wine mixture back to a boil, and then reduce the heat to medium and simmer until the shallot mixture is like a wet purée (20 to 30 minutes); watch carefully, as the last 5 minutes of the reduction go quickly. Discard the thyme. Transfer the wine and shallot mixture to a small bowl, cover, and refrigerate for an hour (or until cold).

When the salmon is cold, place it in a medium bowl and flake it with a fork. Mix in the smoked salmon. Add the mayonnaise and gently mix with the fork to combine; you don't want to

FRESH AND SMOKED SALMON RILLETTES *continued...*

mush it up. Gradually add the shallot mixture, tasting as you go to make sure the flavor isn't too strong. Season with salt and pepper. Mix in the parsley. Refrigerate the rillette until well chilled.

To serve, spoon the salmon into small Weck jars or ramekins and serve with toasted pumpernickel soldiers (see note).

The salmon rillettes can be refrigerated for 4 days.

NOTE
Pumpernickel soldiers are thin strips of toast but can be made with any kind of bread you like. You can also serve this dish with toast triangles or whatever pleases you.

CIOPPINO, AKA FISHERMEN'S STEW

This hearty, warming dish comes together pretty quickly once the broth is prepared. It's closely related to both Italian cioppino and French bouillabaisse, but since it's made with fewer varieties of fish, it's really more of a classic fishermen's stew.

SERVES 4

3 tablespoons extra virgin olive oil

1 small yellow onion, sliced

1 large carrot, sliced

1 celery stalk, sliced

1 Idaho potato, peeled and sliced into ¼-inch half-moons and halved again

3 garlic cloves, grated

Pinch saffron (optional)

1 medium tomato, coarsely chopped (1 cup)

½ cup tomato purée

½ cup dry white wine

Herb bundle: 5 parsley stems, 3 large basil leaves, 2 thyme sprigs, and 1 bay leaf tied together

1 quart Fish Fumet (page 341)

Kosher salt and fresh ground black pepper

Rouille (recipe follows)

4 slices toasted baguette slices (cut on a 4-inch-long bias), plus more for dipping (optional)

12 pieces large shrimp, peeled and deveined, tails left on

12 pieces mussels, scrubbed

8 pieces small clams, scrubbed

1 pound cleaned cod fillet, cut into 1–1½-inch chunks

2 teaspoons finely cut flat-leaf parsley

In a large enameled cast-iron casserole or heavy-bottomed pot, heat the oil over medium heat. Add the onion, carrot, celery, potato, garlic, and saffron (if using) and cook, stirring often, until softened (10 to 12 minutes). Add the tomato, tomato purée, white wine, and herb bundle and bring to a simmer for 5 minutes to blend the flavors.

CIOPPINO, AKA FISHERMEN'S STEW

continued . . .

Add the fish fumet and simmer for 10 minutes. Season with salt and pepper, and discard the herb bundle.

Preheat the broiler. Spread or drizzle some of the rouille on the baguettes and brown quickly; set aside.

Add the shrimp, mussels, and clams to the hot broth, and then add the cod last. Spoon some of the hot liquid over the seafood, and then cover and simmer over medium heat for about 4 minutes (or until all the mussels and clams have opened). Discard unopened ones.

Divide the seafood into four large bowls and ladle the broth over the top. Garnish with parsley and serve with baguette slices.

ROUILLE

An authentic rouille—the thick French sauce that's served with fish soup—is rich and garlicky with hints of saffron and a trace of heat. It's so good with the soup that you won't regret toasting extra baguette slices for dipping.

MAKES 1 CUP

2 large egg yolks

1 tablespoon roasted red pepper from a jar, finely chopped

1 teaspoon fresh lemon juice

1 garlic clove, smashed

Pinch cayenne pepper

Small pinch saffron

¾ cup extra virgin olive oil

Kosher salt and fresh ground black pepper

In the bowl of a food processor or using an immersion blender, combine the egg yolks, red pepper, lemon juice, garlic, cayenne, and saffron. Pulse until smooth, and then slowly drizzle in the oil and process continuously until the mixture thickens. Season with salt and pepper to taste and use immediately.

GRILLED WHOLE FISH WITH A RUSTIC VINAIGRETTE

This chunky vinaigrette is spooned right up the belly of the butterflied fish, and when it hits the hot branzino, it melds right into the fish, infusing it with the vibrant flavors of onions, capers, olives, mustard, and lemon. Branzino is used, but it can be any other round fin fish (red snapper, black sea bass, striped bass, to name a few). Have your fishmonger clean the fish—scaled and all bones out.

SERVES 4

3 tablespoons plus 2 teaspoons extra virgin olive oil

1 large fresh fennel bulb, thinly shaved

1 small red onion, thinly shaved

1 cup whole artichoke hearts from a can, patted dry and quartered

2 tablespoons grated lemon zest

Kosher salt and fresh ground black pepper

2 teaspoons finely cut flat-leaf parsley

Oil, for the grill

Two 2-pound whole branzino, scaled, butterflied, and deboned

2 lemons, halved

Rustic Vinaigrette (recipe follows)

In a large skillet, heat 1 tablespoon of olive oil. Add the fennel, onion, and artichokes and cook over medium heat until softened and heated through. Stir in half the lemon zest and season with salt and pepper. Set aside and keep warm. Stir in the parsley before serving.

Light a grill or preheat a grill pan over medium heat. Oil the grill to prevent the fish from sticking. On a baking sheet, open the fish. Rub each fish with 2 teaspoons of olive oil, season with salt and pepper, and sprinkle with the remaining zest. Close the fish and rub each on the outside with an additional 2 teaspoons of oil. Grill fish on each side for about 6 minutes (or until cooked through). While the fish cooks, add the lemon halves to the grill cut side down and cook until lightly browned.

Spread the vegetables on a platter and place the fish on top. Drizzle with the vinaigrette and serve with the grilled lemon halves.

RUSTIC VINAIGRETTE

⅓ cup red wine vinegar

2 teaspoons Dijon mustard

¼ cup extra virgin olive oil

¼ cup canola oil

2 tablespoons red onion,
finely chopped

1 tablespoon capers,
finely chopped

1 tablespoon slivered green olives

1 teaspoon finely cut
flat-leaf parsley

½ teaspoon grated lemon zest

Kosher salt and fresh
ground black pepper

In a small bowl or in a jar, whisk (or cover and shake the jar) to combine the vinegar, mustard, and oils. Stir in the remaining ingredients, and season with salt and pepper.

The vinaigrette can be refrigerated for 2 weeks.

NOTE

Pickled Wild Ramps (recipe in the "Pantry" section) can be added to the fennel and artichoke hearts for an added zing.

CARAMELIZED RACK OF LAMB

These succulent lamb chops have an unbeatable glaze that's a simple combination of Dijon mustard, honey, and fresh thyme. They are delicious served with Creamed Spinach (page 333) and Potato Gratin (page 334) or Mashed Potatoes (page 29).

SERVES 4

1 teaspoon canola oil

Two 8-bone racks of lamb, about 2 pounds each (have your butcher french the bones and save the trimmings for the sauce)

Kosher salt and fresh ground black pepper

1 large shallot, chopped

1 garlic clove, smashed

1 cup Veal Stock (page 344)

1 rosemary sprig

1 tablespoon all-purpose flour

2 tablespoons Dijon mustard

1 tablespoon honey

½ teaspoon fresh thyme leaves

Preheat the oven to 450°F. In a very large ovenproof skillet, heat the oil over medium-high heat until shimmering. Season the lamb all over with salt and pepper and sear until browned on both sides (about 7 minutes). Add the lamb trimmings to the pan and set the lamb racks on top. Transfer to the oven and roast for about 13 minutes (or until a thermometer inserted in the thickest part of a rack reaches 130°F for medium-rare). Transfer the lamb racks to a plate and tent loosely with foil to keep warm.

Turn on the broiler. Add the shallot and garlic to the skillet and broil, browning lightly with the fat and juices in the skillet (about 3 minutes). Remove from the broiler and carefully pour off any fat in the skillet. Add the stock and rosemary to the skillet and simmer over medium heat for 3 minutes. Mix the flour with about 2 teaspoons of water to make a slurry, and then whisk this mixture into the veal stock; simmer for about 10 minutes until thickened. Season with salt and pepper and discard the rosemary sprig, and then strain with a fine-mesh strainer.

Meanwhile, in a small bowl, combine the mustard, honey, and thyme leaves. Brush this mixture over the lamb and let stand for 5 minutes. Broil the lamb racks until they bubble and begin to caramelize (about 2 minutes). Cut between the bones and serve with the sauce.

ROASTED BEET RISOTTO

Chef Peet loves beets and their deep earthy flavor, which makes them ideal for ramping up salads and other dishes. Beets can be somewhat polarizing, but Chef says that this rich, creamy risotto can convert even die-hard beet haters. It also makes a great vegetarian meal.

SERVES 4 TO 6

2 medium beets, trimmed

6 cups Vegetable Stock (page 341) or low-sodium broth

5 tablespoons unsalted butter

1 tablespoon extra virgin olive oil

1 medium yellow onion, minced

1½ cups arborio rice

1½ cups Parmigiano-Reggiano, grated (any kind of Parmesan cheese can be substituted)

Kosher salt and fresh ground black pepper

1 bunch watercress, washed and stemmed

Preheat the oven to 400°F. Wrap the beets loosely in foil and roast for about 55 minutes (or until easily pierced with the tip of a knife). When cool enough to handle, finely chop the beets and reserve with any beet juices accumulated in the foil and cutting board. You will need 1 cup of the chopped beets along with any reserved beet juices for the risotto.

In a medium saucepan, bring the stock to a low simmer.

In a large enameled cast-iron casserole or saucepot, melt 2 tablespoons of the butter in the oil over medium heat. Add the onion and cook, stirring often, until transparent (about 10 minutes). Add the rice and cook, stirring often, for 3 minutes; do not let it brown. Add 3 cups of the hot vegetable stock and cook, stirring, just until the stock is absorbed (about 7 minutes).

Add another 2 cups of stock and cook, stirring often, until the stock is absorbed (5 to 7 minutes). Add the remaining stock and cook, stirring, until creamy and absorbed (about 4 minutes longer). The rice should be cooked through but still have a little bite to it.

Add the beets and any beet juice and stir well. Remove from the heat and stir in the remaining 3 tablespoons of butter and the cheese. Season with salt and pepper. Transfer to bowls, top with the fresh watercress, and serve right away.

BITTERSWEET CHOCOLATE MOUSSE

This creamy, decadent, billowy mousse, developed by Chef Peet when he was sous chef and pastry chef at Manhattan's legendary Lutèce, was called out in the restaurant's four-star *New York Times* review and remains a staple during Peet's holiday season.

The mousse is not difficult to make, but it does require a bit of organization (and a few very large bowls). It's essentially four components made separately and then folded together. Because it can be made ahead, it's perfect for a party. The coffee and rum are subtle, but they definitely add that special something. If you loved Fudgsicles as a kid, you will love this mousse!

SERVES 8

FOR THE EGG WHITES:

1 cup/180g granulated sugar

¼ cup/80g light corn syrup

¼ cup water

5 large egg whites

FOR THE EGG YOLKS:

1¼ cups/240g granulated sugar

¼ cup/80g light corn syrup

¼ cup water

5 large egg yolks

1 large whole egg

FOR THE MOUSSE:

10 ounces/283g
unsweetened chocolate

3 tablespoons/42g
unsalted butter

1 tablespoon instant coffee

¼ cup dark rum

1 quart chilled heavy cream,
lightly whipped to soft peaks
(set aside in the fridge)

Orange Tuiles, for serving
(page 287)

Make the egg whites. In a medium saucepan fitted with a candy thermometer, combine the sugar, corn syrup, and ¼ cup water. Bring to a boil over medium-high heat, stirring once or twice to dissolve the sugar. Lower the heat and simmer undisturbed until the syrup reaches a "soft crack" stage (270°F to 290°F)—7 to 10 minutes.

Meanwhile, in the bowl of a stand mixer fitted with the whisk attachment, whip the egg whites on high speed until stiff peaks form (7 to 9 minutes). With the machine on, carefully drizzle the hot sugar syrup down the side of the bowl; avoid getting the syrup directly on the whip. Continue whipping on high speed until the egg whites are shiny and have cooled to room temperature (10 to 12 minutes). Set the whipped whites aside.

Make the egg yolks. In a medium saucepan fitted with a candy thermometer, combine the sugar, corn syrup, and ¼ cup water. Bring to a boil

BITTERSWEET CHOCOLATE MOUSSE

continued . . .

over medium-high heat, stirring once or twice to dissolve the sugar. Lower the heat and simmer undisturbed until the syrup reaches a "soft crack" stage (270°F to 290°F)—7 to 10 minutes.

Meanwhile, in the clean bowl of a stand mixer fitted with the whisk attachment, whip the egg yolks and whole egg on high speed until lightened in color and doubled in volume (about 5 minutes). With the machine on, carefully drizzle the hot sugar syrup down the side of the bowl; avoid getting the syrup directly on the whip. Continue whipping on high speed until pale yellow and thickened (10 to 12 minutes).

Make the mousse. In a microwave-safe bowl, melt the chocolate with the butter in 20-second increments, stirring between. In a small bowl, stir the instant coffee into the rum to dissolve it.

Using a large rubber spatula, stir the dissolved coffee into the whipped egg yolks, and then fold in the melted chocolate until thoroughly combined. Fold in the whipped egg whites, and then fold in the whipped heavy cream until no white steaks remain.

Transfer the chocolate mousse to containers and refrigerate until set (at least 3 to 4 hours). Serve cold.

The mousse can be refrigerated for 1 week.

ORANGE TUILES

These pretty, lacy orange tuiles are a nice complement to the Bittersweet Chocolate Mousse (page 285) and would go well with lots of other desserts too, even just a simple scoop of ice cream or sorbet.

½ cup/52g blanched sliced almonds

1 cup/113g confectioners' sugar

⅓ cup/43g all-purpose flour

Finely grated zest of ½ orange (about 1 teaspoon)

½ stick/56g unsalted butter

¼ cup orange juice

In the bowl of a food processor, chop the almonds using quick pulses until they resemble very coarsely ground coffee. Transfer to a bowl and whisk the almonds with the confectioners' sugar, flour, and zest.

In a small saucepan, melt the butter over medium heat and cook until the butter starts to brown and smell nutty (7 to 8 minutes). Add the orange juice, and then whisk into the almond mixture just to combine. Refrigerate for at least 2 hours.

Preheat the oven to 350°F. Spray two large, rimmed baking sheets with cooking spray and cover with parchment paper. Scoop 1 teaspoon of the batter and shape into a ball; repeat to form eight balls. Arrange four balls, leaving about 4 inches between, as the tuiles spread a lot, on each prepared sheet. Bake for 6 to 8 minutes, until flat and golden brown. Cool for 5 minutes on the baking sheets, and then carefully transfer to a rack to cool completely. Repeat to bake the remaining tuiles.

The tuiles can be stored in an airtight container for up to 1 week.

NOTES

- The rounder the tuile batter is before it's baked, the more you will be rewarded with a perfectly round, lacy tuile.
- To make a classic curved/rounded tuile shape, after removing from the oven, let the tuiles sit on the baking sheet for 30 seconds. While the tuile is still warm and pliable, use an offset spatula to drape the tuile over a rolling pin, pressing it gently around the pin. Let cool for a few minutes to firm up, and then carefully transfer to a storage container.

PEANUT BRITTLE

For the best results when making this sweet, nutty, crunchy brittle, premeasure the peanuts as well as the butter, vanilla, baking soda, and salt so they can be quickly added to the saucepan and nothing gets overcooked. This brittle is perfect to put in a jar or tin and give as a holiday gift.

MAKES ABOUT 1 POUND

¾ cup plus 2 tablespoons granulated sugar

½ cup light corn syrup

3 tablespoons water

1 cup shelled roasted peanuts

1½ tablespoons unsalted butter

½ teaspoon vanilla extract

½ teaspoon baking soda

⅛ teaspoon kosher salt

Spray a large, rimmed baking sheet with cooking spray. In a heavy-bottomed medium saucepan fitted with a candy thermometer, combine the sugar and corn syrup and add 3 tablespoons of water; it should look like wet sand. Bring to a boil over medium heat and cook for 8 minutes; brush down the side of the pot with a wet pastry brush to keep the sugar from burning. Continue to simmer, undisturbed, until a light amber color forms (about 20 minutes).

Add the peanuts and stir slowly to combine without splashing the sugar up the side of the pot. Cook, stirring occasionally, until the temperature reaches 300°F to 310°F and a nice honey color forms (about 4 minutes). Remove from the heat and quickly stir in the butter, vanilla, baking soda, and salt. Immediately pour the mixture onto the prepared baking sheet and use the back of a spoon or a spatula to spread it in a thin, even layer. While it is still very hot, use 2 forks to stretch the mixture as thinly as possible, and then turn it over so the peanuts are well suspended in the candy mixture.

Let cool until completely hard (about 20 minutes). With the back of a spoon, break the brittle into pieces before serving.

The brittle can be stored in an airtight container for 1 month.

DAY OF

THANKSGIVING

On Thanksgiving Day,
Chef Peet arrives at the Tavern at
4:00 a.m., driving a circuitous route
through the neighborhood because
the Tavern entrance on
Central Park West is closed.

Chef Peet's first task is to set up coffee and pastries in the Horseshoe Bar area for members of the New York City Police Department. Throughout the day, detectives, ranking officers, and patrol officers will meet in the Tavern to coordinate their holiday enforcement plan. The first shift arrives at 5:30 a.m. The sweets and caffeine are a goodwill gesture on the part of the Tavern. "This is how we give back—to provide food and hospitality. These people may be having a rough day. They can come in here to take a break," Chef says.

Chef Peet's staff begins to arrive at 5:00 a.m., walking to the restaurant from the southern and eastern sections of the park to avoid the chaos of Central Park West. There is a lot to do before 11:00 a.m., when the restaurant opens for Thanksgiving Day guests and will likely serve more than fifteen hundred meals (not to mention more than two thousand portions of cornbread!).

Yet preparations began three weeks earlier, when Chef Peet shared his critical path strategy with the cooking staff. He tacked it to a kitchen wall to keep everyone on course throughout November. "We look at it every day, we talk about what's coming up. You know what we can do ahead of time and what we can't," Chef Peet says.

CHEF PEET'S CRITICAL PATH ON THANKSGIVING DAY

A bit of history: The Tavern keeps two refrigerated sea boxes on site. One is for cases of produce, big cuts of meat and fish, and other foods needed for daily operations. (Delicate menu items are kept in the restaurant.) The second is for beer and wine. The outdoor boxes replaced a long room tacked onto the back of the kitchen after it was torn down to restore the site to its original footprint. At this time of year, the Tavern rents a refrigerated trailer to hold all the food and turkeys for the holidays. It is kept until January.

Two truck trailers are also behind the Tavern. One stores the equipment needed for events; the other is for the restaurant's dry supplies, such as paper goods. One trailer is also home to six 55-gallon heavy-duty garbage cans with lids that are used for brining the turkeys. The staff drag out the cans, clean them, and then pour in brine once the turkeys arrive. Only breasts will be brined; thighs will be seasoned and then cooked in duck fat. The French method, confit, infuses meat with fat and flavor. The thighs are boned after cooking and set up to slice.

Three weeks out, the staff starts to cut the bread for stuffing; they will go through more than two hundred loaves of bread. Two-thirds is challah, which holds its shape when liquid is added. One-third is brioche, which breaks down with liquid. When the brioche starts to crumble, it creates what Chef Peet calls "the mortar that holds it all together."

The cut bread is toasted, and then every morsel must cool before being stored in large plastic containers called Lexans. The bread must be dry so that it won't grow moldy. The containers are carried into the steel sea box shipping container that sits in the circular drive behind the restaurant.

Two weeks out, a turkey farm delivers the stars of the Thanksgiving show: 190 or so fresh organic, heirloom, grass-fed turkeys, which will be stored on rolling racks in the refrigerated trailer until the big day. They arrive very chilled, so they need to completely defrost before their preparation begins.

One week out, the staff begins working on the turkeys. Breasts are placed in brine—a mix of salt, water, a few aromatics, and a sugar solution—for 24 hours. This step adds moisture to breast meat so that it doesn't dry out when cooked. But after the brine bath, the breasts are removed and will sit for 24 to 48 hours to allow excess liquid to seep out. At this stage, the staff changes the trays a couple of times to air-dry the skin, which roasts better when dry.

The mirepoix vegetables (carrots, onions, and celery) are cleaned and roasted. A large 40-gallon steam kettle is used to make stock for turkey gravy. That process finishes on Tuesday, when Brussels sprouts and carrots are prepared.

Also prepared this week are the 130 gallons of Thanksgiving Day soup. The day before the holiday, there is still more to do: The turkeys must be roasted and then broken down. Whole breasts are removed from the bone and then sliced like a roast. Meanwhile, the turkey bones roast to flavor the stock.

Potatoes are peeled and cleaned on Wednesday but prepared on Thursday.

On Thanksgiving Day, certain critical tasks are top of the list because some side dishes can be made only on the holiday, such as mashed potatoes and sweet potatoes baked until soft.

Endless trays of cornbread must also be baked so that every table receives a generous helping with whipped honey butter. The pastry chef, Juan Olguin, begins prepping and baking desserts at 5:00 a.m.

By 8:30 a.m., Chef Peet serves a full Thanksgiving meal for cooks and staff: turkey, stuffing, gravy, mashed potatoes, sweet potatoes, cranberry, carrots, and Brussels sprouts. An hour later, he and his chefs perform a "food show" for the staff, describing every dish and discussing allergies, as well as the gluten-free, vegetarian, and vegan dishes on the menu.

Before the Tavern opens, the turkeys are sliced into appropriate servings and daubed with butter and stock. Two 30-pound partially roasted turkeys are placed on display near the entrance. As Chef Peet explains it, "Everything that we do here at Thanksgiving is what I would do at home; it's just on a much bigger scale."

MUSHROOM AND BLACK LENTIL SOUP

At Thanksgiving everyone gets soup, and Benito Martinez, who has worked with Chef Peet since 1996, makes about 130 gallons of this soup just for the day. It's hearty, full of flavor, and easy to make. Small black beluga lentils are a nice change from more common brown or green lentils, but you can also use French green lentils. For an extra special touch, this soup can be further garnished with a drop or two of black truffle oil.

SERVES 4

4 tablespoons unsalted butter

1 large onion, cut into small dice

2 cups (about 5 ounces) white button mushrooms, cut into small dice

2 carrots, cut into small dice

2 celery stalks, cut into small dice

2 garlic cloves, minced

Kosher salt and fresh ground black pepper

1 cup black beluga lentils, rinsed and drained

6 cups Vegetable Stock (page 341) or low-sodium broth

1 bay leaf

1 sprig thyme

3 tablespoons finely cut flat-leaf parsley

In a large, heavy-bottomed pot or Dutch oven, melt the butter over medium heat. Add the onion, mushrooms, carrots, celery, and garlic and season with salt and pepper. Cook, stirring occasionally, until the vegetables are softened (10 to 12 minutes).

Add the lentils and stir to combine. Add the vegetable stock, bay leaf, and thyme sprig. Bring to a boil over medium-high heat, and then lower the heat to medium and simmer until the lentils are softened (about 25 minutes). Discard the bay leaf and thyme sprig, and season the soup with salt and pepper. Add the parsley and serve.

The soup can be refrigerated for 3 days.

CORNBREAD with WHIPPED HONEY BUTTER

This super-moist cornbread, speckled with delicious little bites of corn, is not overly sweet. Feel free to use thawed frozen corn kernels, drained canned corn, or fresh kernels cut straight off the cob when corn is in season.

MAKES ONE 9-BY-13-INCH PAN

2½ cups/350g all-purpose flour

1½ cups/225g fine cornmeal

½ cup/100g granulated sugar

3 teaspoons baking powder

¾ teaspoon baking soda

1¼ teaspoons kosher salt

1½ cups corn kernels

2½ cups whole milk

2 sticks unsalted butter, melted and cooled

2 large eggs

¼ cup chopped pickled jalapeños (optional)

Preheat the oven to 375°F. Lightly grease a 9-by-13-inch baking pan and line the pan with parchment paper; grease the parchment paper.

In a large bowl, whisk the flour, cornmeal, sugar, baking powder, baking soda, and salt. Stir in the corn. In another bowl, whisk the milk, melted butter, eggs, and jalapeños (if using). Make a well in the dry ingredients and pour in the wet ingredients, stirring quickly and gently until just combined. Do not overmix.

Pour the batter into the prepared pan and spread the top. Bake for 30 to 40 minutes (until the edges turn golden and begin to pull away from the pan and a cake tester inserted in the center comes out clean). Transfer to a rack to cool for 10 minutes. Cut into squares and serve warm with the Whipped Honey Butter.

The cornbread can be made up to 3 days ahead. Rewarm before serving.

NOTE

The cornbread can be baked into jumbo muffins, which will be a little sturdier than cornbread squares. Add about ⅔ cup batter in each cup of lightly greased molds and bake for 20 to 25 minutes. Makes about 15 jumbo muffins.

WHIPPED HONEY BUTTER

MAKES ABOUT 1 CUP

2 sticks salted butter,
at room temperature

2 tablespoons honey

In the bowl of a stand mixer fitted with the paddle attachment or using a hand mixer, whip the butter and honey until smooth, scraping down the side of the bowl with a rubber spatula once or twice (about 1 minute). Serve.

THANKSGIVING TURKEY

When it comes to the big day, Chef Peet suggests keeping a to-do list and crossing items off as they are prepared. Regarding the bird, he shares his thoughts on how to make the best version:

Stuff the turkey just before it goes into the oven. The cool stuffing keeps the bird from overcooking, and the drippings from the turkey cavity add a ton of flavor to the stuffing.

Slice up vegetables (the ratio should be about 50% onions, 25% carrots, and 25% celery) and use these as a bed for the turkey in the roasting pan. The vegetables are also used in the gravy for flavor. Place the neck and wing tips (roughly chopped with the heel of the knife) plus the gizzards and heart around the turkey in the roasting pan. These are also used in gravy. The heart and gizzards are used as a garnish for the finished gravy.

SERVES 6 TO 8

2 celery stalks, roughly chopped

1 large onion, roughly chopped

1 large carrot, roughly chopped

One 12–14-pound turkey, wing tips clipped and chopped, neck bone chopped, gizzards and heart reserved

2 tablespoons unsalted butter, melted

Kosher salt and fresh ground black pepper

Rustic Sage and Sausage Stuffing (page 301, optional)

3 tablespoons all-purpose flour

2 cups Chicken Stock (page 342) or low-sodium broth

3 thyme sprigs

1 sage sprig

Preheat the oven to 450°F. In a large roasting pan, arrange the chopped vegetables, wing tips, and neckbone roughly where the footprint of the bird will be; lay the turkey on top. Scatter the gizzards and heart around the perimeter of the pan. Brush the melted butter over the entire surface of the bird and season generously inside and out with salt and pepper.

If you are stuffing the turkey, place the cold stuffing in the cavity, being careful not to overstuff it. Roast the turkey, uncovered, for 45 minutes at 450°F. Then turn the oven temperature down to 350°F and roast, basting with the pan juices every 15 minutes or so. Doing so gives the turkey a crisp skin. Cook the turkey until a thermometer inserted in the thickest part of the bird reaches 155°F (150°F if the bird isn't stuffed)—about 12 minutes per pound if stuffed and 10 minutes per pound if not stuffed. If you notice the turkey is getting too dark while roasting, tent it loosely with foil.

THANKSGIVING TURKEY *continued...*

Remove from the oven, carefully transfer to a carving board, and cover with a sheet of heavy foil. Let the turkey rest for at least 30 minutes before carving; it will continue to cook as it sits.

Meanwhile, carefully strain the roasting pan juices into a small bowl or measuring cup and let the liquid settle and separate. Skim the fat off the top, reserving 3 tablespoons. Reserve the pan juices.

Add the vegetables, gizzards, heart, and bones back to the roasting pan. Over medium heat, mix in the reserved fat and sprinkle the flour over everything. Cook, stirring constantly, to brown the vegetables (about 5 minutes). Add the stock, pan juices, and herb sprigs and cook, scraping up the browned bits on the bottom of the pan. Bring to a boil, and then simmer for about 10 minutes until the gravy thickens; skim off any fat that rises to the top.

Strain again, picking out the gizzards and heart; dice and add back to the gravy. Season with salt and pepper. Remove the stuffing from the cavity. Carve the turkey, removing the legs first and then slicing the meat off the thighs. Serve the drumsticks whole. Remove the breasts in one piece and slice them like a roast. Serve with the gravy and stuffing.

TIPS

- Heat up the plates before the food hits the table and serve all the food on warm platters and bowls.
- When reheating the turkey, use a little gravy to keep it moist. It also heats up faster.

RUSTIC SAGE AND SAUSAGE STUFFING

This fantastic stuffing recipe is prepared with the Tavern's homemade sage sausage, but it can easily be prepared with store-bought breakfast sausage that's sold in a log (without the casing). If you like stuffing cooked in your turkey, the result will be deliciously savory and soft. The remaining stuffing (of which there will likely be a lot) can be baked in two smaller casserole dishes and will give you a crunchy, well-toasted topping interspersed with moist filling.

MAKES TWO 9X13-INCH CASSEROLES

2 loaves country white bread with crust (about 1 pound each), cut into ½-inch cubes

1½ pounds Tavern's Homemade Sage Sausage (recipe follows) or bulk breakfast sausage, broken up

1 stick unsalted butter, plus more for greasing the dishes

2 medium onions, finely chopped

6 large celery stalks, finely chopped

4 garlic cloves, finely chopped

¼ cup fresh sage, finely chopped

2 tablespoons rubbed sage

4 cups Chicken Stock (page 342) or low-sodium broth

Kosher salt and fresh ground black pepper

Preheat the oven to 350°F. Spread the bread cubes in an even layer on two large, rimmed baking sheets and toast until golden brown, tossing halfway through for even browning (about 15 minutes). Transfer to a very large bowl. Increase the oven temperature to 425°F.

In a large, nonstick skillet, cook the sausage over medium heat, breaking it up with a wooden spoon, until fully cooked (about 10 minutes). Using a slotted spoon, transfer the sausage to the bread bowl, leaving the fat in the skillet.

Melt half of the butter in the skillet. Add the onions, celery, and garlic and cook over medium heat, stirring occasionally, until the vegetables are softened (about 10 minutes). Stir in the fresh and rubbed sage for about 1 minute, and then add the vegetables to the bread bowl.

RUSTIC SAGE AND SAUSAGE STUFFING *continued…*

Meanwhile, bring the chicken stock to a simmer. Pour the hot stock over the bread mixture, folding gently with a large spatula and being careful not to break up the bread cubes too much. Season with salt and pepper.

Generously butter two 9-by-13-inch casserole dishes. Transfer the stuffing to the casseroles and dot the top with the remaining 4 tablespoons of butter. Cover the casserole with foil and bake for 25 minutes, and then remove the foil and bake for 20 to 25 minutes longer, until golden and crusty. Serve hot.

The unbaked stuffing can be covered and refrigerated in the casserole overnight. The cooked stuffing can be refrigerated for 3 days.

THE TAVERN'S HOMEMADE SAGE SAUSAGE

This nicely spiced sausage isn't just for Thanksgiving; it can be shaped into patties and pan-fried for breakfast, too.

MAKES 1½ POUNDS

1½ pounds ground pork butt

¼ cup warm water

1½ teaspoons rubbed sage

1 teaspoon kosher salt

1 teaspoon fresh ground
black pepper

¾ teaspoon dried marjoram

¼ teaspoon dried savory

⅛ teaspoon fresh
ground nutmeg

¼ cup warm water

In a medium bowl, using your hands, mix all the ingredients until thoroughly combined.

The raw sausage can be refrigerated for 3 days.

WHIPPED POTATOES

You can't go wrong with these creamy whipped potatoes. At the restaurant, Chef Peet keeps the recipe basic, but he says you can infuse the potatoes with other flavors. To do so, add a few springs of thyme or sage to the cream while it's warming (or even a Parmesan rind or roasted garlic), and then let the cream sit for about 15 minutes. Strain and make sure the cream is heated again before mixing it into the potatoes.

SERVES 6 TO 8

2½ pounds Idaho potatoes, peeled and cut into 2-inch chunks (about 8 medium potatoes)

Kosher salt

1 stick unsalted butter, at room temperature

1½ cups heavy cream, heated

Fresh ground white pepper

Put the potatoes in a large pot and add enough water to cover by 2 inches. Add ½ teaspoon of kosher salt. Boil the potatoes over medium-high heat until they are very tender when pierced with a knife (15 to 20 minutes).

Strain the potatoes and return to the pot. Using a heavy-duty wire whisk, break up the potatoes, leaving no big pieces. Gradually add the butter and heated heavy cream, whipping vigorously until smooth. Season with salt and pepper and serve.

The whipped potatoes can be made a day ahead. To reheat, heat a little extra cream or whole milk in a pot and stir into the potatoes to warm through.

MAPLE-INFUSED SWEET POTATO MASH

This unusual and totally delicious mash is inspired by a dish in Ecuador, which Chef Peet learned to make from a former sous chef named Cesar Riera.

SERVES 8

6 large sweet potatoes,
washed and pricked with a fork

2 small ripe bananas, peeled,
one banana cut into 8 chunks

1 orange with skin,
cut into 8 wedges

1 vanilla bean, split lengthwise

2 cups maple syrup

1 stick unsalted butter,
at room temperature

½ cup heavy cream, heated

Kosher salt and fresh
ground black pepper

Preheat the oven to 400°F. Bake the sweet potatoes on a parchment-paper-lined baking sheet until they can be easily pierced (about an hour). When cool enough to handle, peel the potatoes and transfer the flesh to a large bowl.

While the potatoes cool, light the broiler and position the rack 6 inches from the heat source. In a medium ovenproof sauté pan, combine the banana chunks and orange wedges (cut sides up) with the vanilla bean. Broil for 2 minutes, and then remove the vanilla bean. Turn the banana and orange and continue to broil for about 5 minutes, until golden brown and aromatic; watch carefully, as you don't want to burn them.

Transfer the pan to the stovetop and add the maple syrup and toasted vanilla bean. Bring to a boil over medium-high heat, and then reduce heat to medium and simmer, stirring occasionally (about 3 minutes). Strain into a bowl. Discard the solids.

Mash the potatoes with the remaining banana, and then add the butter, cream, and infused maple syrup to taste to achieve your desired sweetness. Season with salt and pepper and serve warm.

GLAZED CARROTS

The kitchen easily goes through ten bags of carrots for Thanksgiving: ten bags that each weigh fifty pounds! Chef Peet says everyone wants extras on the holiday, so they have to prepare for that.

1 stick unsalted butter

¼ cup light brown sugar

1 cup water

Kosher salt

2 pounds carrots, peeled and cut on the bias into ½-inch pieces

Fresh ground black pepper

2 teaspoons finely cut flat-leaf parsley

In a large sauté pan, combine the butter and brown sugar with 1 cup of water and a good pinch of salt. Bring to a boil, and then stir in the carrots. Lower the heat to medium, cover, and simmer until the carrots are almost tender (8 to 10 minutes).

Using a slotted spoon, transfer the carrots to a plate. Return the pan to medium heat and simmer, stirring occasionally, until the liquid is reduced to a glaze (12 to 15 minutes); you should be able to leave a trail on the bottom of the pan with a rubber spatula or spoon.

Add the carrots back to the pan and toss to coat. Season with pepper and more salt, if necessary. Add the parsley and serve hot.

The glazed carrots can be refrigerated for 2 days.

SUN-DRIED CRANBERRY CONSERVES

Unlike many cranberry sauce recipes, these chunky cranberry conserves aren't too sweet. The contrast of firm fresh cranberries with chewy dried cranberries is very appealing. The conserves will last well after Thanksgiving, making its versatility a real boon. Chef Peet mixes this item into buttery sauces, serves it with fried foods, puts it on cheese plates, and adds it to mayonnaise to slather on grilled chicken sandwiches.

MAKES 8 CUPS

2 cups cranberry juice

2 cups granulated sugar

Large zest strips from two cleaned oranges

2 pounds fresh or frozen cranberries

2 cups unsweetened sun-dried cranberries

In a large saucepan, bring the cranberry juice, sugar, and orange zest to a boil over medium-high heat and simmer, stirring occasionally, until the sugar dissolves (about 5 minutes). Add the fresh and dried cranberries and simmer over medium heat, stirring frequently, until the fresh cranberries begin to burst and the mixture thickens slightly (5 to 7 minutes). Remove from the heat and cool completely, and then discard the zest. Refrigerate until fully chilled.

The conserves can be refrigerated for 4 weeks.

STICKY PECAN TARTS

As a student at the Culinary Institute of America, Chef Peet learned a dessert called Pecan Diamonds from one of his favorite instructors, George Metropolis. Chef reworked the recipe from a confection to a tart, and now it's very popular at the Tavern. If you prefer, it can be made into a larger tart using a pie shell.

MAKES 8 TARTS

FOR THE TART SHELLS:

2¼ cups plus 2 tablespoons/325g Wondra flour, chilled, plus more for rolling

2 sticks/228g unsalted butter, cubed and frozen

3 tablespoons plus 1 teaspoon/40g granulated sugar

¼ teaspoon kosher salt

½ cup ice water

¼ teaspoon pure vanilla extract

FOR THE FILLING:

6 tablespoons unsalted butter

3 tablespoons honey

½ cup dark brown sugar

2 tablespoons granulated sugar

2 tablespoons heavy cream

1½ cups pecan halves, lightly toasted

Whipped cream, for serving

To make the tart shells, in the bowl of a food processor, pulse the flour, butter, sugar, and salt until the butter resembles small crumbs. In a small bowl or measuring cup, mix the ice water and vanilla. With the processor running, add the water and vanilla in a steady stream until just incorporated. The mixture will look dry but should hold together when pinched. Transfer the dough to a work surface and pat into a thick square. Wrap in plastic and refrigerate for an hour.

Spray eight jumbo muffin pan slots with cooking spray. On a lightly floured surface, roll out the dough ¼ inch thick. Cut out eight 5-inch rounds. Lay each round into a muffin cup and press the dough into the corners. Refrigerate for 20 minutes.

STICKY PECAN TARTS *continued...*

Preheat the oven to 350°F. Roll up eight balls of aluminum foil, one to fill each muffin cup. Delicately place each foil ball into the prepared dough cups, being careful not to poke any holes in the dough. Bake for 8 minutes (or until the tart shells are set and start to brown just slightly). Gently lift out the foil balls and bake another for 12 to 15 minutes longer, until the dough is fully baked and golden brown. Raise the oven temperature to 375°F.

To make the filling, in a heavy medium saucepan, combine the butter, honey, and both sugars and bring to a low boil over medium heat, and then simmer for 2 minutes. Stir in the heavy cream, followed by the pecans. Bring back to a low boil, stir, and then remove from the heat and let stand for 5 minutes. Working quickly, divide the filling evenly between the tart shells, making sure the nuts are facing flat side up; press the nuts down into the sauce.

Bake for 8 to 10 minutes, until the filling starts to bubble slightly. Let cool in the pan on the counter for 15 to 20 minutes.

Remove the tarts from the pan and transfer to a plate. Refrigerate for at least 2 hours. Serve with a dollop of whipped cream on each tart.

The tarts can be refrigerated for 3 days.

PUMPKIN POTS DE CRÈME

As a kid, Chef Peet always loved chocolate pudding and the skin that formed on the top. Once he started making desserts in restaurants, he researched many recipes looking for that perfect pudding. The best recipe was for pot de crème, which is silky and more refined than a traditional pudding. This is because unlike pudding, which is often thickened with a starch, pot de crème is baked and set with eggs, giving it a rich, pure flavor and velvety-smooth texture.

SERVES 6

4 cups half-and-half

1 cup/200g granulated sugar

½ cup/128g pumpkin purée

1 tablespoon dark rum

1 teaspoon pure vanilla extract

½ teaspoon cinnamon

¼ teaspoon ground ginger

¼ teaspoon ground nutmeg

¼ teaspoon ground cloves

4 large eggs

4 large egg yolks

Kosher salt

Lightly sweetened whipped cream, for serving

Preheat the oven to 325°F. Set six 8-ounce ramekins in a roasting pan and place a kettle of water on to boil.

In a medium saucepan, whisk the half-and-half with the sugar, pumpkin, rum, vanilla, and spices and bring to a simmer over medium-high heat, stirring occasionally (about 10 minutes). Cover and set aside for 15 minutes.

In a large bowl, whisk the whole eggs and yolks with a pinch of salt. Bring the half-and-half mixture just back to a simmer. While whisking constantly, slowly pour the half-and-half mixture into the eggs until fully combined. Strain the custard through a fine-mesh strainer into a clean bowl.

Ladle the custard into the ramekins set in the roasting pan (about ¾ cup per ramekin). Fill the roasting pan with boiling water so it comes halfway up the sides of the ramekins. Cover the pan lightly with foil and bake until just set and slightly jiggly in the centers (40 to 45 minutes).

Cool in the roasting pan for an hour, and then remove from the water. Cover each pot de crème with plastic wrap and refrigerate overnight. Serve with a spoonful of lightly sweetened whipped cream.

The pots de crème can be covered and refrigerated for 2 days.

DECEMBER

The final month of the year overflows with parties and celebrations with a menu to match, as cold winter days lead to the annual triumvirate of Christmas Eve, Christmas Day, and New Year's Eve.

There is no holding back in December, and indulgent starters range from silky Cauliflower Velouté and Coconut Lobster Bisque to Smoked Salmon Salad with Potato Chive Galettes. Award-Winning Short Rib Meatballs with Creamy Horseradish Sauce share the table as well.

If diners are not already full from the abundance of rich appetizers, they move on to decadent mains, such as a Grilled Filet Mignon Salad that comes piled high with crispy buttermilk onion rings. Other holiday mains include Chardonnay Braised Lamb Shanks with Creamy Goat Cheese Polenta, Pan-Roasted Veal Chops with delightfully crunchy Duck Fat Lyonnaise Potatoes and Braised Red Cabbage, and Honey Roasted Christmas Duck with Wild Rice with Sun-Dried Cherries and Creamed Spinach.

'Tis the season of giving , so every grand meal finishes with Eggnog Crème Brûlée served with adorably irresistible Gingerbread Cookies, or perhaps one might opt for Decadent Hot Chocolate topped with a pillow of freshly whipped cream.

December is a very special month. There is a snappy zip in the air. As soon as Thanksgiving ends, the Tavern team turns the restaurant into a holiday wonderland. Outdoors, green and red lights shine and beckon, while inside white lights, holly boughs, and red velvet bows adorn the rooms and the fireplace roars. A giant gingerbread house replica of the Tavern—lit from within—sits on a table in the entryway, made with every candy imaginable, from gumdrops and nonpareils to Skittles, peppermint drops to jellybeans. The template for the house was created by Chef Peet's son, Tim, who is an architectural model maker. Each year the pastry team bakes and assembles the gingerbread house to be ready the day after Thanksgiving. Multiple miniature "Do Not Eat" signs surround the house: Kids have a hard time staying away!

The Tavern hosts a big tree-lighting party in the courtyard early in December, welcoming people aged one to one hundred, locals and tourists alike. A stage is set up for live holiday jazz and Christmas carolers from nearby Juilliard School of Music. Steaming cups of hot chocolate and hot cider are handed out, and Chef Peet's team sends out plates of hors d'oeuvres for everyone. At 7:00 p.m. sharp, the countdown begins to the tree lighting. It's a festive and joyous evening that sets the tone for the whole month.

CAULIFLOWER VELOUTÉ

This snow-white, velvety smooth soup is a perfect warming way to start your holiday meal. It's a bit indulgent, with both crème fraîche and heavy cream, but the crème fraîche keeps the soup light tasting with its natural tang. Truffle oil adds yet another layer of flavor and a pretty green swirl—a must for all the truffle lovers out there.

SERVES 4 TO 6

1 small head cauliflower

2 tablespoons unsalted butter

1 small yellow onion, thinly sliced

Kosher salt and fresh ground white pepper

2 small Idaho potatoes, peeled and cut into a large dice

4 cups Vegetable Stock (page 341) or low-sodium broth

1 cup crème fraîche

½ cup heavy cream

Truffle oil for garnish (optional)

Trim the cauliflower and set aside 1½ cups of florets for the garnish. Chop the remaining cauliflower.

In a heavy-bottomed stockpot, melt the butter over medium heat. Add the onion, season with salt and pepper, and cook until transparent (about 5 minutes). Add the chopped cauliflower, potatoes, and stock and bring to a boil over high heat. Lower the heat to medium and simmer until the potatoes and cauliflower are tender (about 25 minutes).

Meanwhile, in a small pot of water fitted with a steamer insert, steam the reserved cauliflower florets until just tender. Remove from the steamer and set aside.

Using an immersion blender or in batches in a standard blender, purée the soup. If using a blender, return the soup to the pot. Stir in the crème fraîche and cream and bring back just to a simmer. Season with salt and pepper. Serve the soup hot, garnished with the steamed cauliflower florets. Drizzle with a little truffle oil (if using).

The soup can be refrigerated for 3 days.

COCONUT LOBSTER BISQUE

The deep, rich flavor in this velvety, creamy bisque comes from incorporating the lobster shells into the recipe. It's an extra step that home cooks might not typically take, but it's worth the effort. Coconut milk and lemongrass infuses the soup with a lovely whisp of Thai flavor that makes it even more special.

SERVES 4 TO 6

2 tablespoons canola oil

One 1¼-pound live lobster (see note)

1 medium onion, thinly sliced

1 small carrot, chopped

1 small celery stalk, chopped

2 garlic cloves, smashed

1 lemongrass stalk, smashed and chopped

1 tarragon sprig, leaves finely chopped, stem reserved

2 tablespoons brandy

½ cup/4 ounces tomato paste

1 cup coconut milk

1 cup heavy cream

3¼ cups Vegetable Stock (page 341) or low-sodium broth

1 tablespoons arrowroot

Kosher salt and fresh ground black pepper

½ teaspoon finely cut flat-leaf parsley

In a large saucepot or Dutch oven, heat the canola oil over medium heat. Add the lobster pieces and cook, stirring frequently, until they start to turn red (about 5 minutes). Add the onion, carrot, celery, garlic, lemongrass, and tarragon stem and cook, stirring frequently, until the onions are soft and transparent (about 5 minutes). Add the brandy, stirring to scrape up any browned bits from the bottom of the pot (about 1 minute). Stir in the tomato paste.

Add the coconut milk and cream, increase the heat to medium high, and bring just to a boil. Add 3 cups of the stock and bring back just to a boil. Do not boil for more than 30 seconds. Remove from the heat.

Using tongs, transfer the lobster pieces to a bowl. Remove the meat from the shells, transfer to a small bowl, and cover loosely with plastic wrap. Add the shells back to the pot and simmer over medium-low heat for 20 minutes, stirring frequently.

Meanwhile, in a small bowl, stir the remaining ¼ cup of stock with the arrowroot until completely smooth. Drizzle the arrowroot mixture into the simmering soup, stirring to incorporate it; let simmer for 3 minutes to thicken.

COCONUT LOBSTER BISQUE *continued...*

Using tongs, remove and discard the lobster shells. Strain the soup through a fine strainer into another saucepot, pushing with the back of a spoon or ladle to extract as much liquid as possible. Bring the soup back to a simmer and season with salt and pepper. Cut the lobster meat into ½-inch dice and distribute between hot bowls. Add the soup, sprinkle with tarragon and parsley, and serve.

The soup and lobster meat can be refrigerated separately for 2 days.

NOTE

This recipe requires killing and cutting up a live lobster. You can ask your fishmonger to do this, if you prefer, or you can do it yourself. To cut up the lobster, using a large, sharp knife, starting from the back of the head, split the head in half. Cut through the body lengthwise, through the tail (you can also use sharp kitchen shears for this step). Twist off the tail. Remove the claws and knuckles and crack them with the back of a knife. Clean out the head and remove the intestines from the body.

SMOKED SALMON SALAD WITH POTATO CHIVE GALETTES

Even though this is primarily a smoked salmon salad, this dish was created as a way of repurposing mashed potatoes. Chef Peet made a large potato pancake with chives and then built a very composed smoked salmon salad to serve on top of it. He incorporated horseradish, crème fraîche, and pickled red onions into the dish, but the really fun part is actually the variety of herbs and greens: Every bite reveals a different flavor, from mint and tarragon to celery, watercress, and dill.

SERVES 4

1 cup leftover Mashed Potatoes
(page 29)

1 large egg

1 tablespoon all-purpose flour

1 teaspoon finely chopped chives

Kosher salt and fresh
 ground black pepper

2 teaspoons canola oil

¼ cup crème fraîche

1 tablespoon prepared
horseradish

2 packed cups mixed herbs and
greens, such as baby arugula,
baby watercress, tarragon leaves,
flat-leaf parsley leaves, yellow
inner celery leaves, dill fronds,
torn mint leaves, and red-veined
sorrel leaves

2 tablespoons extra virgin
olive oil

1 tablespoon apple cider vinegar

¼ cup Pickled Red Onions,
drained (page 208)

Sea salt

8 ounces thinly sliced smoked
salmon, julienned

SMOKED SALMON SALAD WITH POTATO CHIVE GALETTES *continued...*

In a medium bowl, mix the mashed potatoes, egg, and flour with a fork; stir in the chives and season with salt and pepper. Divide into four cakes.

In a large nonstick skillet, heat the canola oil over medium-low heat. Add the potato cakes and press each with a spatula to thin them slightly. Cook undisturbed for 4 to 5 minutes per side, until golden brown. Transfer to a plate and keep warm.

Meanwhile, in a small bowl, stir the crème fraîche with the horseradish. In a medium bowl, toss the herbs and greens with the olive oil, vinegar, and pickled onions and season with sea salt. Gently toss in the salmon.

Put the warm galettes onto four plates. Mound the salad over each galette, fluffing it up a little. Drizzle the horseradish crème fraîche around the plate and serve immediately.

AWARD-WINNING SHORT RIB MEATBALLS WITH CREAMY HORSERADISH SAUCE

Chef Peet came up with this recipe when he participated in a meatball contest sponsored by the Meatball Shop. With many chefs competing, the contest required that he really think outside the box. Chef Peet thought back to a Dutch cook he used to work with, who taught him a popular dish called bitterballen, which is a breaded and fried beef croquette. With that as a starting point, Chef Peet used his delicious short rib recipe as a base, alongside pickled red onions. And he won the contest!

MAKES 8 LARGE MEATBALLS

2 cups leftover Dark Beer Braised
Short Ribs (page 27), chopped,
plus 1¼ cups sauce

3 tablespoons Pickled Red
Onions (page 208)

1 teaspoon finely cut
flat-leaf parsley

Kosher salt and fresh
ground black pepper

2 large eggs

½ cup all-purpose flour

¾ cup panko breadcrumbs

2 cups canola oil

2 teaspoons Creamy Horseradish Sauce (recipe follows)

In a small saucepan, simmer 1 cup of the short rib sauce over medium heat until reduced by half (about 15 minutes). Put the chopped short ribs into a bowl and mix with the reduced sauce to moisten.

Chop 1 tablespoon of the pickled onions and add to the meat, along with the parsley. Season with salt and pepper. Cover and refrigerate for at least 3 hours (or overnight).

Roll the meat into eight equal balls and refrigerate for 15 minutes. Meanwhile, beat the eggs in a small bowl. Place the flour and panko into two separate bowls.

Roll the meatballs in the flour, tapping to remove any excess. Dip in the beaten eggs, letting any excess drip back into the bowl. Roll in the panko. Dip the meatballs once more in the eggs and dredge a second time in the panko. Transfer to a paper-towel-lined plate.

Meanwhile, in a medium saucepan, heat the oil over medium heat; it's ready when a few breadcrumbs sprinkled in bubble and brown. Working in batches, gently lay the breaded meatballs in the oil and lightly fry, turning now

AWARD-WINNING SHORT RIB MEATBALLS WITH CREAMY HORSERADISH SAUCE *continued...*

and then, until golden brown and cooked through. Transfer to a paper-towel-lined plate and season with salt and pepper. Keep warm.

Heat the reserved short rib sauce. Put the meatballs onto four plates and drizzle with the sauce. Top with horseradish sauce and the remaining pickled onions and serve immediately.

CREAMY HORSERADISH SAUCE

This versatile sauce has a nice kick to it and pairs well with everything from beef and crudites to shrimp and salmon.

MAKES ABOUT 1 CUP

1 cup sour cream

¼ cup freshly grated horseradish

1 tablespoon Dijon mustard

1 teaspoon white wine vinegar

Kosher salt and fresh
ground black pepper

In a small bowl, stir all the ingredients and season with salt and pepper. Refrigerate for at least 2 hours to meld the flavors. Serve cold.

The sauce can be refrigerated for 1 week.

GRILLED FILET MIGNON SALAD WITH CHIPOTLE VINAIGRETTE AND ONION RINGS

The combination of filet mignon and onion rings in this irresistible salad is a perfect high/low marriage. You can't go wrong with filet mignon if you don't overcook the meat, and these grill up perfectly tender and juicy.

SERVES 4

Four 6-ounce filet mignon steaks, trimmed

1 tablespoon canola oil

Kosher salt and fresh ground black pepper

2 packed cups kale, cut into 1-inch pieces

2 packed cups escarole, cut into 1-inch pieces

1 cup treviso, cut into ½-inch slices

½ cup Chipotle Vinaigrette (recipe follows)

2 plum tomatoes, seeded and julienned (see note)

Buttermilk Onion Rings (recipe follows)

Heat a grill pan over a medium-high heat. Rub the steaks with oil and season with salt and pepper. Grill on one side until browned (4 to 5 minutes), and then turn and grill for another 4 to 5 minutes, until browned and a thermometer inserted in the thickest part of a steak registers 130°F to 135°F for medium-rare. Remove from the heat and let rest while you prepare the salad.

In a large bowl, toss the kale, escarole, and treviso with half of the vinaigrette and season with salt and pepper. Divide the greens into four large bowls and top with the tomatoes. Slice the steaks and arrange around each mound of salad. Drizzle the rest of the vinaigrette over the sliced beef and salad, top with onion rings, and serve immediately.

GRILLED FILET MIGNON SALAD WITH CHIPOTLE VINAIGRETTE AND ONION RINGS *continued...*

NOTE

To julienne tomatoes, quarter them lengthwise, and then run the knife between the seeds and flesh, discarding the seeds. Cut the remaining tomato into ¼-inch slices.

CHIPOTLE VINAIGRETTE

MAKES 1 CUP

¼ cup white wine vinegar

2 teaspoons adobo sauce from a can of chipotle peppers

1 teaspoon Dijon mustard

¾ cup extra virgin olive oil

Kosher salt and fresh ground black pepper

In a small bowl or in a jar, whisk (or cover and shake the jar) to combine the vinegar, adobo sauce, mustard, and oil. Season with salt and pepper.

The vinaigrette can be refrigerated for 3 weeks.

BUTTERMILK ONION RINGS

MAKES 12 RINGS

1 large Spanish onion, cut into four ¾-inch-thick slices

1 cup buttermilk

1 cup Wondra flour

2 cups canola oil

Kosher salt and fresh ground black pepper

Push out the inner layers of onion and separate the largest 12 rings. Place the rings in a bowl and pour the buttermilk over them. Put the flour in another bowl.

Remove and drain the onion rings for 15 seconds or so. One by one, dredge the wet rings in the flour. Transfer to a paper-towel-lined plate and refrigerate for at least 30 minutes. (The crust will fry better after being refrigerated.)

In a 2-quart saucepan, heat the oil to 365°F. Fry a few onion rings at a time until golden brown. Drain on a paper-towel-lined plate, season with salt and pepper, and keep warm until ready to serve.

CHARDONNAY BRAISED LAMB SHANKS WITH CREAMY GOAT CHEESE POLENTA

These slow-braised lamb shanks are fall-off-the-bone delicious, and with all the vegetables in the sauce, the dish comes together as an easy but impressive one-pot meal. The polenta is the perfect canvas to soak up the gravy-like sauce. If you like, parsley and lemon zest make a perfect garnish to brighten up the dish.

SERVES 4

¼ cup canola oil

4 lamb shanks,
1 to 1¼ pounds each

Kosher salt and fresh ground
black pepper

2 large onions, cut into large dice
(about 3 cups)

5 carrots, cut into large dice
(about 2 cups)

4 large celery stalks, cut into
large dice (about 2 cups)

4 garlic cloves, smashed

¼ cup tomato paste

½ cup all-purpose flour

2 cups chardonnay

4 cups Vegetable Stock (page
341) or broth

2 fresh thyme sprigs

1 bay leaf

Creamy Goat Cheese Polenta
(recipe follows)

Preheat the oven to 325°F. In a large Dutch oven, heat the oil over medium heat until shimmering. Season the shanks with salt and pepper and sear until browned on all sides (about 2 minutes per side). Transfer to a plate and set aside. (Depending on the size of your Dutch oven, you may have to brown the shanks in batches for the best sear; you do not need to add more oil between batches.)

Add the onions, carrots, celery, and garlic to the pot and cook, stirring often, until the vegetables start to brown (5 to 7 minutes); season with salt and pepper. Stir in the tomato paste and then the flour, cooking until slightly browned (about 2 minutes). Add the wine and cook, scraping up the browned bits from the bottom of the pot, until the wine is reduced by half (about 2 minutes). Add the stock, thyme, and bay leaf and bring to a boil. Return the lamb to the pot. Cover, transfer to the oven, and cook for 2 to 2½ hours, until the meat is fork tender.

Transfer the lamb shanks to a plate and cover tightly with aluminum foil to keep warm.

CHARDONNAY BRAISED LAMB SHANKS WITH CREAMY GOAT CHEESE POLENTA *continued…*

Skim off any fat on the surface of the braising liquid. Simmer the liquid for 10 minutes over medium heat to thicken it slightly. Season with salt and pepper.

Return the lamb to the sauce to gently reheat over medium-low heat, stirring occasionally (about 10 minutes). Serve the lamb with the vegetables; discard the thyme sprigs and bay leaf before serving. Serve this dish with a large spoonful of the polenta, drizzling a little sauce over it.

The lamb shanks can be refrigerated for 3 days.

CREAMY GOAT CHEESE POLENTA

SERVES 4

Kosher salt and fresh ground black pepper

1 cup polenta

¼ packed cup crumbled goat cheese

In a medium saucepan, bring 2½ cups of water to a boil with 1 teaspoon of salt. Whisk the polenta into the boiling water in a steady stream. Once the polenta comes to a boil, reduce the heat to the lowest setting and cook, stirring constantly with a wooden spoon, until thick, creamy, and lump free; the time will vary depending on your polenta, so cook according to the package directions. Stir in the goat cheese until melted and completely incorporated. Season with salt and pepper and serve hot.

PAN-ROASTED VEAL CHOPS WITH DUCK FAT LYONNAISE POTATOES AND BRAISED RED CABBAGE

Veal used to be very popular, but it isn't as common as it once was. These big chops are perfect to prepare and cut off the bone to serve, though you'd be remiss not to serve the bones alongside—the meat on the bone is the sweetest, and, for some folks, it's the best part of the dish!

SERVES 4

2 teaspoons extra virgin olive oil

1 garlic clove,
grated on a microplane

Leaves from 1 thyme sprig

2 veal chops
(about 20 to 22 ounces each)

1 tablespoon canola oil

Kosher salt and fresh ground
black pepper

1 tablespoon unsalted butter,
cut in half

½ cup dry white wine

1 cup Veal Demi-Glace Sauce
(page 345)

Braised Red Cabbage
(recipe follows)

Duck Fat Lyonnaise Potatoes
(recipe follows)

In a small bowl, combine the olive oil, garlic, and thyme. Rub over the veal chops and let stand at room temperature for 30 minutes.

Preheat the oven to 400°F. In a large cast-iron skillet, heat the oil over medium-high heat until it starts to shimmer. Season the veal all over with salt and pepper and cook until browned (3 to 4 minutes). Turn the chops over and place a piece of the butter on each chop. Transfer the skillet to the oven and cook until a thermometer inserted

PAN-ROASTED VEAL CHOPS WITH DUCK FAT LYONNAISE POTATOES AND BRAISED RED CABBAGE *continued...*

in the thickest part of a chop registers 130°F (10 to 14 minutes); baste the chops with the fat in the pan once or twice while roasting.

Transfer the chops to a plate and tent with foil to keep warm. Carefully pour the juices from the hot skillet into a small bowl. Separate the fat and discard it.

Put the hot skillet back on the stove top (do not wipe it out). Reheat the skillet over medium heat, allowing the bits in the pan to brown. Add the white wine and cook, scraping up the browned bits with a wooden spoon. Bring to a simmer and reduce the wine by three-fourths. Add the demi-glace and bring to a boil with the reserved pan juices (and any juices from the resting meat plate). Simmer until the sauce coats the back of a spoon (6 to 8 minutes). Season with salt and pepper.

Remove the bones from the veal chops and cut the meat against the grain into ½-inch slices. Transfer to a platter and surround with the bones. Serve with the red cabbage and potatoes, along with the reserved sauce.

BRAISED RED CABBAGE

This braised cabbage is a wonderful contrast in textures and flavors—tender and crunchy, a little sour and a little sweet from the fruity Beaujolais, and just a hint of earthiness from the duck fat. It's a perfect winter side dish when serving a rich, hearty main.

SERVES 4 TO 6

½ cup duck fat

1 large onion, thinly sliced

1 small head red cabbage, cored and thinly sliced

1 cup red wine, preferably Beaujolais

½ cup red wine vinegar

Kosher salt and fresh ground black pepper

Preheat the oven to 400°F. In a heavy cast-iron casserole or Dutch oven, heat the duck fat over medium heat. Add the onion and cook, stirring occasionally, until transparent (5 to 7 minutes). Add the cabbage, wine, vinegar, and a bit of salt and pepper and stir well.

Cover the cabbage directly with a round of parchment paper and cover the pot. Bake until the cabbage starts to lose its crunch (about 40 minutes). Season with salt and pepper and serve hot.

DUCK FAT LYONNAISE POTATOES

Lyonnaise potatoes hail from Lyon, France. They are golden, crispy, and tender, and lovely paired with a variety of meat or game, but they're exceptionally good alongside veal or duck. In fact, what makes this version so delicious is the fact that potatoes are cooked in duck fat, which has a uniquely rich and meaty taste. If you have some duck fat left over, try frying French fries in it—you won't be disappointed.

SERVES 4 TO 6

Kosher salt

1 bay leaf

Four 12-ounce Idaho potatoes

⅓ cup duck fat (store-bought or reserved from Duck Confit, page 243, or Honey Roasted Christmas Duck, page 331)

1 large onion, thinly sliced

1 fresh thyme sprig

Fresh ground black pepper

2 teaspoons finely cut flat-leaf parsley

Bring a large pot of lightly salted water to a boil with the bay leaf. Add the whole potatoes and simmer just until a paring knife easily pierces a potato but meets some resistance (about 30 minutes). Remove from the water and refrigerate for at least 2 hours.

Peel the potatoes with a knife. Slice them lengthwise, and then cut into ¼-inch-thick slices.

In a large cast-iron skillet, melt half of the duck fat over medium heat until it starts to shimmer. Carefully add half the potatoes in a single layer, if possible, and cook undisturbed for 5 minutes. Turn the potatoes and continue to cook, turning now and then, until the potatoes are lightly browned (5 to 7 minutes longer). Using a slotted spoon, transfer the potatoes to a plate.

Add the remaining duck fat to the skillet and fry the rest of the potatoes as before. Once they're browned, add the reserved potatoes, onion, and thyme and cook over medium heat, stirring occasionally, until the onions are cooked and start to brown around the edges (5 to 6 minutes). Discard the thyme sprig and season with salt and pepper. Sprinkle with parsley and serve.

HONEY ROASTED CHRISTMAS DUCK WITH WILD RICE WITH SUN-DRIED CHERRIES AND CREAMED SPINACH

Chef Peet is used to having whole roasted duck on his menus—duck that is roasted long and slow to allow the fat to render and the bird to develop a super-crisp skin. This type of slow-cooked whole duck, carved tableside, is increasingly hard to find in restaurants.

SERVES 4

One 5–6-pound whole duckling, defrosted if frozen, cleaned, and patted dry, wings removed

Kosher salt and fresh ground black pepper

1 orange, quartered

1½ cups Brown Chicken Stock (page 343)

1 fresh thyme sprig

1 tablespoon honey

1 tablespoon all-purpose flour

2 tablespoons cold water

Wild Rice with Sun-Dried Cherries (recipe follows)

Creamed Spinach (recipe follows)

Season the duck cavity with salt and pepper. Prick the skin all over with a roasting fork or a fork with very sharp tines. (A bamboo skewer works as well.) Be careful to prick only the skin and not

the meat below the skin. Looking at the breast from the cavity end, cut 6 slits in the skin on the breast on each side of the breastbone. Slice in a downward motion away from the breastbone; do not cut through to the meat. Season the skin liberally with salt and pepper. Place the quartered orange inside the cavity.

Preheat the oven to 450°F. Place the duck breast side up on a rack in a roasting pan. Place the wings, neck, giblets, and heart in the bottom of the roasting pan. Roast the duck for 15 minutes,

HONEY ROASTED CHRISTMAS DUCK WITH WILD RICE WITH SUN-DRIED CHERRIES AND CREAMED SPINACH *continued...*

and then reduce the heat to 375°F and continue roasting for about 1½ hours longer, pouring off most of the fat in the pan and basting with the remaining fat every 15 minutes or so.

After an hour or so, remove the browned heart and gizzards and place in a medium saucepan. Add the stock and thyme and simmer, covered, for an hour.

The duck is done when the juices that run out of the cavity are clear and a thermometer inserted in the thigh registers 155°F to 160°F. In the final 20 minutes of roasting, brush the honey over the skin. Transfer the duck to a platter, tent loosely with foil, and keep warm.

Pour off the fat in the roasting pan (reserve this for another use) and discard the wings and neck. Add ¼ cup water to the pan and scrape up any browned bits with a wooden spoon. Add the pan juices to the simmering stock. Mix the flour with 2 tablespoons water and add to the pan. Cook for 10 minutes to thicken, and then strain into a bowl and season with salt and pepper. Carve the duck and serve with the sauce, wild rice, and creamed spinach.

WILD RICE WITH SUN-DRIED CHERRIES

Wild rice is an aquatic grass seed that's high in protein, fiber, and antioxidants, and it also happens to be gluten-free. With its nutty, earthy flavor, it's perfect alongside duck, turkey, and game. Cherries add a nice hit of sweetness to complement the poultry and game, but feel free to swap in dried apricots or cranberries if preferred.

SERVES 4 TO 6

1 tablespoon canola oil

1 small onion, finely chopped

Kosher salt and fresh ground black pepper

1 cup wild rice

½ cup sun-dried cherries

1 fresh thyme sprig

1 bay leaf

2 cups Vegetable Stock (page 341) or low-sodium broth

1 tablespoon unsalted butter

2 teaspoons finely cut flat-leaf parsley

Preheat the oven to 375°F. In a medium oven-safe saucepan with a lid, heat the canola oil over medium heat. Add the onion, season with salt, and cook until the onion is transparent (about 5 minutes).

Add the rice and stir to cover the rice with the oil. Add the cherries, thyme, and bay leaf. Pour in the stock and bring to a boil; then cover the saucepan and transfer to the oven.

Bake for 50 to 55 minutes, until the rice starts to burst a bit and the liquid is absorbed. Discard the thyme sprig and bay leaf. Stir in the butter and parsley, season with salt and pepper, and serve.

CREAMED SPINACH

SERVES 4 TO 6

2 tablespoons unsalted butter

2 tablespoons all-purpose flour

½ cup half-and-half

¼ cup (2 ounces) cream cheese

Pinch grated nutmeg

1 tablespoon canola oil

1 tablespoon finely chopped onion

1 large garlic clove, minced or grated

One 10-ounce box frozen chopped spinach, defrosted and squeezed dry

2 tablespoons freshly grated Parmesan cheese

Kosher salt and fresh ground black pepper

In a small saucepan, melt the butter over medium-low heat. When it starts to foam and sputter (about 4 minutes), add the flour. Cook for 4 minutes, stirring often. Whisk in the half-and-half, and then whisk in the cream cheese; continue whisking until the mixture is thick and smooth (3 to 4 minutes). Add the nutmeg. Remove from heat and set aside.

In a large skillet, heat the oil over medium heat. Add the onion and garlic and cook, stirring often, until transparent (about 3 minutes). Reduce heat to low, add the spinach and 2 tablespoons of water, cover, and cook, stirring occasionally, until the spinach is cooked (about 6 minutes).

Stir the Parmesan and white sauce into the spinach until thoroughly combined. Season with salt and pepper and serve hot.

The creamed spinach can be refrigerated for 2 days. Reheat gently before serving.

POTATO GRATIN

Chef Peet always like offering a few decadent side dishes on the holiday table, whether it's at the restaurant or at home, and this potato gratin is one of his go-to choices (especially with the Caramelized Rack of Lamb, page 281, or Honey Roasted Christmas Duck, page 331). The secret to a supremely creamy and rich gratin like this one is to cook the potatoes twice: first in the cream on top of the stove, and then again in the oven.

SERVES 6

6 cups heavy cream

4 garlic cloves, thinly sliced

Kosher salt and fresh ground black pepper

4 pounds Idaho potatoes, peeled and sliced ¼-inch thick

2 tablespoons unsalted butter, at room temperature

⅔ cup freshly grated Parmesan cheese, or more to taste

In a large saucepan, bring the cream and garlic to a simmer over medium-high heat. Lower the heat slightly and simmer to reduce the cream a bit and infuse the garlic flavor (about 7 minutes). Season the cream with salt and pepper.

Add the potatoes to the cream and cook over medium heat, stirring frequently, until the potatoes are nearly cooked through (about 25 minutes).

Preheat the oven to 350°F. Butter a 2½- or 3-quart casserole dish. Using a slotted spoon, layer the potatoes into the casserole; sprinkle Parmesan between the layers and set some aside for topping the casserole before it goes into the oven.

Reduce the cream in the saucepan over medium heat until thickened slightly (about 5 minutes). Pour the cream over the potatoes. Sprinkle the remaining Parmesan on top.

Set the casserole on a foil-lined baking sheet. Cover with foil and bake for 50 minutes, and then remove the foil and bake for about 15 minutes longer, until the potatoes are golden brown. Serve hot.

The gratin can be refrigerated for 3 days.

ROASTED WILD STRIPED BASS WITH CRUSHED FINGERLING POTATOES

When Chef Peet goes freshwater fishing in the spring, he seeks out wild ramps and brings them home to eat alongside trout, but they are equally delicious in this recipe, alongside thick and meaty wild striped bass. When ramps are not in season, he opts for scallions, which add finesse to the overall dish. The truffle butter and veal demi-glace contribute a bit of richness and umami to what is an otherwise fresh and light dish.

SERVES 4

8 wild ramps or scallions, trimmed and washed

1 pound fingerling potatoes, skin on

2 tablespoons unsalted butter, at room temperature

½ teaspoon sea salt, preferably Maldon

1 tablespoon canola oil

Four 7–8-ounce wild striped bass fillets with skin

Kosher salt and fresh ground black pepper

2 tablespoons black truffle butter, at room temperature (see note)

½ cup warm Veal Demi-Glace Sauce (page 345)

1 teaspoon finely cut flat-leaf parsley

ROASTED WILD STRIPED BASS WITH CRUSHED FINGERLING POTATOES

continued . . .

Preheat the oven to 400°F. Bring a medium pot of water to a boil and blanch the ramps for 2 minutes, until softened. Using tongs, transfer to a strainer and drain, and then refrigerate for 15 minutes to stop them from cooking further.

Add the potatoes to the boiling water and boil for about 8 minutes (or until tender when pierced with a knife). Drain thoroughly and return to the pot. Using the back of a fork, crush the potatoes. Mix in the butter and season with the sea salt. Cover with foil or a lid and keep hot.

Meanwhile, heat the oil in a large nonstick oven-safe skillet over medium-high heat. Season the skin side of the fillets with salt and pepper. When the oil is shimmering, add the fillets, skin side down. Cook undisturbed for 6 to 7 minutes (or until the skin is crisp and starting to brown); the fish is ready to flip when it releases easily from the bottom of the pan.

Season the fillets and flip them. Add the ramps to the perimeter of the pan, transfer to the oven, and cook for 3 to 4 minutes, until the fish is cooked through.

Divide the potatoes into four large, wide bowls. Wind up the ramps and place two on the potatoes in each bowl. Top with the fish, pushing down gently to secure the fish on the potatoes. Divide the black truffle butter over the hot fish and pour the demi-glace around the bowls. Sprinkle with parsley and serve.

NOTE

Black truffle butter is a simple compound butter made by mixing unsalted butter with grated fresh black truffles and salt. It's available at gourmet markets and online.

EGGNOG CRÈME BRÛLÉE

Chef Peet is a big fan of store-bought eggnog, which is eggy and rich and redolent with warming spices like nutmeg and cloves. In a nod to the holidays, one of Chef Peet's pastry chefs thought up this clever recipe, and now it's on the dessert menu every year around Christmas. For fans of eggnog, it's a must-have, as are the creative eggnog cocktails the Tavern bartenders make for toasting the season.

SERVES 6

1 cup eggnog

1 cup heavy cream

½ cup whole milk

¼ teaspoon ground nutmeg

7 large egg yolks

½ cup granulated sugar

Pinch kosher salt

½ cup turbinado sugar
(Sugar in the Raw)

6 Gingerbread Cookies
(page 338)

Preheat the oven to 300°F. In a medium saucepan, bring the eggnog, cream, milk, and nutmeg to a simmer over medium heat, stirring occasionally with a rubber spatula to keep the bottom from scorching (about 13 minutes). Remove from the heat and let stand for 5 minutes.

At the same time, in a medium bowl, whisk the yolks, granulated sugar, and salt until the eggs are pale (1 to 2 minutes).

While whisking constantly, gradually pour the hot cream into the egg mixture. Continue whisking until completely combined. Strain the custard through a fine-mesh strainer into a clean bowl.

Set six crème brûlée dishes in a roasting pan. Pour the custard into the dishes. Pour hot water into the pan to reach halfway up the sides of the dishes. Carefully slide the pan into the oven and bake for 35 to 40 minutes, until the crème brûlées no longer jiggle when gently shaken.

Gently remove the crème brûlées from the water bath and let cool for an hour; then refrigerate for at least an hour (or until fully chilled).

Sprinkle the turbinado in a thin layer over the surface of each crème brûlée. Using a torch, brown each dish until the sugar melts and browns evenly. Alternately, broil the custards as close to the heat source just until the sugar is browned. Serve immediately with Gingerbread Cookies.

The baked crème brûlées can be covered and refrigerated for 3 days. Brûlée the tops just before serving.

GINGERBREAD COOKIES

These gingerbread cookies are loved by all who eat at Tavern during the holidays. The little people adorn the Eggnog Crème Brûlée and also guard the gingerbread replica of Tavern on the Green, made with the same gingerbread, that is displayed at the entrance.

MAKES 40 TO 60 COOKIES

FOR THE COOKIES:

1½ sticks/170g unsalted butter

¾ cup plus 2 tablespoons/180g dark brown sugar

½ cup/160g unsulfured molasses

2 teaspoons ground ginger

1 teaspoon cinnamon

½ teaspoon grated nutmeg

¼ teaspoon ground cloves

3 cups/425g all-purpose flour, plus more for dusting

1 teaspoon baking soda

¼ teaspoon kosher salt

1 large egg, lightly beaten

FOR THE ROYAL ICING:

3 large eggs whites (90g)

1 pound/454g confectioners' sugar

To make the cookies, in a medium saucepan, combine the butter, sugar, molasses, and spices over medium-high heat and bring just to a boil, stirring occasionally, until the sugar is dissolved and the spices have bloomed (4 to 6 minutes). Transfer to a bowl and let cool to room temperature.

In a large bowl, whisk the flour, baking soda, and salt. Create a well in the dry ingredients and pour the wet ingredients in along with the egg. Stir well to combine.

Turn the dough out onto a lightly floured surface and knead a few times until smooth. Divide into two pieces, flatten each into a disk, and wrap in plastic wrap. Chill for an hour.

Preheat the oven to 350°F. Line two baking sheets with parchment paper. On a well-floured surface, and working with one piece of dough at a time, roll the dough ¼ inch thick. Use a classic gingerbread man cutter (or whatever shape or size cutter you like) to cut out shapes. The dough is easiest to work with when it's chilled, so if it starts to get too sticky, put it back in the fridge for about 15 minutes. Transfer to the prepared baking sheets. You will have to bake the cookies in a few batches.

Bake the cookies, rotating the baking sheets halfway through, until crisp—about 10 minutes (for a softer cookie, bake closer to 8 minutes).

Transfer the cookies to a wire rack to cool completely before decorating.

To make the royal icing, in the bowl of a stand mixer or in a large bowl using a hand mixer, whip the egg whites and sugar for 5 minutes, until combined. Transfer to a piping bag fitted with an extra fine tip and decorate as you like. Let the decorated cookies dry for at least an hour to harden the icing.

The gingerbread cookies can be stored in an airtight container for 3 weeks.

DECADENT HOT CHOCOLATE

For many years around Christmas, Tavern on the Green used to take part in a holiday food market near Lincoln Center that celebrated local restaurants. This rich hot chocolate was always served, alongside fresh fried apple cider donut rounds.

SERVES 4

2 cups whole milk

¼ cup sugar

2 tablespoons unsweetened Dutch-processed cocoa powder

Kosher salt

1 cup chopped bittersweet chocolate

1 teaspoon pure vanilla extract

Whipped cream, for serving

In a small saucepan, bring the milk to a simmer over medium heat. Whisk in the sugar, cocoa, and a very small pinch of salt until no lumps remain. Stir in the chopped chocolate and vanilla extract until completely melted. Remove the pot from the heat and divide the hot chocolate into four mugs. Top with whipped cream and serve immediately.

IN THE
PANTRY
A few more essential recipes . . .

VEGETABLE STOCK

MAKES 3 QUARTS

2 large yellow onions,
unpeeled and chopped

2 carrots, chopped

1 celery stalk, chopped

3 garlic cloves,
peeled and smashed

½ cup fresh fennel, chopped

3 quarts cold water

4 to 6 parsley stems (no leaves)

2 bay leaves

1 fresh thyme sprig

8 crushed black peppercorns

1 tablespoon kosher salt

Place the onions, carrots, celery, garlic, and fennel in a large stockpot. Cover with the cold water. Bring to a boil, and then lower the heat to a simmer.

Meanwhile, make a bouquet garni by tying the parsley stems, bay leaves, and thyme into a bundle with kitchen twine. Add to the pot, along with the peppercorns and salt.

Cover halfway and simmer for about 90 minutes (or until the vegetables are completely cooked).

Use a fine-mesh strainer to strain out the vegetables (or pour the stock through a fine-mesh strainer into another pot to cool). Discard the vegetables.

Once cooled, refrigerate the stock.

The vegetable stock can be refrigerated for 3 weeks or frozen for 6 months.

FISH FUMET

MAKES ABOUT 1½ QUARTS

2 tablespoons canola oil

2 celery stalks, diced

1 large Spanish onion, diced

1 medium leek, green and white parts, thinly sliced and cleaned

½ cup sliced white mushrooms

2 garlic cloves, smashed

2 parsley stems

Kosher salt

2 pounds white fish bones, rinsed of blood and scales and soaked in cold water for 30 minutes

1 cup dry white wine

2 quarts cold water

10 black peppercorns

1 bay leaf

In a large stockpot or Dutch oven, heat the oil over medium-high heat. Stir in the celery, onion, leek, mushrooms, garlic, and parsley; season with a bit of salt. Cook for 5 minutes, stirring often. Stir in the fish bones and cook, stirring, for 3 minutes. Add the wine and bring to a boil; let simmer for about 5 minutes, stirring once or twice.

FISH FUMET *continued...*

Add the cold water and stir to combine; add 1 teaspoon of salt. Bring to a boil, and then lower the heat to a simmer. With a ladle or shallow spoon, skim off any foam or other impurities that float to the surface. Add the peppercorns and bay leaf and simmer, uncovered, for 30 minutes.

Remove from the heat. Set a large colander into a bowl. Using a slotted spoon, transfer the bones and vegetables to the colander. Strain the fumet through a fine-mesh strainer into a medium bowl; when you see any debris in the pot, stop pouring and discard. Add the extra broth from the drained bones to the bowl; discard the bones and vegetables. Let the fumet cool for an hour, and then transfer to a container, cover, and keep refrigerated.

The fumet can be refrigerated for 5 days or frozen for 4 months.

CHICKEN STOCK

MAKES ABOUT 4 QUARTS

2 to 3 parsley stems

1 fresh thyme sprig

1 bay leaf

5 pounds raw chicken wings and bones, rinsed

1 yellow onion, coarsely chopped

1 carrot, coarsely chopped

1 small celery stalk, coarsely chopped

5 quarts cold water

4 black peppercorns, crushed

½ teaspoon kosher salt

Make a bouquet garni by tying the parsley, thyme, and bay leaf into a bundle with kitchen twine.

Place the chicken, chopped vegetables, and bouquet garni in a very large stockpot. Add the cold water. Slowly bring up to a boil over medium-high heat. Just before it comes to a rapid boil, lower the heat to a simmer. Add the peppercorns and salt. Simmer over low heat for about 2 hours, until the vegetables are well cooked; skim off any fat and scum that rises to the surface.

Let the stock sit off the heat for 20 minutes, and then skim off any additional fat and scum from the surface. Strain the stock through a coarse sieve and then through a fine-mesh strainer. Let cool; then transfer to containers and refrigerate.

The stock can be refrigerated for 4 days or frozen for 4 months.

BROWN CHICKEN STOCK

MAKES 1 QUART

1 pound raw chicken
wings and bones

1 small onion, chopped

1 small carrot, chopped

1 celery stalk, chopped

1 tablespoon canola oil

1 teaspoon tomato paste

1 fresh thyme sprig

1 bay leaf

6 cups water

4 black peppercorns, crushed

½ teaspoon kosher salt

Preheat the oven to 400°F. Rinse the chicken bones under cold water and remove any large pieces of fat. Dry with paper towels.

In a large ovenproof pan, toss the chicken bones and chopped vegetables with the canola oil. Roast for 20 to 25 minutes, stirring now and then, until the bones and vegetables are well browned. Stir in the tomato paste and roast until slightly browned (about 5 minutes).

Transfer the chicken and vegetables to a large saucepan along with the thyme and bay leaf. Add 1 cup of water to the pan that was used to roast the bones and vegetables. Using a wooden spoon, scrape up all the brown residue stuck to the pan and add the liquid to the saucepan along with 5 cups of cold water.

Slowly bring just up to a boil, skimming off any fat and scum that rises to the surface. Add the peppercorns and salt and simmer over medium-low heat, uncovered, for an hour. Remove from the heat and let stand for 20 minutes.

Skim off any fat and scum from the surface, and then strain the stock through a fine-mesh strainer into a bowl; discard the solids. Cool before refrigerating or freezing.

The stock can be refrigerated for 4 days or frozen for 3 months.

VEAL STOCK

MAKES 4 QUARTS

2 tablespoons canola oil

5 pounds veal knuckle bones, broken up (see note)

1 yellow onion, peeled and chopped

1 carrot, chopped

½ celery stalk, chopped

½ split head of garlic

1 tablespoon tomato paste

5 quarts plus 2 cups cold water

3 parsley stems, leaves removed

1 fresh thyme sprig

1 bay leaf

4 crushed black peppercorns

½ teaspoon kosher salt

Preheat the oven to 450°F. Place a heavy roasting pan in the hot oven for 10 minutes to heat. When hot, add the canola oil, veal bones, onion, carrot, celery, and garlic and stir to coat with the oil. Roast for about 15 minutes (or until the vegetables start browning). Remove from the oven, add the tomato paste, and mix thoroughly. Return the pan to the oven for another 20 minutes and give everything a good stir. Continue roasting until the bones and vegetables are very browned (another 20 to 30 minutes).

Transfer the browned bones and vegetables to a very large stockpot. Over low heat, heat up the roasting pan and add 2 cups of cold water. Simmer, scraping up the browned bits on the bottom of the pan with a wooden spoon. Pour this mixture into the stockpot.

Add the 5 quarts of cold water and bring to a boil over medium-high heat. Reduce the heat to a simmer. Skim off the foam that rises to the surface.

Meanwhile, make a bouquet garni by tying the parsley stems, thyme, and bay leaf into a bundle with kitchen twine. Add to the pot along with the peppercorns and salt. Simmer over very low heat for about 6 hours, skimming off the foam that rises to the top now and then.

When the stock is done, use a slotted spoon to transfer the bones and vegetables to a colander set over a bowl to catch any drippings. Skim the fat from the stock and discard it. Ladle the stock through a fine-mesh strainer into another pot to cool; strain the drippings from the bowl into the pot as well. Discard the bones and vegetables.

Once cooled, refrigerate the stock. After it is completely cooled, the fat can be lifted off the liquid and discarded.

The stock can be refrigerated for 4 days or frozen for 6 months.

NOTE

Ask your butcher to break the bones into smaller pieces. The more surface area that is exposed during simmering, the more flavor is extracted into the stock.

VEAL DEMI-GLACE SAUCE

Many chefs reduce veal stock until it is the thickness they are looking for, but Chef Peet thinks the sauce loses a lot of its identity when it's reduced too much. Instead, he likes to thicken it slightly with flour and then reduce it to the right consistency. The result is more flavor and not just a syrupy product.

MAKES 2 CUPS

1 quart Veal Stock (page 344)

¼ cup dry white wine

2 tablespoons all-purpose flour

1 fresh thyme sprig

Kosher salt and fresh ground black pepper

In a medium saucepot, bring the stock to a boil over medium-high heat. In a small bowl, mix the wine with the flour and whisk into the boiling stock. Reduce the heat to a simmer and add the thyme sprig. Simmer the veal stock until it has reduced by half, stirring occasionally (about 90 minutes); skim off any fat or impurities that float to the top.

Strain the thickened stock through a fine-mesh strainer. Season with salt and pepper while the sauce is hot.

The sauce can be refrigerated for 1 week or frozen for up to 6 months. It's convenient to freeze in 4-ounce portions to pull out of the freezer whenever you need.

BRINE FOR POULTRY AND PORK

This all-purpose brine brings a nice hit of sweet and salty flavor to chicken and pork. It also makes the meat juicier. As a rule of thumb, Chef Peet brines chicken breasts for 5 hours, whole chicken for 12 hours, turkey for 24 hours, and pork chops for 6 to 12 hours, depending on their size.

MAKES 1 GALLON

1 gallon water

½ cup kosher salt

¼ cup dark brown sugar

2 tablespoons honey

1 tablespoon pickling spice

In a large pot, combine all the ingredients and bring to a boil to dissolve the salt and sugar. Let cool before using.

PICKLED WILD RAMPS

Native to eastern North America, ramps are a kind of wild onion or garlic; sometimes they're called wild leeks. They pop up at farmers markets as a sign that spring has begun. To preserve their aromatic and delicious flavor, Chef Peet pickles them so they can be used well past their brief growing season. These ramps will last for quite a long time in the refrigerator. They are great to add to some of the recipes in this book—a little goes a long way. Recipes that would benefit from an addition would be Soft-Shell Crabs (page 119), Charred Octopus and Chorizo Salad (page 73), Veggie Burgers (page 149), Grilled Whole Fish (page 277), and Grilled Chicken Salad (page 195).

MAKES ABOUT 1½ CUPS

1 pound wild ramps, cleaned

½ cup white wine vinegar

½ cup granulated sugar

1 teaspoon kosher salt

½ cup water

1 bay leaf

½ teaspoon mustard seed

½ teaspoon coriander seed

½ teaspoon fennel seed

½ teaspoon white peppercorns

In a large pot of simmering water, blanch the ramps for 2 minutes, and then drain and let cool. Place the ramps in a large, clean mason jar. Meanwhile, in a small saucepan, bring the vinegar, sugar, salt, and water to a boil. Add the bay leaf, seeds, and peppercorns and simmer for 3 minutes. Pour the hot mixture over the ramps in the jar and let cool. Seal and refrigerate for up to 6 months.

NOTE

Be sure to sterilize your jar and follow proper procedures for safe pickling.

SLOW-COOKED TOMATO JAM

This recipe is ideal when you find yourself with less-than-perfect tomatoes. Depending on the taste of the tomatoes you use, you should feel comfortable adjusting the amount of vinegar; Chef Peet sometimes adds a touch of balsamic vinegar at the end for a sweet and tangy effect. The jam is very good added to pasta and can be used as a sandwich spread for a surprise hit of flavor. This jam can be used with the Tavern Burger (page 117) and the Lamb Meatball Sliders (page 141).

MAKES ⅔ CUP

¼ cup extra virgin olive oil

1 shallot, finely sliced

1 garlic clove, peeled and smashed

Kosher salt

4 ripe plum tomatoes (about 14 ounces), peeled, seeded, and chopped

1 fresh thyme sprig

¼ cup aged sherry vinegar

Fresh ground black pepper

1 teaspoon finely cut flat-leaf parsley

Balsamic vinegar (optional)

In a medium saucepot with a lid, heat the olive oil over medium-low heat. Add the shallot and garlic and sprinkle in a little salt. Cover and cook, stirring once or twice, until the shallot and garlic are transparent but not browned (8 to 10 minutes). Add the tomatoes and thyme, and then cover and cook until the tomatoes have broken down (25 to 30 minutes). Remove the lid and simmer for 15 to 20 minutes (or until much of the extra liquid is evaporated).

Add the sherry vinegar and simmer, stirring once or twice, until jam-like and a deep, rusty red (about 30 minutes). Discard the thyme sprig, and season with salt and pepper. Stir in the parsley and add a touch of balsamic (if desired).

The jam can be refrigerated for 1 week. Serve hot or at room temperature.

BALSAMIC VINAIGRETTE

This is a go-to vinaigrette that works on a variety of salads. At the Tavern, Chef Peet makes a giant batch using an industrial-sized immersion blender. This recipe is scaled down for home cooks, yielding a cup of vinaigrette that can be made by hand. Feel free to double or triple the recipe if you want to keep it handy, as it can be kept in the fridge for months. This vinaigrette is a great alternative to a few of the other vinaigrettes in the book, and it can be used with the Salt-Roasted Golden Beet Salad (page 239) or drizzled over the Pan-Roasted Baby Black Sea Bass (page 75).

MAKES 1 CUP

2½ tablespoons balsamic vinegar

1 tablespoon Dijon mustard

¼ teaspoon sugar

1½ tablespoons water

¾ cup canola oil

Kosher salt and fresh ground black pepper

In a medium bowl or tall container, whisk (or cover and shake the container) to combine the balsamic, mustard, sugar, water, and oil. Season with salt and pepper.

The vinaigrette can be refrigerated for 3 months.

TIP Make sure all your ingredients are at room temperature so the vinaigrette comes together perfectly.

ACKNOWLEDGMENTS

BILL PEET

To my best friend and partner in crime, my wife, Anna Maria, for her unconditional love and support. She was there through it all—the long hours, the personal sacrifices. Thank you for pushing me in high school to fill out my application for the Culinary Institute of America.

To my children, Will and Tim, you gave me purpose. I'm thankful that with a chef's schedule I was able to take the time to be there and share all of your accomplishments. I am so proud of the men you have become. To the daughter we never had but love as if we did, our daughter-in-law, Aldry, thank you for your straightforward love of the family.

To my chef and mentor, my second father, my teacher, and, most of all, my friend, André Soltner. Not only am I the chef I am today because of André, but I am the person I am because of him. I am so thankful for having had his encouragement for almost forty-five years.

To Christian Bertrand, my chef de cuisine at Lutèce, who made me think about everything I cooked. The descriptive way he broke down and explained recipes and cooking procedures has stuck with me over the years. I try to carry on and teach the same way.

To my friends and sous chefs who were my backbone at Tavern, Juan Mendez and Juan Morales—you are appreciated more than you will ever know.

To my friend Benito Martinez, who was an integral part of every restaurant I worked in since 1997—your soups and sauces truly elevated the dining experience.

To my grandmother, Mildred McCoy, for teaching me the value of patience, to appreciate all the small stuff, and to always have a positive outlook.

To my sous chefs over the years who supported me without question and made our restaurants much better: Chris Gillis, Elvis Jimenez, Paul Ragan, Brian Peterson, Sean Rembold, Mark Longo, Tom Keyes, Ryan Walker, Michael Kogan, Eric Korsh, and Ed Simmons.

To my friend and purchaser extraordinaire, Cheo Leon. If I could imagine it, he could get it.

To my boss and friend, David Salama, for his continued support and believing in me and this book.

To our agents, Beth and Tricia Davey, for their positive guidance and support.

To Kate Heddings for transcribing my thoughts and stories into the written page.

To our recipe tester, Tricia Davey, for translating my recipes and her valuable insight when testing and tasting the recipes.

To our photographer, Deborah Whitlaw Llewellyn, for her beautiful images that bring the food to life.

To Douglas Glenn Clark for his early work on the proposal for the book—you got the ball rolling.

For the countless cooks who worked with me over the years and whom I always considered my other family—I am extremely proud of what we accomplished. Thank you.

Courtesy of Cole Wilson

DAVID SALAMA and JIM CAIOLA

Tavern on the Green wouldn't be what it is today without the incredible team whose hard work, talent, and dedication made the restaurant's reopening and ongoing success possible. After years of planning and extensive renovations, we transformed a neglected structure into the vibrant space that it is now.

From the very beginning, we worked tirelessly to bring our vision to life—one that has enabled the restaurant to become known for its lavish galas, festive parade celebrations, and iconic marathon-day events. Every step of this journey has been fueled by teamwork, perseverance, and a shared belief in what we were creating.

This cookbook is more than a collection of recipes; it's a tribute to the people behind it—chefs, servers, dishwashers, managers, and every team member who showed up, gave their best, and helped bring our dream to life.

Thank you for your dedication, your passion, and your trust in the process. This accomplishment is as much yours as it is ours.

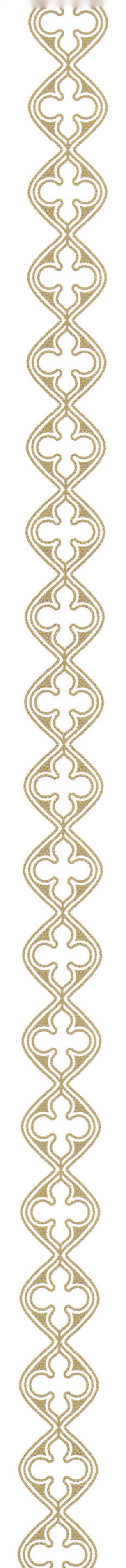

INDEX

ABOUT THE AUTHORS

BILL PEET came to Tavern on the Green in 2016 as their executive chef with more than thirty-five years of New York City fine-dining experience. During his extensive career, he has worked in an array of iconic restaurants. Bill spent fifteen years as sous chef and pastry chef at the legendary Lutèce with André Soltner. Following his departure from Lutèce, Bill was the chef/owner of the critically acclaimed restaurant La Petite Rose in Westfield, New Jersey. He has also held the positions of corporate executive chef with ARK Restaurant Group, overseeing twenty-eight restaurants, and executive chef at many renowned restaurants, such as Asia de Cuba, Café des Artistes, Patroon, and Restaurant "44" at the Royalton Hotel. Inspired by the reputation of New York City's most iconic restaurant—Tavern on the Green—this is the perfect match with his experience.

DAVID SALAMA was born in Cochabamba, Bolivia, and holds a BFA in graphic design from the Tyler School of Art. He studied in Rome during college, which sparked his interest in the culinary arts. Years later in Philadelphia, David combined his restoration, design, carpentry, painting, and culinary skills to open Creperie Beau Monde and L'Etage with Jim Caiola, successfully creating not only lauded restaurants but also distinct ambiance. David employed these talents once again when reopening Tavern on the Green to restore the beloved, welcoming atmosphere of the landmark restaurant.

JIM CAIOLA is an award-winning filmmaker and holds a degree in hotel restaurant management from Johnson & Wales University. Jim and his partner David Salama opened Creperie Beau Monde in Philadelphia in 1998, where they brought national attention to the culinary renaissance in the city for almost two decades. In 2003, they also opened L'Etage, a bar-lounge and performance space. Jim first fell in love with Tavern on the Green as a Lee Strasberg acting student in the early 1980s and returned to New York with David to reopen the restaurant in 2014. Jim and David revived Tavern on the Green with the vision of the original landmark—a warm, celebratory gathering space that captures the spirit of Central Park and the energy of New York City.